W9-ATT-424

The Politics of Hate

The Politics
of HATE

*Anti-Semitism, History, and the
Holocaust in Modern Europe*

JOHN WEISS

Ivan R. Dee

CHICAGO

THE POLITICS OF HATE. Copyright © 2003 by John Weiss. All rights reserved, including the right to reproduce this book or portions thereof in any form. For information, address: Ivan R. Dee, Publisher, 1332 North Halsted Street, Chicago 60622. Manufactured in the United States of America and printed on acid-free paper.

Library of Congress Cataloging-in-Publication Data:
Weiss, John, 1927–
     The politics of hate : anti-Semitism, history, and the Holocaust in modern Europe / John Weiss.
          p. cm.
     Includes bibliographical references and index.
     ISBN 1-56663-492-X (alk. paper)
     1. Antisemitism—Europe—History—20th century. 2. Europe—Ethnic relations. 3. Holocaust, Jewish (1939–1945)—Causes. I. Title: Anti-semitism, history, and the Holocaust in modern Europe. II. Title.

DS146.E85 W45 2003
305.892'404'09041—dc21   2002031398

For Barbara Hart Weiss

Acknowledgments

I WISH TO THANK the following for providing me with a forum to present my ideas: Norman Shaifer of the National Institute of the Arts; Sheldon Grebstein of the Westchester Holocaust Commission; Frederick M. Schweitzer of the Holocaust Resource Center of Manhattan College; Professor Hubert G. Locke, and Franklin and Marcia S. Littell of the Scholar's Conference on the Holocaust and the Churches; and Father Michael O'Keefe.

Barbara Hart Weiss has given me perceptive and excellent editorial advice. Thanks to Vicki Hsu for her editorial assistance. Ivan Dee is that rarity nowadays, a truly skillful editor and publisher who is dedicated to quality.

Contents

The Politics of Hate

ONE

The Origins of European Anti-Semitism

FOR MORE THAN a thousand years Jews have been accused of following a false and immoral religion and preferring deceitful commercial practices and usurious moneylending to honest work in field and factory. Jews have been accused of being loyal only to their own people and to enemies of any nation foolish enough to grant them hospitality or citizenship. The most extreme anti-Semites have insisted that throughout history the Jews have waged war against Gentiles, that they are international conspirators whose depraved traits are innate, "racial," and unchangeable. Such stereotypes still exist, of course, but only among those who, in the West at least, rate lowest in education, achievement, and political power. Consequently it is extremely difficult for educated and tolerant Westerners to imagine the dangerous power that anti-Semitism has enjoyed in modern Europe and impossible to grasp how it could have led to the unique and unimaginable horrors of the Holocaust.

A study of the origins and history of anti-Semitism by itself helps but little. To fully grasp the dangerous potential of racism we must also know the relationships between the fantasies of the anti-Semites and the long-term historical development of various nations, relationships that gave or denied racists the power to harm their Jewish communities. It is important to witness and remember, but it is essential to explain. Without more knowledge of its long-term historical causes, the Holocaust may well end as an inexplicable enigma, a searing and bitter memory of horror kept alive chiefly within the Jewish community. As such, the Holocaust will offer little help to those who hope to learn from its causes possible ways to avoid future if lesser mass murders with different killers and victims.

In European civilization there were five major sources of anti-Semitism. Christian anti-Semitism was the first, though today the vast majority of Christians reject it, and hostility to Jews was obviously never the message of Christ. As he said, it is not enough to love your neighbor, "You must love your enemies . . ." (Matthew 5:44–46). And of course he never thought of his own people as his enemies, only some of their religious leaders. The earliest Christians were Jews who believed that Jesus was the Messiah promised by the Hebrew Scriptures, the Christian Old Testament. They followed Jewish law, attended synagogue, and hoped to persuade their coreligionists that Christ was the awaited Messiah whose sacrifice on the cross would redeem the sins of all who accepted him as their savior.

The breach between the two communities began when St. Paul preached that obedience to Jewish law was futile without faith in Christ. By the end of the second century, Gentiles dominated the church and ignored Jewish law, but they did not believe Christianity was a new religion. For them Jesus was the culmination of Judaism, and those who accepted him were the new chosen people. The vast majority of Jews rejected Christ, of course, and thus the seeds of antagonism were sown, for the truth of Christianity seemed to depend on Old Testament prophecy, yet the Jewish community regarded Christ as a heretic and false Messiah.

In those days history seemed to be a scenario written by God, as the extreme fundamentalists and ultra-orthodox of the major religions still believe. Thus the failure of the Jews to accept Christ, St. Paul contended, must be the work of the Lord

Himself; mere men could not possibly resist his divine truth. Until the Jews converted, they would suffer a bitter fate, a lesson to all who refused to accept Christ. Eventually the Lord would bring the Jews to convert, the ultimate proof of Christianity and a necessary prelude to Judgment Day.

The first Christians expected the conversion of the Jews and Christ's Second Coming momentarily. But by the third and fourth centuries after Christ, many of the most famous and saintly Christian leaders found no insult too gross to hurl at the Jews, denouncing them as an obstinate, arrogant people who denied their own God, dangerous examples to Christians if allowed to live among them. With time, the fury of the Christian masses intensified, for the truth of Christianity still seemed to depend on the conversion of the Jews. By the tenth century ordinary Christians, priests, and many higher clergy believed the Jews were literally a satanic people. Where else could they gain the power to resist the will of their own Messiah? Had they not called for Christ's death after a Jewish court convicted him of heresy? (There is no evidence that these events actually occurred. The Gospels are theology, not history, and were written long after Christ's death by persons who could not have known him.)

It did not help to tell ordinary Christians, as church leaders did, that the fate of the Jews must be left to the Lord, for they also taught that the Lord works through the deeds of mankind. Yet according to Christian theology, Christ's death was not caused by human will; the Lord foreordained his crucifixion and the miracle of his resurrection. In addition, during Christ's lifetime most Jews did not live in Palestine and had never heard of Christ. Too, his apostles were Jews, and the Gospels tell of large crowds greeting him when he entered Palestine. Nevertheless to ordinary Christians unaccustomed to theological niceties, the charge of "Christ-killers" echoed down through the ages to cause the Jews countless miseries. Thus the burst of religious passion that brought the Crusades of the later Middle

Ages nearly destroyed the Jewish communities of Western Europe.

In the latter half of the twentieth century even those mainstream Christian leaders who believed Judaism to be a false religion no longer accused "the Jews" of having killed Christ; liberal Christian theologians now reject the idea out of hand. Wherever strong traditions of toleration and humanism prevail, the clergy of all but a few obscure cults today oppose harming Jews. Nor should Christian anti-Semites be confused with those who believe Jews to be innately evil because of their "blood" or "race." Even during the Crusades, Jews could save themselves by converting, something racists do not admit. And during the Holocaust, innumerable Christians of all denominations protested the killings, and thousands risked death to aid the Jews of Europe. Still, in the nineteenth century Christian hostility reinforced racist anti-Semitic movements, and in some nations—notably Poland and Austria—it helped create a culture that allowed them to flourish.

A second major source of anti-Semitism in Europe was commercial. Jews were plagued for centuries by accusations that they innately preferred to exploit and manipulate others through dishonest commercial practices and usurious moneylending. The accusations confuse the results of oppression with alleged racial traits. Jews originally migrated to Europe as traders from the advanced civilizations of the East. As centuries passed, many became peasants, warriors, craftsmen, and even nobles—as Jews were in the East. But after the fall of Rome, the dominant European feudal authorities, influenced by the clergy, gradually excluded Jews from state and military service and landowning. Heretics and Christ-killers, clerics insisted, could not hold positions of power over Christians.

Jews were also forbidden to join artisans' guilds. Composed of skilled craftsmen and small merchants, the guilds were the dominant form of enterprise in pre-industrial Europe, authorized to license those who entered a trade and to control market share, prices, wages, and product quality. Although the guilds had Christian patron saints and rituals, their basic motive was to restrict Jewish competition and persuade rulers to support the restrictions. In medieval Europe and later, Christian small businessmen could rarely compete with Jewish traders who had maintained mercantile and linguistic connections with the East, where the most desired products and commercial skills were located. Consequently European Jews were gradually limited to petty commerce and moneylending, barring a handful who served as financial agents for princes. The general population, illiterate and ignorant, easily confused the results of past oppression with innate Jewish traits. By the seventeenth century, ghettos were common and Jews assumed to be fit only for the lowest forms of commerce.

The eighteenth-century Enlightenment challenged traditional attitudes toward Jews. Basing their ideas on the new science of the seventeenth century, the new thinkers inferred that religious mythology was not divinely revealed but a human creation. Hence they argued for religious toleration and the separation of church and state. They believed that environment, experience, and education, not innate or "racial" traits, formed character. They valued free enterprise and wanted entrepreneurs freed from guild restrictions. Increasingly a burgeoning and pragmatic middle class in France, Great Britain, Italy, Scandinavia, and colonial America supported these ideas. Inspired by the Enlightenment, the leaders of the French Revolution of 1789 legislated equality before the law and attacked the old order of absolute monarchs, privileged aristocrats, guild monopolies, serfdom, and the extensive secular powers of a wealthy church. When the Revolution turned more radical in 1791, the Jews of France were liberated from all legal disabilities. By the 1860s the Jews of Western Europe were liberated, though still subject to much informal discrimination.

The association of Jews with liberal and progressive movements in modern Europe was a third source of anti-Semitism.

Secular liberalism offered Jews freedom from religious persecution while their new status as free citizens offered the prospect of eventual full assimilation in a future democratic society. Aided by liberal free enterprise, Jews were no longer limited to marginal economic pursuits. They easily adapted to the new commercial expansion because of their extensive experience in commerce and trade.

In the 1870s and later, aristocrats, clergy, and guilds organized to defend their powers and values against the threatened rise of an urban, commercial, and democratic social order, and often held Jews responsible because of their prominence in commerce, the professions, and liberal and progressive movements. Royalists, aristocratic landowners, high civil servants, and military officers discriminated against Jews and used anti-Semitism to gain popular support. In Austria, Germany, and Eastern Europe, guild artisans supported extremist anti-Semitic movements, blaming Jews for the threat that free enterprise posed to their old monopolies and the new technology that made their traditional skills obsolete. Excluded from guilds, Jews had pioneered in new products, sales techniques, and large-scale merchandising beyond guild control. Small-scale merchants and handicraft shops often lacked the capital, the capability, or the will to adjust. When liberal politicians denounced guild restrictions that hindered economic growth, conservatives defended them as necessary for economic stability. By the 1800s, anti-Semitic movements tried to boycott, limit, or outlaw Jewish enterprises. But many progressives welcomed new enterprises because they lowered consumer prices and helped them challenge the power and privileges of their aristocratic opponents.

In the later nineteenth century, subsistence peasants and small landowners found it difficult to adjust to the opening of national and international markets created by railways and ocean transport. In Germany and Eastern Europe, Jews—for centuries excluded from landowning—were often dealers in cattle, farm machinery, fertilizer, and agrarian products. The naturally antagonistic relationship between buyers and sellers easily translated into anti-Semitism when hard times brought low prices for farm products and high prices for farm needs, and when cheap agrarian imports flooded the market. Peasants often fell into debt to finance the production of cash crops for new markets, and established bankers found it far too risky to lend to them. Consequently middlemen—often Jewish—were lenders of last resort, and charged high interest to cover their many losses through defaults, reinforcing the image of the usurious Jew.

The strong presence of Jews in the modern sectors of the new capitalist economies also made it convenient for anti-Semites to persuade those with no knowledge of economic complexities that Jews were responsible for depressions. But the small number of Jews—about 1 percent (excluding the Austrian Empire with just over 4 percent)—made it impossible for them to dominate the economy, and in any event capitalists follow the laws of the market, not unique ethnic or religious rules.

Physicians, lawyers, and students often supported anti-Semitism when faced with strong competition from Jewish students who, liberated from the ghetto, flocked to the study of law and medicine. Private practice freed them from the discrimination often found in state and corporate bureaucracies, the military, teaching, and the judiciary. Science and mathematics also attracted Jewish students. Scientific skills are portable and hard to ignore; the language of math and physics is international, not ethnic. But the study of history and literature was strongly nationalistic in the nineteenth century, and many academics refused to believe that a Jew could truly understand the historical or literary expression of the unique spirit of Christian peoples. Hence the predominance of assimilated German and Hungarian Jews in physics and mathematics at the turn of the century, and the prominence of assimilated European Jews among winners of the Nobel prize.

Anthropology was a fourth source of European anti-

Semitism and racism in the nineteenth century. Academics and best-selling writers believed there were different races with different physical characteristics and inborn intellectual and even moral capacities. They ignored the force of thousands of years of group isolation, sexual selection, climatic influences, and the power of society, experience, and upbringing on character, intelligence, and morality. Geneticists now know that differences between ethnic groups are tiny, including IQ, as compared to the vast variations within ethnic groups. Ethnic differences in test scores, for example, are either marginal or the result of individual inheritance as well as education, class advantage, social experience, and family influence. But only since the 1950s have most intellectuals and cultural leaders discredited the idea of fixed races with inherent traits. Historical experience has also forced changes. In Israel, for example, Jews work in almost every occupation and trade and possess the widest possible range of abilities, incomes, and physical types of perhaps any nation.

But in the later nineteenth century, anthropology gave scientific validity to educated people who wished to use racism to justify imperialism, competitive capitalism, discrimination, segregation, slavery, and conquest in war—the ultimate struggle for survival of the "most favored races." Long before the Nazis, anthropologists popularized invidious comparisons between, among others, Semites and Aryans. Textbooks often featured such ideas, and in some nations—notably Germany, Austria, and Eastern Europe—university students and high school teachers were quite prominent among the leaders and followers of anti-Semitic movements. Those who read the textbooks of the time do not wonder why so many well-educated people could support racism and anti-Semitism.

The fifth source of anti-Semitism, especially powerful in Central and Eastern Europe, was ethnic nationalism. Until the 1850s the French Revolution had determined that demands for national liberation would be accompanied by calls for human rights and democratic reforms. But when revolutionary and idealistic liberal nationalists in the East were defeated by the armies of the Ottoman, Austrian, and Russian empires, many intellectuals among the oppressed minority nations turned to an exclusive and harshly militant ethnic nationalism. Reviving the ancient language, culture, and customs of their peoples, they lauded their ancestors as a race of sturdy peasants and valiant warriors who battled to forge a free nation against tyrannical imperialists. Popular writers enshrined these idealized heroic deeds and names in stirring and bloody epics, poems, and songs; many are used still today to inspire "ethnic cleansers" in the Balkans. Ancient claims to a "greater Serbia," a "greater Hungary," or a "greater Poland," among others, were resurrected. But such claims and counterclaims necessarily encompassed territories containing other ethnic minorities with their own demands for independence. With the decay of the tsarist, Habsburg, and Ottoman empires, ethnic conflicts against them gave way to ethnic struggles among the minorities themselves, as newly free ethnic groups sought to assimilate minorities within their territories by force.

Jews were more vulnerable than other ethnic groups. They could claim no territories of their own, followed a despised religion, composed only about 10 percent of the population in the East, and were extremely prominent in the modern sectors of the economy. Consequently ethnic nationalists denounced the influence of Jewish financiers, bankers, merchants, teachers, journalists, and cultural activists, reviling the Jews' alleged rootless urban cosmopolitanism, subversive values, and pacifism. Above all they insisted that the blood of the people must be kept pure—an impossible notion with fatal implications. Jews were even more at risk in the 1914–1918 war and after when governments inflamed all kinds of ethnic antagonisms to justify terrible civilian sacrifices, while postwar border settlements inevitably favored one ethnic group at the expense of another.

Democratic socialism, influential by the 1890s, was a counterforce to ethnic nationalism and religious discrimination. Defiantly secular, socialists blamed the capitalist system, not any ethnic group, for social misery and rejected ethnic nationalism as a delusion. Although he was an anti-Semite in his youth, Karl Marx did not embody anti-Semitism in Marxism, and he also rejected nationalism. As he wrote in the Communist Manifesto, "The Proletariat has no Fatherland." In 1890 Friedrich Engels, Marx's partner, declared anti-Semitism a reactionary attempt to divert attention away from the evils of capitalism—the official Marxist and Social Democratic position. Reactionaries, as Hitler would later do, insisted that socialism was an invention of unpatriotic and rootless Jews who manipulated honest "Aryan" workers in order to subvert and dominate traditional society. To make the case, one had to ignore the fact that some 90 percent of Western European Jewry supported liberal—not socialist—parties except in the Austrian Empire and the East, where liberalism was effectively dead long before 1914 because of raging ethnic conflicts.

With the important exception of Italian fascism, the most extreme anti-Semites in Europe tended to join fascist movements. The basis for fascist ideology was created in late-nineteenth-century Germany, Austria, and Eastern Europe. Race and blood, nationalists held, determined that they were descended from forest tribes composed of noble warriors and productive peasants. Semites were their natural enemies, a people that originated in the hostile and sterile deserts of the Middle East and were therefore drawn to the city and "parasitic" commerce. As revolutionary reactionaries, fascists hoped to launch violent and ultra-nationalist attacks against liberalism, democracy, socialism, and communism—condemned as the work of subversive Jews hoping to destroy traditional values and even pollute the blood of Aryans through racial mixing.

Like almost everyone except socialists, fascists despised women's liberation and homosexuality, but they blamed both on leftist "Hebrew women" and cowardly Jewish males trying to destroy the patriarchal institutions needed for a stable society and a strong military. Gypsies were (and still are) despised, but fascists believed them to be a degenerate race unworthy of life; the Nazis tried to exterminate both Gypsies and homosexuals. When Bolsheviks overthrew the new democratic Russian government in 1917, anti-Semites, not only fascists, added "Judeo-bolshevism" to the stereotype of the evil Jew. But fascists should not be confused with authoritarian nationalist leaders, men like Francisco Franco of Spain or Miklos Horthy of Hungary. Unlike authoritarian nationalists, including Benito Mussolini, fascists wished to reduce Jews to a ghetto existence, drive them from the nation, or worse. When threats to the powers and interests of traditional reactionary elites arose, however, authoritarian nationalists often supported fascism.

Fascists did not, as is commonly thought, regard the Jews as subhuman but as a powerful, cunning, and dangerous race who had survived and even prospered in spite of centuries of Christian persecution. German, Austrian, Romanian, Hungarian, Polish, and Croatian fascists alike insisted that the inevitable racial war against the Jews could be won only by ignoring traditional humanitarian illusions in order to destroy a people that would otherwise create and inevitably dominate a degenerate democratic, liberal, and commercial society. For fascists, war embodied heroic idealism and the nobility of sacrifice for the common good, as opposed to the liberal bourgeois desire for individualism, creature comforts, and endless ignoble compromises with their antagonists. Peace was seen as a despicable notion of Jewish merchants and leftists who knew they could never conquer "Aryans" except by economic manipulation and political subversion. Consequently many military officers and veterans supported fascist movements—men who, like Hitler, viewed politics as a military confrontation with enemies who must be destroyed.

Those who have grown up in liberal societies find the grisly terror of Nazis, fascists, and contemporary "ethnic cleansers" impossible to understand; thus we often view the murderers as small groups of psychotic criminals. Many even argue that all of us have the same potential for evil. True or not, it still takes specific historical circumstances to foster this alleged potential. Others attribute the murderous crimes of fascists to the rise to power in times of social trauma of a few obsessed, charismatic leaders who can manipulate hatreds. But this does not explain why such high percentages of the population in the 1930s—one-third in Germany, and more in Austria and Eastern Europe— eagerly believed that the Jews were responsible for all social and economic ills, and wanted them stopped, one way or another. However difficult it may be, we must recognize that even the Nazis were not psychotic brutes but often highly educated, sincere believers who led ordinary lives in spite of their unbelievably bloody deeds against "racial" enemies.

Whatever the myths or goals of anti-Semites and fascists, their hope for political power was directly related to the general history of the nation in which they lived, including, of course, the history and place of the Jewish community within it. It is not enough simply to narrate the history of anti-Semitic ideas or estimate how many believed them. Nor are different forms of anti-Semitism of equal impact. Christian anti-Semitism, for example, was distinctly unpopular among the Lutheran and Calvinist clergy of Scandinavian nations, and racism was rejected by the majority of Christians, including Pope Pius XI, though Judaism was not accepted as a valid religion. Nor do ethnic hatreds thrive simply because they have a long history; they must be encouraged by demagogues and manipulated by politicians. Even where millions of anti-Semites exist, as in France and the United States from 1919 to 1939, they often belong to groups and classes that cannot unite or gain access to power. Above all, anti-Semitism can thrive only where the ideas and values that oppose it are too weak to oppose the racism of rulers and electorates.

That is why we must know the relationships between political anti-Semitism, fascism, and the general history of nations. Therein lie the answers to our questions: Why did Germany initiate the Holocaust? Why did Austrians supply so many killers? Why is it that a million French fascists could not gain sufficient power to help destroy the Jews until the German conquest put the Vichy government in power? Why did fascist Italy not cooperate in the massacre of the Jews until Mussolini had lost the war? Why was anti-Semitism, as Poland illustrates, far stronger in Eastern than in Western Europe? The answers will help us understand why the politics of racial hate succeeds, and what can be done about it. The Holocaust was unique, but its historical origins tell us much that can help us in the battle against present and future horrors by other perpetrators with different victims.

Germany to 1914

W<small>HY</small> <small>WAS</small> <small>IT</small> that Germans initiated the Holocaust? After all, there were millions of vicious anti-Semites in many nations, some with a larger proportion of their population—notably Austria, Poland, Romania, and the Ukraine. A half-million non-Germans volunteered for the SS, and thousands more voluntarily helped with the killings. In fact the majority of Germans opposed harming the Jews, as the historical power of parties that opposed political anti-Semitism demonstrates: National Liberals, Progressives, Social Democrats, and the Catholic Center. In their best year, 1932, the Nazis received 37 percent of the vote while opposition parties received about 60 percent. And from 1933 through 1939, tens of thousands of Germans faced exile, prison, or death for acts of resistance. Fierce terror ended open opposition, but it is obvious that many more Germans were too frightened, and with reason, to oppose the Nazi party publicly.

Many still believe that only Hitler and a few obsessed Nazi leaders wanted to murder the Jews. But dozens of similarly obsessed anti-Semitic paramilitary groups, with hundreds of thousands of supporters and a multitude of similar leaders, sprang up in Germany after 1918. Hitler became the leader because his failed *putsch* (attempted overthrow of the government) of 1923 convinced paramilitaries that he was determined to act, not because he was uniquely anti-Semitic. Some say that Hitler's charismatic harangues persuaded millions of Germans to share his loathing of the Jews. But charismatic speakers succeed only if their slogans excite hatreds and fears already shared by their audience. The old newsreels show a false unanimity. From his earliest days in Munich, Hitler's SA had to throw out those in the crowd—mostly leftists—who shouted him down or heaved beer bottles at the podium. Nor should we make too much of Hitler's psyche. Hundreds of thousands of Germans and Austrians shared his beliefs but not, of course, his psychological profile.

Most Holocaust scholars still think Germany's post–World War I traumas were the primary cause of the rise of the Nazis: the lost war, the Treaty of Versailles, the ravages of a devastating inflation and the Great Depression. Yet the Jews did not lose the war, write the treaty, or cause the economic collapse. One would expect those who suffered to blame the leaders who lost the war, the Allies who wrote the treaty, and the politicians in office during economic disasters. If so many Germans voted for those who insisted the Jews were to blame, it is because a long history of anti-Semitism had prepared them to do so. Certainly without the postwar traumas the Nazis would not have come to power. But without the unique history of anti-Semitism in Germany there would have been no Nazis to take power.

Some believe that only about 12 percent of those who voted for the Nazis did so because they were anti-Semites, and that most voted for them because they were anti-Communist. But for the Nazis and the German Conservative party, communism was Jewish, as their constant use of the phrase "Judeobolshevism" reveals. And all other parties were anti-Communist but did not blame communism on the Jews. Misled by the norms of Western democratic politics, we assume that voters select candidates because of their positions on separate issues. But to extreme racists, all issues are racial. Thus Nazi campaign literature claimed that Jewish bankers set the reparations terms of the treaty, Jewish businesses imported cheap products to ruin German farmers, Jewish speculators destroyed

German currency, and Jewish retail outlets ruined small businessmen by price-cutting. Above all, the Nazis claimed that Jews dominated the Weimar *Judenrepublik* that followed World War I, supported the crimes of their race, and helped the Allies undermine the autocratic and military traditions that had made Germany great.

The Nazis also insisted that international Jewish financiers deliberately caused the Great Depression in order to stimulate revolution and thus help Jewish Communists destroy the nation. We find it irrational to claim that Jewish capitalists and Communists worked together, but for extreme anti-Semites the Jews are a race that uses all its power positions to further its war against "Aryan" civilization. To stop the Jews, Nazi speakers demanded they be driven from their privileged positions and, their wealth confiscated, ultimately forced out of Germany—or worse. The call of "Death to the Jews" was constantly shouted out at Nazi rallies. It was clear to all that a vote for Hitler was a vote to do grievous harm to the Jews.

The significant difference between German and other Western nations with strong anti-Semitic movements was the power of anti-Semitism among the German ruling elites—civil servants, aristocratic landowners, military officers, and educational leaders. From the 1870s onward these groups used anti-Semitism to protect their power, values, and economic interests from growing democratic, liberal, and socialist movements. During the Weimar Republic, as we shall see, anti-Semitism among the prestigious Conservative party intensified to Nazi-like levels because reactionaries feared democratic and progressive threats. Of course Hitler had to gain the votes to make his movement useful to them, but he did so by exploiting popular anti-Semitic ideas extending back to the 1870s and before. In addition, no nation could initiate a Holocaust without a powerful industry and military, able to conquer Poland and western Russia where the bulk of European Jewry lived. Romania, Poland, and Austria were too weak for such ambitions.

To understand why the elites and so many ordinary Germans supported Nazi racism, we must look to the German past. In the sixteenth century Luther founded the German Reformation by denying the Catholic church's claim to possess the divine grace to forgive sinners. Calling the pope the Antichrist, he insisted that nothing the Catholic church could do would assure salvation; only one's personal faith through Jesus could bring eternal life. Various German princes protected him, if only because his doctrines enabled them to seize the considerable wealth of the Roman church, and because, unlike the Vatican, Luther claimed no secular powers and demanded strict obedience to princes.

At first Luther believed he had restored the original truth of Christianity and that the Jews would see this truth and convert. But why would Jews surrender their ancient and complex religious culture merely because of a quarrel between oppressors, both of whom demanded their conversion? Luther's fury at rejection, a result of his intense psychic struggle for certainty about his own salvation, far exceeded that of the popes of the Crusades, who had admonished the faithful not to kill the Jews. "I cannot convert the Jews," Luther wrote. "Our Lord Christ did not succeed in doing so: but I can close their mouths so that there will be nothing for them to do but lie upon the ground." He thus contradicted Christian theology by denying the power of the universal grace of Christ. He and his numerous followers engaged in bitter and literally obscene attacks against the Jews. Burn their synagogues and sacred books, Luther cried, drive them from the land, silence them, for they are the tools of Satan.

For many German intellectuals, the Lutheran Reformation marked the true beginning of modern German history, allegedly freeing man's moral idealism from the ritualistic dogma of Judaism and Catholic Christianity by resting on faith alone. It is important to note that today Lutheran clergy do not support anti-Semitism. Even in Luther's time, in England the proliferation of sectarian movements made relative toleration necessary. Where Calvinism reigned, as in Scotland, Switzerland, and the American colonies, Christian anti-Semitism was muted because Calvinist predetermination emphasized that the death of Christ was divinely preordained and not a result of mere human decisions, Jewish or Roman. Moreover, Calvinists flourished in commercially advanced economies where the "capitalist ethic" of commerce and trade was highly valued. They were not likely to blame Jews for their commercial activities. But Lutheranism became the preferred religion of the Prussians in their militaristic, autocratic, and agrarian state, a state destined to unite and lead the Germanies. Luther himself denounced commerce and the city, insisting that true Germans led a rural life.

The Enlightenment's challenge to Christianity had much less impact on German intellectual and popular culture than elsewhere in the West. The most influential philosophers in Germany—Kant, Hegel, and Fichte, the German Idealists—all opposed the secular humanism of the Enlightenment and incorporated Christian theology into their philosophies. They believed that innate moral impulses, not external experience, governed mankind, and that Lutheran Christianity had attained the highest moral worth by sanctifying an intensely personal relationship with God through Jesus. The history of Western civilization, the Idealists believed, was the manifestation of man's divinely given moral sense gradually reshaping the world.

Each people, the Idealists believed, possessed a unique spirit. The first stage in the realization of the Absolute Spirit was the monotheism of the ancient Hebrews, a mortal challenge to the belief in the semi-human divinities of antiquity. But Christ's message encompassed a higher morality because it made the inner moral spirit primary. Catholicism corrupted Christ's message, but the Jews rejected it altogether, clinging to their primitive belief in the power of ritual and law.

Divine destiny, the Idealists declared, had selected the Teutonic peoples to make the highest contribution to the moral development of mankind through the Reformation, displacing the superficial legalistic spirit of the Roman church and the Latin peoples. The French Revolution of 1789 was bound to end in terror and tyranny, led by a people unchanged by the inner spirituality of Lutheran Christianity. Judaism remained a primitive religion of mere ritual and law without ethical content, rendering the Jews unfit to contribute to a truly moral national community. (Those who know Judaism will understand that such notions betray an ignorance of Judaism's strong emphasis on personal righteousness.) Kant called the Jews a nation of swindlers. Hegel labeled them a moral dunghill. Fichte wanted them thrown out of Germany. Later, many German academics adapted the alleged corruption of the Jewish spirit to the secular racism of corrupted blood.

True, Germany was home to important liberal and progressive groups. But in the main, the Prussian middle classes, with little access to the wealth of imperial markets that brought self-confidence and an independent voice to Westerners, were largely a civil-service class loyal to state and monarch. Unlike the French, they had little reason to resent the aristocracy. French aristocrats lived from state pensions in the sterile idleness of court rituals, but the Prussian aristocracy—the famous Junkers—was a hardworking military and civil-service class. Prussians did not demand the separation of church and state, in part because the Lutheran church possessed neither secular power nor vast wealth, as did the French Catholic church.

In 1807, when Napoleon routed the powerful Prussian army, he imposed many of the reforms of the French Revolution. In helpless fury, aristocratic Prussians watched as their lands were seized, their monopoly on high office broken, and more power granted to the middle classes. Embittered guild-masters lost many of their monopolies in the name of free enterprise. Shocked clergy saw the troops of the "Antichrist" tear down the ghetto walls and establish freedom of religion and occupation for the Jews. Napoleon assumed that a productive and grateful German middle class would support him, and many did welcome the reforms. But they also hoped to rid themselves of Napoleon's tyranny and create a unified and liberal Germany on their own.

To the dismay of older aristocrats, young Prussian bureaucrats and military officers supported many of the French emperor's reforms, believing that reform gave Napoleon's troops the admirable fervor of a truly national army backed by a grateful and patriotic people. Prussia's forced peasant recruits could not compete. Thus Prussian reformers proceeded to free the serfs, introduce moderate free enterprise, and limit the aristocratic monopoly on the officer corps and civil service. Shocked, aristocratic landowners petitioned the reformers, complaining that such "Jewish and French" reforms would turn Prussia into a "newfangled Jewish state" dominated by a materialistic people lacking Christian morality and warrior virtues. Free the serfs and the inherently inferior peasants would become useless as soldiers, no longer obedient to their natural aristocratic masters. Replace the stable economic system of the guilds with free enterprise, and usurious and destructive "Jewish" free competition would reign. End aristocratic monopolies over military and bureaucratic positions, and the source of the traditional might of old Prussia would be destroyed.

Conservatives believed that the battle against Napoleon and his reforms was a struggle to defend a unique and superior Germanic spirit. Fichte, the most extreme of the Idealists, was the intellectual leader of the nationalist war of liberation against Napoleon. For him, Napoleon's reforms were mortal dangers to the Germanic peoples' destiny to bring Luther's moral vision to full realization. A new Germany united in spirit and body could arise only if it protected itself from all foreign influences—especially the Jews: "It is you Germans, who, of all peoples, possess most clearly the germ of human perfectibility, and to whom belongs the leadership in the development of mankind. . . . If you sink, then mankind sinks with you, with no hope of resurrection."

In Germany, universities were branches of the civil service. Only a small percentage of the relevant age groups attended—mainly the children of elites, who were the future rulers of Germany, and the upper middle class. Founded in 1809 to counter foreign influence, the University of Berlin, whose first provost was Fichte, was the most distinguished. Excluding the exact sciences, its departments stressed the Germanic spirit of German literature and history and its alleged superiority to the cosmopolitanism of "Jewish and French liberalism." Academics often believed, consequently, that Jews could neither understand nor teach German history or literature, and excluded them when possible.

After the defeat of Napoleon, university students glorified the demagogues Friedrich Ludwig Jahn and Ernst Moritz Arndt (both later listed as worthy predecessors by the Nazis). Arndt believed the Jews to be a degenerate, worthless race; both sought to resurrect the pre-Christian religion and customs of the Germanic tribes, alternatives to the "decadent" Latin world and a Christianity corrupted by its Jewish origins. Important academics and intellectuals made invidious racial distinctions between Aryan and Semite, as did learned men elsewhere. But such ideas were more popular in Germany and more often accompanied by an emphasis on the "science" of eugenics, that is, the hope of cultivating a pure and superior race by selective breeding.

Nevertheless liberalism continued to advance. The king of Prussia wanted to force the Jews back into the ghetto after Napoleon was defeated, but in the name of economic progress his advisers prevented him from doing so. Guild masters regained only some of their former monopolies. Entrepreneurs and professionals flourished as the market economy advanced, and they tended to support liberal values. In the Revolutions of

1848 almost every German state elected liberals to a parliament at Frankfurt formed to create a liberal and united Germany. Their proposed constitution included freedom of trade and speech, parliamentary government, and the liberation of the Jews from all civic disabilities. But, fearful of the example of Robespierre and the Terror that followed the French Revolution, they did not try to wrest power by force from the swiftly regrouping princes. Moreover, most of those who originally supported the revolutions with violence were artisans and peasants. Artisans detested free enterprise, of course, and peasants scorned the liberals' refusal to seize and redistribute aristocratic estates because of their concern for the sanctity of private property. Peasants and artisans both grumbled about "Jewish liberalism." A parliamentary delegation offered the king of Prussia the crown of a united Germany, but he detested liberals and would not offend his fellow princes—and hostile foreign powers—by incorporating German territories into Prussia. And because a prominent Jew headed the delegation offering the crown, the king refused, saying he could not accept an offer from the gutter.

The Prussian army easily disbanded the revolutionaries, but the king created a Prussian parliament to meet liberal demands. To maintain aristocratic control, strict suffrage requirements favored the very wealthy. Nevertheless the Prussian middle class swiftly outpaced the aristocracy in wealth. In the elections of 1861 the Liberal party of Prussia shocked the Conservatives by winning 256 delegates to 15; only strict limits to parliamentary power allowed the old guard to retain control. Frightened, the Prussian High Command vowed to stem the liberal tide by force if necessary and persuaded the king to call Otto von Bismarck as minister-president of Prussia. Known as the "red reactionary," he had opposed any royal concessions in 1849, including the constitution, and declared he could never serve under a Jewish civil servant. He began his campaign against the liberals in 1862 by violating the constitutional rights of parliament and passing a budget over its objections.

In 1866 Bismarck maneuvered Austria into war; victory was swift. In 1870 the Prussian army defeated France almost as easily. With successes over its two major enemies, the Prussian army had accomplished the greatest single achievement in modern German history: the unification of the different German states into a single nation. The prestige of army and autocracy soared. A flood of pamphlets and sermons praised the "Prussian God of Battles" and, with Social Darwinist ideas, boasted of the superiority of the Prussian warrior race. The Liberals renamed themselves the National Liberal party and legalized after the fact Bismarck's violations of their constitutional rights, granting him honors and wealth as well. The Prussian upper middle classes began to imitate the ways and attitudes of the aristocracy and the military, including their hostility toward the Jews.

Bismarck needed the National Liberals. Only they could create the industrial wealth required if Germany were to be a truly great power. Consequently Bismarck created a constitution for the new united Germany with a Reichstag elected by universal manhood suffrage; but he added an upper house and other provisions to assure the dominance of the Prussian ruling class. The former king of Prussia, now Kaiser Wilhelm I, ruled what was in fact a Prussian Empire, not a democratic Germany—the Second Reich. In accord with the demands of the National Liberals, Bismarck ended restrictions on investment capital by limiting the liability of investors, thereby freeing capital for new industries. Speculators founded corporations and issued fraudulent claims of success to attract the unsuspecting, however, and thousands of small investors were ruined. Because of a handful of fraudulent Jewish speculators, a chorus of anti-Semites attacked the Jews as a whole, even though thousands of Jewish investors were also ruined. Bismarck and his cabinet, Christians all, had approved the measures, and many aristocrats were involved in the frauds. In fact, two leading Jewish members of the National Liberals were the first to expose the scandals and demand regulations to prevent them.

In 1874, before the economic crisis reached its peak, the liberal parties trounced the conservatives yet again in national elections. To counterattack, in 1876 the elites formed the German Conservative party. Its reactionary wing demanded that the party officially adopt anti-Semitism. In a series of articles in the most popular middle-class magazine, a leading conservative, Otto Glagau, contributed an essay with the title that became famous: "The Social Problem Is the Jewish Problem." Complete with false statistics, Glagau blamed the Jews for the economic collapse and joined others in accusing Bismarck of allowing Germany to become a "new Palestine," supported by the "Party of the Jews," the National Liberals.

In the 1870s Bismarck, with Liberal support, passed a series of laws to weaken the Catholic church because he feared that the millions of Catholics added to the new Germany through unification would be allies of the Vatican and rivals to the Protestant conservative establishment. Liberals cooperated with Bismarck because it seemed a step toward the separation of church and state. Jewish religious leaders withheld support, fearing they might be next. Nevertheless the leading German Catholic newspaper published a series of anti-Semitic articles both from conviction and to prove its loyalty. As a depression took hold and the votes of the National Liberal party declined, Bismarck retracted the more tyrannical of his anti-Catholic laws and made peace with the Vatican. He encouraged his ministers to shift the blame to Jewish liberals in the Reichstag. Bismarck also purged the civil service of liberals and Jews to reestablish his credentials with conservatives who had often denounced his cooperation with both.

By 1879 the left wing of the National Liberals had split off to form the Progressive party. And another threat faced Bismarck and the establishment: the Marxist Social Democrats. Supported by the industrial proletariat, they scoffed at religion, German nationalism, Prussian autocrats, Bismarck, and the kaiser himself. Among those shocked by the Social Democrats' lack of patriotism was Pastor Adolf Stoecker, a rigid fundamentalist, defender of Prussian virtues, and military chaplain in conquered Alsace-Lorraine, where the German army had brutally driven out thousands of Jews. The kaiser honored him by appointing him court chaplain. Stoecker, hoping to persuade the proletariat to desert socialism and affirm loyalty to throne and altar, founded the Christian Social Workers party in 1878 and ran for the Prussian parliament from Berlin. He advocated a return to the guild system, limits on workers' hours, social insurance policies for the unemployed and victims of industrial accidents, and a ban on usury. But he gained only a handful of votes. Most Berliners voted for the Progressives, followed closely by the Social Democrats. The Conservatives trailed far behind.

During the 1878 campaign anarchists, many of them Jewish, heckled Stoecker as a reactionary priest whose halfway measures were a meaningless façade to mask the exploitation of the workers. His predominantly lower-middle-class audiences shouted out demands that he speak against the real cause of Germany's ills, the Jews. Consequently, in a second campaign in 1879, Stoecker spoke of the evil influence of the Jews, deniers of Christ who had even deserted their own religion for secular liberalism in order to give free rein to their materialism and greed. The Jews threatened all that was decent and Germanic, he insisted. They must convert and end their destructive economic practices, or Germans would have to limit their activities and rights severely. Only a state governed by the New Testament, Stoecker thundered, could survive. In the heat of the campaign he called the Jews a separate "tribe" whose defects were innate; even conversion might not improve them. Hailed as a new Luther by his supporters, this time Stoecker won handily.

Conservative candidates also attacked the Jews and immediately doubled their seats in Berlin. The Progressives and Social Democrats, both of whom scorned anti-Semitism, took heavy losses. Elected to the Reichstag in 1881, Stoecker, the "King of Berlin" as he was called, became a powerful voice in the reactionary and racist wing of the German Conservative party, now regularly running anti-Semitic candidates. But his votes came from the lower middle class, not the industrial proletariat he had hoped to win for Prussian autocracy.

In 1879 Wilhelm Marr, inventor of the term "anti-Semitism," published a best-seller that sold out twelve editions in its first year. He claimed that blood determined the Jews' "anti-social" traits. Literally born enemies of all idealism, commerce and money were their only gods. Conversion simply enabled them to subvert society anonymously; Christian anti-Judaism could not stop this cunning and devious race. Jews supported liberalism only because toleration and unfettered capitalism allowed them the freedom to conquer their host societies. Socialism was merely a Jewish front to deceive the workers into believing that Christian German industrialists were their enemies, not Jewish international financiers. This "demonic race" had already conquered German society, Marr declared. They dominated Bismarck's vaunted Reich, and Germans had lost the will to fight back. Germany was fated to become the first Jewish world power. Fatalism aside, Marr joined with reactionary backers to found an anti-Semitic society that called for the boycott of Jewish stores and a refusal to vote for Jews and politicians who supported "Jewish liberalism." They must be stopped by any means, he asserted, for it was impossible for a race to change its behavior.

In the 1880s Bismarck encouraged anti-Semitism, though he wished to limit the attack to Jewish leftists. He also tried to abolish the Social Democrats with trumped-up charges of assassination attempts on the kaiser. When that failed, he contemplated a *putsch* against parliament but had to be satisfied with putting socialist leaders in prison and raising legal obstacles to prevent them from campaigning. In 1881 anti-Semites drew up a petition demanding that Jews be banished from all positions of authority in Germany, above all in education. In a few months in Berlin a quarter of a million persons signed it, including more than half the students at the University of Berlin—Germany's future rulers. Inspired by the most popular historian in Germany, Heinrich von Treitschke, a boundless admirer of the Prussian warrior autocracy, students founded their own Anti-Semitic League. Treitschke wrote the famous phrase "The Jews are our misfortune"; it would appear later on the masthead of the Nazi Julius Streicher's virulent racist paper *Der Stuermer.*

But industrial Germany continued to create forces that the old rulers were unable to master, and in 1890 the right suffered a series of setbacks. The new kaiser forced Bismarck to resign and even toyed with ideas for social reform. In 1890, elections almost wiped out Stoecker's party and doubled the Reichstag seats of the Progressives. Worst of all, the Social Democrats won the largest popular vote of any party in the history of the Reich, as well as a majority on the Berlin city council, partly because they supported consumer interests and worked for peaceful and democratic reform, not revolution. To the fury of the Conservatives, they now had a voice on all parliamentary committees, including the military, whose leaders despised the opinions of civilians, let alone socialists.

The final blow fell when the kaiser's new chancellor, General von Caprivi, surprised even the kaiser by attempting to make Germany more democratic, end the dominance of Prussia in the Reich, and even cooperate with the Social Democrats. He also adopted a more conciliatory foreign policy and lowered grain tariffs that favored aristocratic landowners at consumers' expense. He even dared to cut the sacred budget of the army. Although Caprivi was a member of the German Conservative party, he shocked his colleagues by condemning their use of anti-Semitism as dangerous and self-defeating. Meanwhile the Progressives and Social Democrats attacked the informal, unconstitutional, and severe discrimination of the government, the civil service, and the army against Jews, but to no avail.

In rural Prussia, anti-Semitism grew among Protestant peasants, especially those still engaged in subsistence farming like their ancestors. The national market system of a unified Germany, bound together by railroads and unprotected by previous customs barriers, required that peasants develop new skills and find capital to produce cash crops. Banks avoided such risky loans, and moneylenders naturally charged high interest to cover numerous defaults. In much of rural Germany, Jews were moneylenders as well as cattle and fertilizer dealers, the main personal contact between peasants and the harsh imperatives of free competition in a national market. Hence peasants blamed Jews for usury, low crop prices, and the high price of new agrarian machinery and fertilizers. Capitalist-funded technology also made many traditional artisans' skills obsolete, as did free access to the crafts. As early as the 1840s artisans blamed Jewish politicians and entrepreneurs for both, especially in the textile industry, the first where handicraft skills were made obsolete.

Peasants and artisans who could not adjust were ruined. They could not understand the complexities of an economic system that was national in scope and managed from Berlin by non-Jews. Nor were they aware that previous discrimination had limited Jews to middlemen functions and moneylending, or that credit rates are not determined by ethnic or religious norms. (In Italy, for example, moneylenders were Italian Catholics; hence the naturally antagonistic relationship was without ethnic or religious implications.) Consequently in the 1890s small "single-issue" anti-Semitic parties emerged among rural folk in the north, and in 1893 they won sixteen seats in the Reichstag, close to 5 percent of the vote. In 1899 the most important such party called for a "final solution" by "annihilation." Although weak, the new parties began to attract voters away from the Conservative party, persuading more Conservative candidates to stress their anti-Semitism in future campaigns.

The German Conservative party was the most prestigious party in Germany, the party of military officers, high civil servants, aristocratic landowners, and the kaiser's court. Conservatives in the Prussian parliament had already voted 95 to 1 to support anti-Semitism. In 1892 the national leadership of the party took the same decision, responding to the demands of their constituencies, the threats posed by Caprivi, and the rise of Progressives and Social Democrats. Led by Pastor Stoecker and over Caprivi's objections, they adopted a sweeping platform intended to fight the "aggressive, decomposing, and arrogant" power of Jewry, demanding that Jews be banned from the civil service, the judiciary, and the teaching of non-Jews, with strict limits on other economic and cultural activities. Also in 1892 Conservative party leaders founded the most powerful and wealthy anti-Semitic lobby in Europe, the Agrarian Bund, and joined or supported the Pan German League, an anti-Semitic lobby for German imperialism. About one-third of the leaders of Pan German chapters were high school teachers, who always played a prominent role in reactionary politics and anti-Semitic agitation, indoctrinating their students as well.

The prestige of the Conservative party made anti-Semitic vituperation highly respectable. Because of their smallness, the populist anti-Semitic parties could vote but not speak in the Reichstag without their allies in the Conservative party giving permission. In 1895 the Conservatives allowed Hermann Ahlwardt, populist leader, Reichstag delegate, and publisher of anti-Semitic lies, to call for the extermination of the Jews. Discrimination had left only twelve Jewish teachers in all of Prussia—and Prussians constituted something like three-fifths of all Germans. The generation that came of age in the 1890s and 1900s—the one that included those who joined or supported the Nazis—studied under outspoken anti-Semites at all levels.

We would not be so surprised that a highly educated nation spawned the Nazis if we looked at the reading lists and textbooks in the schools that preceded them. University students enshrined the Prussian warrior ethic in their famed dueling fraternities and banned Jewish students, who promptly formed their own. The general and severe discrimination meant that Germans would not see Jews as teachers, academics, military officers, or civil servants, thus reinforcing inherited stereotypes by a self-fulfilling prophecy.

The most important white-collar organization, eager to identify with the elites, published vicious anti-Semitic literature through its own publishing house. Many middle-class students adopted reactionary anti-Semitism for the same reason, and because they feared Jewish competition in medicine or law. Once liberated, Jewish youth had rushed to qualify for both professions. Private practice protected them from institutional discrimination by public and private bureaucracies. Consequently the proportion of Jewish students in law and medicine was extremely high, usually about 30 percent.

In the elections of 1893, Conservative campaign literature insisted that Jews had no place in a Christian government. Caprivi's colleagues ostracized him for betraying autocratic ideals, and the moderate wing of the Conservative party lost their seats to reactionaries supported by racist demagogues. All together some 25 percent of the electorate voted for anti-Semites of different parties. Caprivi resigned. At a secret meeting of Conservative party leaders, Count Eulenberg, the reactionary and virulent anti-Semitic minister-president of Prussia, agreed to replace Caprivi, but only if universal suffrage were abolished. The kaiser consented, as did most of his colleagues, but Eulenberg refused because the vote was not unanimous. A true autocrat, the count would not submit himself to democratic votes. The party selected a political hack who would not toy with reform.

As demands for democracy and social reform increased, so

too did anti-Semitism. In the 1890s Heinrich von Treitschke, appointed royal historiographer by the kaiser because of his pro-Prussian and reactionary *History of Germany*—must reading for the middle and upper classes—lectured at the University of Berlin. The lecture hall was crowded with diplomats, aristocrats, military officers, and high civil servants who enthusiastically applauded as he praised Prussian autocracy; denounced liberalism, democracy, universal education, and socialist "treason"; and expressed his hope that one day Germany would defeat France and England and conquer the Slavic East. In the 1870s he had grudgingly admitted there were some good Jews; in the 1890s he accused them of collective guilt for Germany's subversive liberal and socialist trend. Calling Jews fierce opponents of Christian civilization and disseminators of "moral filth," he demanded that they be forbidden to serve in government, teaching, or the law. The Nazis distributed books including his words to German soldiers in World War II.

From the 1860s ugly stereotypes of Jews had appeared in extremely popular novels as well as nonfiction, including the fairy tales of the reactionary, ultra-nationalist brothers Grimm—edited out after 1945. Theodor Fritsch was possibly the most influential prewar anti-Semitic writer among the German lower middle classes. He owned an anti-Semitic publishing house, and his *Anti-Semitic Catechism* of 1896 warned Germans not to associate with Jews or read their liberal press, and above all to shun them: "Keep your blood pure" was one of the ten commandments of his book. Later titled *The Handbook of Anti-Semitism*, it appeared in thirty-seven editions by 1914; another eleven followed. His Hammerbund had a half-million supporters in 1913, and some important industrialists supported his attacks against "Jewish socialism" and labor unions. In the 1920s he translated the famous anti-Semitic articles of the automobile tycoon Henry Ford, but complained that Ford was wrong to think there were some good Jews. At Fritsch's funeral in 1933, Hitler himself gave the eulogy.

In the 1890s two German intellectuals, Paul de Lagarde and Julius Langbehn, wrote runaway best-sellers in which they insisted that Jewish influence had made Germany spiritually empty, bereft of ideals, a weak cosmopolitan democracy with a degenerate culture. The Jews worshiped only money, the god that destroyed all gods and reduced all values to market value. Both wanted a dictator to deal with them and abolish the Reichstag, a strongman who intuited the needs of the Volk (the people) as Hitler later claimed to do. Both hoped for a return to the tribal Teutonic warrior spirit in order to conquer republican France, home of the subversive principles of 1789, and launch a war for *Lebensraum* (living space) to resettle Germans in the East. Should the Russians object, they too must feel the wrath of the German sword. Both Lagarde and Langbehn wrote campaign propaganda for the Conservative party. Lagarde wrote of the Slavs: "The sooner they perish, the better it will be for them and us." Langbehn called for world domination. As for the Jews, "Destroy these usurious vermin. With bacteria one does not negotiate, one exterminates them as quickly and thoroughly as possible."

In 1899 H. S. Chamberlain published his instant best-seller *The Foundations of the Nineteenth Century*, idealizing all things Prussian. The only mistake of the ancient Teutonic tribes, he wrote, had been their failure to destroy all other peoples within reach. We must breed for superior types to defeat the Jews, he insisted. Other peoples were merely inferior; the Jews were uniquely evil and powerful. Enlightenment humanitarianism was simply a Jewish attempt to bring about the spiritual conquest of all true "Aryan" or Germanic civilization. The race that produced a Luther could destroy these money changers, but only if it purged itself of everything Jewish and began a racial war to the death.

Chamberlain enjoyed a lengthy personal correspondence of mutual Aryan admiration with Kaiser Wilhelm II—a privilege granted to few. Married into the Wagner family, Chamberlain met an admiring Hitler in Bayreuth in 1927. For Chamberlain, racism was a religion, and Wagner provided the sacred music. Wagner's public support of virulent anti-Semitic movements was crucial. For much of the German middle-class public and critics, he was much more than a great musician; he was the personification of the profundity of Aryan culture. His praise for the Aryan race brought a circle of sycophantic anti-Semites to Bayreuth to do homage; it was they who wrote the anti-Semitic petition of 1881, and with his blessing.

Chamberlain, Lagarde, and Langbehn, unlike many anti-Semites in the West, did not write for the ignorant, the uneducated, or the powerless. Their admirers came from the highest ranks of German society, including the kaiser, his military officers, and the aristocracy. Countless schoolteachers and academics were avid readers, as were members of German student organizations, middle-class youth movements, the Pan German League, the Agrarian Bund, the German Conservative party, and leaders of a variety of anti-Semitic movements. Their vicious attacks anticipated nearly all the ideas of Hitler and the Nazis.

From 1890 to 1914 German industry soared ahead of all European nations, with a corresponding increase in industrial workers and further erosion of rural conservative constituencies. From the 1890s forward, Progressives and especially Social Democrats dominated elections. In the elections of 1912, Conservatives lost nearly 30 percent of their seats, falling to 57; the small anti-Semitic parties lost half of theirs. But most spectacular was the rise of the Social Democrats from 43 to 110 seats; one-third of all German voters had given the Social Democrats one-fourth of all Reichstag seats.

Conservatives panicked. A parliamentary democracy would have had to form a new government from a coalition of socialists, Progressives, and National Liberals. But the kaiser ignored the electorate. Advised by generals, high civil servants, and industrialists, he appointed their creature, Theobald von

Bethmann-Hollweg, as chancellor, the last prime minister in Europe to appear before parliament in military uniform. He bypassed a Reichstag he could not control, but he and his masters knew that without public support, sooner or later they would lose their autocratic privileges and power.

The Conservative party responded to the shock of the 1912 elections with even more venomous anti-Semitism. Selecting a violent racist as publicity director, and joined by the Pan Germans and the Agrarian Bund, it called for a military dictatorship to punish Jews and socialists, and new groups added their voice. Jewish gold bought the elections; we must abolish the "Jewish" Reichstag, forbid Jewish political activities, or drive them out of Germany altogether. Heinrich Class, head of the elite Pan German League, published an extremely popular pamphlet demanding all this and more. There were no innocent Jews, he wrote. One day we will have to throw them out of Germany—indeed, "they might have to be wholly eliminated. . . . It is a matter of saving the German soul." The kaiser contemplated a military *putsch* and declared that Jews and socialists ought to be strung up. The Jews, fewer than 1 percent of the population, were trapped in a political struggle for Germany's future they could not influence. But the strength of the liberal and left opposition in the Reichstag prevented anti-Semitic legislation, and the elections of the 1890s and 1912 seemed to indicate that the power of the right would fade.

Unfortunately foreign policy was still the prerogative of the kaiser's ministers and generals, many of whom hoped to defeat their opponents by rallying Germans for a preventive war against Russia. Germany would become a true world power, and the old rulers would regain the prestige and admiration they had enjoyed after the defeat of France in 1870. The army demanded a huge increase in the military budget. The kaiser's advisers spoke of a reckoning of accounts with Jews and socialists, and the kaiser predicted a bloodbath against both if war came. During the intricate diplomatic maneuvers following the assassination of the Austrian Archduke Franz Ferdinand, the kaiser and the High Command assured Austria they would support any action needed to punish Serbia. Even Chancellor Bethmann-Hollweg feared his masters were going too far in their attempt to destroy the Progressives and socialists. The representatives of the people in the Reichstag were not informed, let alone consulted, about the warlike decisions. The government encouraged the press to describe Austria as the innocent victim of Serb terror, and France and Russia as joint conspirators out to destroy the Austrian Empire and with it German power in the East. But neither the German High Command nor any European military expert with access to power predicted the horrors of modern industrial warfare or the traumas that would rock Europe in its aftermath, and the intense challenges that would ultimately lead the elites to select Hitler as dictator.

THREE

Germany: Hitler, the Elites, and the Holocaust

B EFORE THE TRAUMAS of a lost war and economic collapse, the long history of anti-Semitism among German elites prepared the way for the rise of the Nazis. But during and just after World War I, when the Nazis did not exist or were still insignificant, the power of racism among leading groups intensified. In 1916 the prestigious *Prussian Yearbook* declared that the real enemy of Germany was international Jewry. In 1917 the Pan German League, Fritsch, and a variety of anti-Semitic organizations insisted that the Jews were deliberately sabotaging the war effort. The German High Command collected statistics hoping to show that Jews had avoided combat, but it did not publish them because they showed that Jewish frontline soldiers exceeded their proportion of the population, perhaps to demonstrate their patriotism after decades of slander. The Jewish businessman Walter Rathenau, in spite of directing the war economy brilliantly, was attacked for allegedly giving lucrative contracts to Jewish businessmen, hiring mainly Jewish firms, and even hindering the war effort. The Conservative party, the Agrarian Bund, and the Catholic Center demanded an investigation. The allegations proved false, yet only Jewish organizations, Progressives, and Social Democrats denounced them.

Cries of Jewish treason arose when the newly formed Independent Socialists, with many Jewish leaders, broke with the Social Democrats in 1917 and demanded an immediate end to the war. Extremists wanted them shot. When the Catholic Center party joined with the Social Democrats and the Progressives in July to propose discussions of peace without annexations, Pan Germans protested that the "Reichstag created by the Jewish vote [1912] wants to make a Jewish peace!" Bethmann-Hollweg was labeled the Chancellor of the Jews for opposing unrestricted submarine warfare; he was replaced by the military dictatorship of Generals Paul von Hindenburg and Erich Ludendorff. Ludendorff, Hitler's coconspirator in the *putsch* of 1923 and a Nazi Reichstag delegate, broke with Hitler later because he thought him too easy on the Jews, and spent his life writing vicious anti-Semitic and anti-Catholic pamphlets.

When the Germans defeated Russia in 1917, Ludendorff and the High Command insisted that bolshevism was Jewish. They planned an empire in the East and aimed to deport Jews and Poles in order to supplant them with German settlers—anticipating the Nazi call for *Lebensraum*. At the armistice, Conservative party publicists wrote of the "stab in the back" of the German army by Jewish pacifists, leftist strikers, and Jewish black marketers. In November 1918, when the High Command informed the kaiser that he must resign, a livid Wilhelm blamed the Jews and lamented they had not been gassed in 1914—as Hitler also wrote in letters from the front and in *Mein Kampf*. Admiral Alfred von Tirpitz founded an anti-Semitic Fatherland's party in 1918 with strong ties to the military and industry; by 1920 it had about a million lower-middle-class members led by military leaders and respected Conservatives.

But threats to the old ruling classes intensified. Councils of Workers and Soldiers sprang up, leftist but democratic, demanding that a voluntary civilian militia replace the German army. The collapse of the Habsburg Empire left Austrians stranded in a tiny and impoverished nation bordered by newly independent, Allied-supported states ruled by the Slavs whom the Germans despised. In January 1919 the new German Communist party, the Spartacists, revolted in Berlin. Karl Liebknecht and Rosa Luxemburg, both of Jewish origin, led the Spartacists, though the overwhelming majority of their followers were Gentiles. Communists, some also of Jewish origin, declared a Bavarian Soviet Republic in February after a rightist assassinated the legally elected Social Democratic leader. Above all, the January 1919 elections to draft a new constitution gave the Social Democrats the highest vote, 38 percent, the new German Democratic party 19 percent, and the Independent Socialists nearly 8 percent; the German Conservative party faded to 10 percent. Democracy threatened to end its privileges and power.

The right swiftly recovered. Rightist volunteers destroyed the Bavarian Soviet, and the government and army easily crushed the Spartacists, whose leaders were arrested and murdered. In May 1919 the newly revealed terms of the dictated Versailles Treaty infuriated nearly all Germans. The Allies had burdened the infant republic with responsibility for a war started by the imperial autocracy, practically abolished the navy, and reduced the army to 100,000 soldiers, stripped of tanks and aircraft. German territories and colonies were seized, depriving her of some three-quarters of her iron ore and one-third of her coal. Immense reparations were demanded. The Social Democratic government refused to sign the suicidal document. When the Allies threatened to invade, the High Command secretly informed the chancellor that Germany could not resist, thus successfully shifting the blame for accepting the hated treaty to the governing Social Democrats they detested.

Racist and anti-Semitic groups now proliferated. The German Conservative party, now renamed the German National People's party (Deutschnationale Volkspartei, or DNVP), allied itself with several smaller and more extremist groups, one of which called for death to the Jews. Count Kuno von Westarp, DNVP leader, found that maligning the Jews brought cheers at meetings of conservative supporters. By the mid-1920s the DNVP campaign propaganda was practically as racist as that of the Nazis. The Agrarian Bund, powerful prewar lobby of the landed aristocracy, declared war against the new Weimar Republic and Jewry. In 1919 the veterans' organization, the Stahlhelm, one million members strong, vowed it would fight to eliminate the "Republic of Jewish traitors." "Kill them, kill them all," declared the leader of the Pan Germans, Heinrich Class, whose directors decided to use the Jews as a "lightning rod" for Germany's suffering in order to divert blame from those who had really started and lost the war. In 1920 a German Racist League for Defense and Attack, with a quarter-million dues-paying members, distributed more than seven million anti-Semitic leaflets. One branch declared, "It is absolutely necessary to kill the Jews."

In 1919, led by General Walther von Luettwitz and Ludendorff, former army officers organized a Freikorps of some 270,000 uniformed fighters, supplied with secret funds and weapons by the army. Battling workers and socialists in Germany, they also invaded the Baltic States and the former Prussian Poland to restore the dominance of German aristocratic landowners and carve out estates for themselves. Eventually they hoped to destroy the republic. Brutal killers, most of their units were as anti-Semitic as the Nazis many later joined. Hundreds of thousands of Germans joined dozens of other armed reactionary anti-Semitic paramilitary groups. In 1920, when Hitler and the Nazis were small and unknown outside Munich, the paramilitary Orgesch counted 300,000 members, 2.5 million rifles, 3,000 artillery pieces, and 30 aircraft. Its second in command, Rudolf Kanzler, wrote, "Our race must unite to eliminate the international Jewish rabble, which sucks the last drop of blood from our veins." The Young German Order, 200,000 strong and allied with the DNVP, fought to return Prussian Poland to German rule, modeling themselves on the Teutonic Knights, the medieval monastic order that sought to convert or slaughter the Slavic peoples and resettle Germans on their lands.

Flaunting the swastika, the Thule Society for Aryans, founded in 1912, met in Munich in 1918. It enjoyed close ties with wealthy Bavarian families, the Bavarian military, and the hundreds of thousands of followers of the Hammerbund of Theodore Fritsch, Germany's most popular anti-Semite. Both groups called for the destruction of the Jews. Many Thule Society members influenced or joined the Nazis, including Alfred Rosenberg, Dietrich Eckart (to whom Hitler dedicated *Mein Kampf*), and Father Bernhard Stempfle, editor of an anti-Semitic paper and Hitler's unnamed coauthor of the book. Influential and wealthy organizations of displaced and anti-Semitic German aristocrats from the Baltic and Russian nobles thrived in Germany. A former tsarist officer published the infamous *Protocols of the Elders of Zion* and wrote in a Berlin newspaper that the "final solution" to the "Jewish problem" was extermination.

In March 1920 Ludendorff and General Luettwitz joined with Wolfgang Kapp, an important civil servant and leader of anti-Semitic groups, to overthrow the republic. The High Command had indicated it would defend the republic only against leftists. It did not join Kapp for fear of a French invasion, but it issued much anti-Semitic propaganda to aid his cause. Business leaders, who despised the democratic republic with its social reforms, stayed neutral. The government fled Weimar, first calling for a general strike and opening government arsenals to the workers. Kapp had to back down. His second in command commented bitterly, "Within our circle there is no enthusiasm left for anything now except anti-Semitic agitation." In Bavaria successful *putschists* led by Gustav von Kahr and Bavarian army units declared they would destroy "Jewish Marxists." Rightist paramilitaries flocked there to fight the Bavarian left, and the Bavarian police enlisted a secret assassination squad called Organization C to help them.

By 1920 only the Social Democrats and the Democrats still believed in the Weimar Republic; to most it was only a forced consequence of defeat. Reactionary groups had hated it from the start, of course, and university academics also attacked the Jews and "their" republic. All national student organizations now barred Jews; physical attacks against Jewish students were common and tolerated by many academics. Catholic student organizations discriminated against converts of Jewish origin in spite of the hierarchy's orders. Lutheran pastors despised the republic, and when it tried to cut their state subsidies, it only reinforced the pastors' Prussian autocratic values. In countless sermons pastors denounced Jews, socialists, and the republic. Racism proved effective. In the elections of June 1920 the Social Democrats lost nearly half their previous votes, the Democrats more than half.

Hitler arrived in Munich in 1919, an army agent who contacted radical right organizations to see if they deserved support with arms and funds—usually directed through Ludendorff. In September Hitler joined the small circle of craftsmen forming the nucleus of the Nazi party. He might not have risen far in the larger organizations led by important officers and politicians. His charismatic speaking attracted those with similar hatreds, and the SA, his brown-shirted storm troopers, battled constantly with leftists. The Nazis received funds from the army, from wealthy Munich families, and 100,000 gold marks from the industrialist Fritz Thyssen. By late 1922 the party numbered some 35,000, the SA 15,000; in 1923 Hitler recruited the SS as his personal bodyguard. Party members were never merely uneducated brutes; some 12 percent came from the upper classes—university students and sons of military officers and higher civil servants. Most of the rest were lower-middle-class craftsmen, white-collar workers, and merchants. Industrial workers remained loyal to the Social Democrats.

Hitler's chance came in 1923 when German currency was destroyed by inflation and the French exploited a minor default in reparations deliveries to invade the Ruhr and separate the Rhineland from Germany. Hitler's famous *putsch* in November failed, but his ensuing trial for high treason in 1924 brought him national fame as the most determined revolutionary of the right. The judges, nationalist reactionaries like the judiciary in general, allowed Hitler to spout political harangues as he claimed full responsibility. They had to find him guilty of treason, but they issued a ridiculously light sentence; he was out of jail in thirteen months. Even so, the DNVP was furious at his conviction, and the bourgeois press gave him favorable coverage. Writing *Mein Kampf* in his comfortable cell, Hitler decided to reorganize the party to compete for votes in the "dirty parliamentary game." In 1925 he reassured the prime minister of Bavaria that he intended no more *putsches*.

From 1893 through 1928, votes for anti-Semitic candidates had ranged from 25 percent to 34 percent. Hitler's singularity lay not in his hatred of the Jews but in his ability to unite those who already shared his hatreds. Prohibited from public speaking until 1927, he placed his loyalists in all important positions. The elections of 1928 shocked the right. The DNVP won only 14.2 percent of the vote, the Nazis a mere 2.6 percent, though about 12 percent went to other racists. The Social Democrats campaigned against government spending for battleships rather than for ordinary Germans and won 30 percent of the vote, more than twice the percentage of any other party. In spite of the lost war, the treaty, and the inflation, the Weimar Republic seemed secure. The Social Democrat Heinrich Mueller became chancellor of a coalition that included the Catholic Center and the German People's party (DVP), a business party led by Gustav Stresemann. Ominously, both the Catholic Center under Father Ludwig Kaas and the DVP were growing more anti-Semitic.

After 1928 Hindenburg, the army, the DNVP, and business leaders desperately hoped to find a way to crush the Social Democrats. Meanwhile Hitler and the Nazi party directorate realized they had been wrong to concentrate on big cities and industrial areas against powerful competition from Social Democratic workers. In 1929 the Nazis began to campaign furiously in rural Germany, where most Germans lived and where many towns and villages had been bastions of anti-Semitism since the 1880s. Conducting seemingly endless political campaigns, the party co-opted local anti-Semitic groups who looked to belong to a united national movement. The Nazis repeated the old falsehoods: Jewish rural middlemen charge high prices for farm needs and pay low prices for farm products; Jewish moneylenders exploit indebted farmers with usurious interest rates; Jewish firms import frozen meat and cheap grain; Jewish speculators buy bankrupt farmers' land and possessions dirt cheap at auction, and the "Jewish Republic" does nothing to help. And it was true that the governments of the republic, Social Democrats and business parties alike, ignored small farmers and rural artisans, believing that they must inevitably succumb to large-scale farming and mass production. Above all, unlike other parties, the Nazis did more than talk. They actively led those who disrupted farm auctions, often going to jail with them.

Nazi campaign propaganda also aimed at middle-class fears of "Jewish socialism" and "Judeo-bolshevism." Trained Nazi speakers insisted that Jewish international bankers had set the reparations terms of the Versailles Treaty and caused the inflation that destroyed so many. Jewish-owned department stores, they declared, ruined small retailers and artisans with cheap prices for shoddy, mass-produced goods. A Nazi poster declared, "Annihilate the gravediggers of the Mittelstand!" To win the Catholic vote, Hitler purged Nazi anti-Catholics, and party leaders raged against the fate of priests under "Jewish" Bolshevik atheists. Like prewar anti-Semites, Nazi propagandists told the industrial proletariat that international Jewish financiers and Jewish socialist leaders, not honest Aryan industrialists, were their real enemies. Nazis did not attract the proletarian vote, but industrialists understood the signal that they were not Nazi targets. The Nazis also denounced as "Cultural and Jewish Bolsheviks" those Weimar leftists who attacked the autocratic and militaristic values of the old rulers. The Nazis despised the bohemian and anarchistic style of Weimar culture and its sexual liberation, highly offensive to most Germans and viewed as an attempt to destroy Christian moral values. Himmler collected lists of homosexuals and pointed out that the Germanic tribes had killed such deviants while now the Social Democrats defended them.

The depression gave Hindenburg the chance to rid himself of the Social Democrats. In 1930 rising unemployment exhausted the unemployment relief fund, and Chancellor Mueller tried to restore benefits with higher taxes and increased contributions from workers and employers. But a storm of protest from businessmen—organized by Alfred Hugenberg, leader of the DNVP, and Hjalmar Schacht, head of the Reichsbank and later Hitler's finance minister—split the coalition government. Corporations demanded government cutbacks in relief and welfare, lower wages, and lower taxes on capital, arguing that increased investment would restart production. But declining purchasing power had reduced the demand for products. Lower taxes on capital would not lead to investment in pointless increased production but would simply deplete public resources. Deficit spending and public works would have eased the depression, as with the American New Deal, or even ended it, as in Social Democratic Sweden, but business groups and the old rulers would not allow it.

Refusing a moderate compromise offered by the Social Democrats, in March 1930 President Hindenburg dismissed the government and appointed as chancellor Heinrich Bruening, a monarchist whose Catholic Center party had received just 12 percent of the vote in 1928. Bruening cut wages and unemployment benefits, fired civil servants or slashed their salaries, increased taxes on lower-income groups, cut taxes on business, subsidized export businesses, and used government powers to side with business in labor disputes. When the Reichstag rejected Bruening's proposals, Hindenburg granted him the emergency powers allowed by the Weimar constitution, powers that Hindenburg had refused the majority Social Democrats he detested. From 1930 on, no chancellor had a parliamentary majority. Three years before Hitler was selected chancellor, parliamentary democracy was ended by those who had always hated it.

From the start of his career, Hitler had favored the influential groups he needed to become chancellor. In return, from 1919 through 1945 the German elites were strongly overrepresented among the Nazis in proportion to their numbers of the population. In 1921 Hitler dropped from the original party program demands for worker profit-sharing and the nationalization of cartels. He prevented attempts to form Nazi trade unions. He forbade Nazis to support Reichstag proposals to tax corporations in order to compensate creditors harmed by anti-inflation measures, demanding instead that the money be seized from Jews. In 1925 some Nazi Reichstag delegates tried to support a Social Democratic attempt to expropriate the great wealth of the many German princes. Calling the proposal a "Jewish-Marxist swindle," Hitler again demanded that Jewish assets be expropriated instead. Princes became large contributors to the Nazis. In his trial in 1924 Hitler assured the army he was their most zealous supporter. When the High Command, mostly DNVP members, complained that younger officers distributed pro-Nazi literature in army barracks, Hitler publicly disavowed his disciples and declared he would never undermine the authority of the generals.

In July 1929 Hitler's efforts won him an invitation to join DNVP conservatives in a meeting to protest a new plan for reparations payments. Among the attendees were Hugenberg and DNVP dignitaries, Heinrich Class and Pan German leaders, the heads of the Stahlhelm and Fatherland's party, representatives of German industry, an assortment of princes and aristocrats, and some 400 delegates from racist groups. They wrote a referendum calling for a "Law Against the Enslavement of the German People," making it treason for any German official to pay reparations; 6 million Germans voted "yes" to it, but 21 million were needed. Yet Hitler had gained respectability among the upper classes and months of free publicity from Hugenberg's media empire of newsreels, newspapers, and films. In May 1930 when Otto Strasser, Hitler's leading party rival, demanded that the Nazis support the nationalization of some industries, Hitler replied, "Do you think I want to destroy the German economy?" When Strasser demanded concessions to the proletariat, Hitler exploded, "We are making a racial not a social revolution!" He expelled Strasser from the party. In 1929 a Nazi election leaflet declared of the Jews: "When we have the power of the state in our hands [we] will thoroughly annihilate this international racial parasite."

Chancellor Bruening, now commonly labeled the "Hunger Chancellor," called for new elections for September 1930 and decreed still more austerity measures. The Hohenzollern crown prince joined the SA and campaigned with Hermann Goering. Hitler ceremoniously dropped a Nazi platform proposal calling for land reform and limits to the size of estates, declaring that only Jewish land would be seized. The Nazis' single-minded campaign against the Jews led to the astounding Nazi vote of 18 percent—in some rural districts they received 40 percent. They were now the second-largest party after the Social Democrats. The DNVP needed Hitler all the more because their vote had sunk to a miserable 7 percent, and they were widely and correctly dismissed as second-rate Nazis interested only in protecting their own wealth. The Social Democrats fell to 25 percent as unemployed workers gave the Communists a new high of 13 percent. The mutual hatred between Socialists and Communists, and Stalin's decree that the reformist Social Democrats merely prolonged capitalism and were worse than the Nazis, prevented cooperation on the left.

Nazi votes offered the establishment a legal way to rid itself of the republic. Two weeks after the elections, Hitler announced that if given power he would replace the constitution and form state tribunals to punish those responsible for Germany's misfortunes—everyone knew who he meant. Hitler also assured the army he would never allow the SA to replace them, as some militant Nazis wished. A leading general remarked that the army almost unanimously desired Hitler in the government. Hugenberg told Hitler that the DNVP agreed with him on everything, including anti-Semitism, but feared he might introduce populist economic policies. In private meetings, Hitler and other Nazi leaders assured businessmen that they believed in private property and profit. In March 1931 the Nazi *Voelkische Beobachter* announced: "The abolition of capitalism has been nothing more than an empty slogan." In the summer of 1931 Hitler made a fund-raising tour. Now that the Nazis were serious contenders for power, significant corporate funds flowed to them.

In October 1931 the Nazis and the DNVP joined in the Harzburg Front in Brunswick, a state governed by a Nazi/DNVP coalition that routinely harassed the Jewish community. Present were Hugenberg, the Stahlhelm chiefs, the Hohenzollern crown prince, Hindenburg, leaders of the Agrarian Bund and Fatherland's party, representatives of Ruhr industrialists, a former president of the Reichsbank, and other prestigious reactionaries. Again Hitler gained much favorable coverage in the conservative press. But he kept a low profile because disgruntled SA members denounced him publicly and even briefly mutinied in Berlin, accusing him of selling out to the upper classes. A week later Hitler publicly attended a mass march of his 225,000 SA to reassure party critics. But Nazi membership increased sevenfold from 1930 through 1932, and half of new members came from the upper classes.

When President Hindenburg's term expired in May 1932, Hitler ran against him, and the DNVP ran Theodor Duesterberg of the Stahlhelm. Hindenburg won 49 percent, Hitler 30 percent, Duesterberg 7 percent. In the runoff vote between Hitler and Hindenburg, the president was enraged because the DNVP instructed its voters to shift to Hitler, deserting their former hero and eager to give Hitler the crucial emergency powers of the presidency. The Social Democrats, desperate to stop Hitler, told their supporters to vote for Hindenburg in order to stop a Hitler dictatorship. Hindenburg then defeated Hitler by 53 percent to 37 percent, but Hitler had picked up the previous DNVP percentage. Some wealthy urban districts deserted to the Nazis rather than support the swiftly collapsing DNVP and business parties. The Nazis also won leading or commanding positions in five state elections. In Prussia, business corporations made heavy contributions to Hitler in order to defeat the Social Democratic government. The Nazis soared from 6 to 162 seats; the socialists sank from 136 to 94—three-fifths of all Germans lived in Prussia. In Bavaria the Nazis equaled the previously dominant and also anti-Semitic Catholic Bavarian People's party—each won one-third of the vote. Two-thirds of Bavarians had voted for anti-Semites. It was obvious that the Nazis would win the next national elections.

When Bruening tried to raise taxes on corporations, his business supporters deserted him. Aristocratic landowners defected when he tried to end the "*osthilfe*" subsidies—millions of marks given to large landowners ostensibly to save German agriculture but criminally spent on personal luxuries. Aristocrats had presented Hindenburg, who owned no land, with a large estate to qualify him for subsidies as well. Hindenburg suddenly discovered that Bruening's government was unpopular, and on May 29, 1932, he harshly dismissed him—the same day the Nazis won 48 percent of the vote in a local election. Hindenburg named as chancellor Franz von Papen, a Catholic monarchist who admired Lueger, the famous Catholic anti-Semitic mayor of prewar Vienna.

Papen ended the threats to corporations and landowners

and added yet more austerity policies at the expense of workers and the middle class. In a deal with Hitler, on June 4 he called for new elections. Even the international press predicted a Nazi victory. After Papen lifted a ban on the SA imposed by Bruening, the SA and Communists battled in the streets; eighty died in Prussia alone. Papen then used an emergency decree to depose the Social Democratic government of Prussia and impose martial law, thus punishing the Social Democrats for the violence of Nazis and Communists. The last obstacle to Nazi rule was gone. The SA marched singing, "Now we will destroy this goddamned Jewish Republic," and upper-class notables campaigned for the Nazis.

In the elections of July 31 the Nazis won 37 percent of the vote and 230 seats to become the largest party in Germany. Nazi votes came from those groups that had tended to be anti-Semitic since the 1870s or before: rural voters, religious fundamentalists, artisans, small businessmen, civil servants, white-collar workers, clerks in state and private bureaucracies, and voters in some wealthy districts. The remaining small anti-Semitic parties lost their votes to the Nazis. The Catholic hierarchy had withdrawn earlier objections to Nazi paganism, and Catholics voted for Hitler in practically the same proportions as Protestants.

Army officers, aristocrats, bureaucrats, church leaders, and many business leaders wanted Hitler named chancellor. In a democracy, Hindenburg would have had to appoint him, as he was head of the largest party. But, still wary of the economic populism and military ambitions of many SA leaders, the president offered him instead the office of vice chancellor. Hitler refused, demanding to be chancellor and with full presidential emergency powers to boot. After a humiliating vote of no confidence, Papen set new elections for November 6, 1932. The Nazis dropped to 33 percent of the vote but remained the largest party; the Social Democrats received 20 percent and the Communists an alarming 16 percent. Still hesitant, in

December 1932 Hindenburg appointed General Kurt von Schleicher chancellor. He was a man with no independent power base who the elites assumed would protect the status quo.

In a radio talk to the nation, Schleicher shocked Hindenburg and the establishment by proposing to ease austerity policies, cooperate with Social Democrats and trade unions, cut the *"osthilfe,"* and seize a million acres of idle land for the poor. He also considered creating public works projects and nationalizing the coal and steel industries. Furious Conservatives denounced this betrayal by the "Red General," and an enraged Hindenburg denied Schleicher the emergency powers he wanted to dissolve the Reichstag, postpone elections for three months, and outlaw both the Nazis and the Communists. The leaders of the highly racist Agrarian Bund, with close to five million members, complained bitterly to Hindenburg about Schleicher's attack on their import quotas.

In December Papen, angry that Schleicher refused to appoint him minister of economics—where he could protect the economic interests of the conservatives—told the upper-class Gentlemen's Club that Schleicher should not outlaw Hitler but bring him into the government. The banker Kurt von Schroeder, head of the club and a DNVP member about to join the Nazis, met with Papen to discuss appointing Hitler chancellor. On January 22 Hitler met privately with the president's son Oskar and may have threatened to publicize the *"osthilfe"* scandals and even impeach Hindenburg. Oskar then declared that Hitler must be chancellor. On January 30, 1933, Hindenburg appointed Hitler.

Hitler immediately silenced criticism of the scandals, gave President Hindenburg thousands of acres of land, promoted Oskar to general, and made Papen vice chancellor and minister of economics. In March, Gustav Krupp and leading businessmen financed another election for Hitler; Goering assured them it was probably the last. The Nazis received 44 percent of the vote, the Conservatives 8 percent. Terrorism kept many oppo-

nents from the polls, but even so, 18 percent voted for the Social Democrats and 12 percent for the Communists.

Some say Hindenburg and the elites appointed Hitler because they feared communism, but any conceivable government
would have easily crushed a Communist uprising, as the Social
Democrats themselves had done in 1919. Others wonder why
Hindenburg and his advisers did not hold off when Hitler's
votes declined in November, but the small decline made Hitler
even more necessary: he was their last hope of destroying the
hated republic. Most think the elites naively believed they
could moderate Hitler's extremism. But they themselves wished
to destroy the Weimar Republic, tear up the Versailles Treaty,
rearm Germany, restore autocratic rule, forge an empire in the
East, destroy the left, and punish the Jews—part of their program since 1892 and of the anti-Semitic organizations they controlled. They did not even try to keep Hitler as chancellor,
where they would have had some control over him; instead they
voted Hitler full dictatorial powers in the famous Enabling Act
of March 1933. Only the socialists, led by the brave Otto Wels,
voted against it. Communist deputies were in jail, underground,
or in exile. The Vatican encouraged the Catholic Center party
to agree to its own dissolution. In June 1934 the High Command informed Hitler that he could combine the office of chancellor and president when Hindenburg died if he agreed to
purge those SA leaders who, led by Ernst Roehm, hoped to replace the army and the establishment in general. Hitler obliged
by having Roehm and his followers murdered—and Schleicher
as well. When Hindenburg died in August, the army swore an
unprecedented oath of personal allegiance to Hitler.

Although many honorable members of the old elites despised Hitler, the bulk of the resistance to the Nazis came from
the left. In the first year alone about 100,000 leftists were
hunted down, tortured, imprisoned, sent to concentration
camps, or killed. Thousands went into exile, and about 800,000
were imprisoned for resistance during the Third Reich. Tens of

thousands of German workers carried out numerous strikes and work slowdowns, interpreted by the Gestapo as disguised anti-Nazi demonstrations. Some generals tried to contact the Allies in 1939 when they thought Hitler would start a war they would lose; but they stopped in 1940 when France was defeated and the English driven from the continent. Two attempts by leftists to assassinate Hitler in the 1930s have received far less attention than the July 1944 effort by military and aristocratic leaders, led by Klaus von Stauffenberg. But by then a powerful Soviet offensive and the Allied landing in France had made it obvious that the war was lost. Moreover the July conspirators—the best of the elites—wanted the Jews removed or at least denied citizenship in any new Germany. Most also wished to preserve some of Hitler's conquests; none thought Poland should be independent.

The extent of anti-Semitism among the old elites is shown by the simple truth that tens of thousands of the old ruling classes voluntarily cooperated with the persecution and murder of the Jews. Careerism played a role, of course, but by itself it cannot explain away complicity in mass murder among the "best" people. For example, one-third of the officers of the *Einsatzgruppen*, the notorious killing squads that murdered some 1.5 million Jews, held university degrees at a time when less than 10 percent of the relevant age groups attended universities. Among the killers, lawyers and the sons of aristocrats, higher civil servants, and military officers were highly overrepresented. The leaders of the German army, aristocrats almost to a man, repeatedly urged their troops to aid the killers. In 1939 a leaflet to all officers from the High Command called the war a conflict with world Jewry "to be fought like a poisonous parasite." Another leaflet informed the troops that "the war is the decisive battle against Jewish world-democracy." In 1941 the High Command wrote of the Bolsheviks, "We would insult the animals if we were to describe these men, who are mostly Jewish, as beasts. . . . [They are] filled with a satanic and insane hatred against the whole of noble humanity." Similar statements abound. Himmler was pleased by the cooperation of the army in the anti-Semitic campaign. When German troop trains rolled into Poland in September, many had "Death to the Jews" scrawled on their sides. The German High Command had agreed in 1939 to help the special killing units.

High civil servants, also from the "best" families, competed for positions in the "racial purification" taking place in the East. Ninety percent of the German judiciary joined the Nazis voluntarily, enforcing Nazi terror on condition that it was legalized—something the regime itself wanted. High officials of the Foreign Office, usually recruited from the aristocracy, spread anti-Semitic propaganda and defended anti-Semitic laws abroad, and helped pressure nations allied with or occupied by Germany to surrender their Jews for the death camps. In Serbia in the spring of 1941, officials from the Foreign Office encouraged the German army to kill thousands of Jews because the camps were not yet ready to kill so many victims.

From 1930 on, university students, most of them children of the elites, supported the Nazis in greater proportion than the German public, and Nazi students controlled all major student organizations. Many academics condoned or ignored student punitive actions against Jewish academics and students. Anthropologists, physicians, and professors of "racial hygiene" helped train SS troops and lectured on racial science to concentration camp guards. Many geneticists, biologists, and physicians who held important positions at leading journals and in professional societies had supported the drive for "racial purity" before the appearance of the Nazis. In 1922 the leading textbook on genetics in Germany had spoken of the noble Aryans and described the innate evils of the "Semitic race." Its three authors later helped plan the killings in the East. Dr. Josef Mengele, the notorious physician of Auschwitz, was not the unique monster civilized Westerners understandably wish to believe. A research professor of genetics at the prestigious Kaiser

Wilhelm Institute in Berlin, in Auschwitz Mengele conducted research on twins and regularly sent back his findings. Many of his fellow scholars competed for similar positions. It is a measure of the sincerity of their racial hatred that after the war a faculty committee cleared Mengele of any wrongdoing at Auschwitz. He fled only when the Americans hunted him. Hundreds of physicians, perhaps thousands, participated in racial selections or murder. Scholars at famous universities used the bodies of camp victims for research and sent graduate students to train the SS in the best methods for killing so as to preserve body parts for study. Physicians and lawyers managed the euthanasia program, helping to murder some 100,000 disabled persons or those assumed to have hereditary diseases; many physicians later worked in the East. Jewish patients in nursing homes were killed even if they did not meet the criteria. Six euthanasia killing centers were located in Germany, and by 1940 it was well known even among German children that people were being gassed or shot there. Months after the war ended, American occupation troops discovered physicians and nurses still killing infants deemed unworthy of life.

The Nazis did not force industrialists, who represented almost all important German firms, to accept slave laborers, as Volkswagen and others still claimed in 2000. In fact industrialists competed for forced and slave labor, and executives bribed Nazi officials for permission to build factories in or near the camps in order to exploit inmate labor. The average slave laborer lasted some three months, but the Nazis did not insist that corporations starve or brutalize them. Corporate management could easily have fed their slave laborers better, justifying the expense as necessary for vital war work, but profits came first, and there were millions more potential workers in the East. Corporate middle managers sometimes recommended that the SS gas workers too sick to work efficiently.

The behavior of the German churches during the Nazi era betrayed their centuries-old claim of moral superiority. The

German Protestant church did not protect even converted Jews, that is, Christians of Jewish origin, though the Confessing Church, which comprised about one-fourth of all Evangelical pastors, tried to. For the Jews themselves, however, neither the Catholic nor the Protestant clergy did anything. Before the war the official handbook for German priests supported the right of a nation to purify its blood, but it recommended methods consistent with Christianity without further specification. Official church writings denounced the Jews as revolutionary Bolsheviks—even though almost all German Jews voted for liberals, and in the East the vast majority of Jews were orthodox or Zionist. Pius XII did not speak out when Jews were murdered, but he also kept silent when the Nazis murdered 18 percent of all Polish Catholic priests. Both the German Protestant and Catholic churches blessed Hitler's war, used forced labor to build churches, congratulated Hitler on escaping assassination in 1944, and prayed for victories in the East though they knew that each day thousands of Jews and other civilians were being slaughtered. German priests followed the army into Russia as missionaries. A handful of religious martyrs spoke out in Germany, but their colleagues usually shunned them as a dangerous embarrassment. Oddly enough, those who sacrificed the most against the Nazis tended to be secular nonbelievers and leftists. But most leading Christians in other nations denounced the Nazis, and many implored the pope to speak out. Thousands of Christians risked their lives to protect Jews in occupied nations.

Although anti-Semitism was stronger elsewhere, only Germany had the industrial might and political will to conquer Poland and western Russia, where the vast majority of Jews lived. The drive for *Lebensraum* in the East was hardly original with the Nazis; it had been the goal of some Prussian rulers well before 1914. For the Nazis, the war and the Holocaust were interconnected. Without destroying the Jews and millions of Poles, Germany would simply conquer new problems instead of raw materials, slave labor, and above all land for "Aryan" settlers. But until Hitler could rebuild the army and stock food-stuffs and war materiel, he needed peace, easily granted by Western leaders who had no need for war and voters who feared a repeat of the horrors of 1914–1918. British Prime Minister Neville Chamberlain unjustly serves as the symbol of appeasement, but all Western leaders, including Franklin Roosevelt, and their voters approved it, excluding the left.

By 1937, with some 74 percent of the budget devoted to rearmament, Germany reached the peak of its capacity for weapons production. Waiting longer would give Germany's foes time to rearm and render German arms obsolete; Hitler told his military and political leaders to prepare to march. The building of Buchenwald began. German troops marched into Austria in March 1938. By 1938 German Jews lived in near ghetto conditions. In July 1938 Roosevelt called the Evian Conference to see if nations would accept German Jewish refugees, but he merely wished to mollify humanitarian opinion. America itself had millions of anti-Semites, some in Congress and the State Department, and no nation wanted a significant number of the approximately 300,000 remaining German Jews. The German press gloated over Western hypocrisy, and Nazi leaders knew that no nation would accept the impoverished Jewish millions of the East.

The Polish government, anxious to rid itself of Jews, tried to stop Polish Jews residing abroad from returning to Poland, requiring them to have their passports revalidated by Polish counsels before November 1938. The Germans abruptly swept up seventeen thousand Poles and dumped them over the Polish border. In Paris, Herschel Grynspan, the son of a family so treated, murdered Ernst vom Rath, a minor German consular official. The Nazi leadership seized this excuse to allow the frustrated SA to attack Jews and burn synagogues during *Kristallnacht* in November. But Hitler believed that pogroms were simply emotional and ineffective. The Jews must be battled systematically, he wrote, with the "ultimate goal . . . the elimination of the Jews altogether." The following week Nazi leaders made plans to eliminate Jews from German society and discussed labor camps, ghettos, and even methods for killing vast numbers in the East. In 1938 the first killing units were organized. In 1939 Hitler told his generals, "Poland will be depopulated and settled with Germans. . . . The fate of Russia will be exactly the same." The killers were already operating in Poland during the Polish campaign in 1939.

Notwithstanding these decisions and activities, many still think the Nazi decision to kill all Jews within Germany's reach came only with the invasion of the Soviet Union. They point out that in the 1930s the Nazis considered shipping German Jews to Madagascar. But nineteenth-century anti-Semites had proposed this idea and assumed that the Jews would not survive there. And why would the SS, which would have supervised any such deportation, treat the Jews differently in Madagascar than in Poland? With the collapse of Poland and the power of the British navy, it was far easier to murder the Jews in Poland. It made no sense to the Nazi leadership to allow millions of Jews, assumed to be mortal enemies, to survive. After all, the Nazis were about to murder tens of thousands of harmless German Gentiles in the euthanasia program. The Jews of Poland would have been eliminated and millions of Poles would have been enslaved or killed even if the Soviet Union had never been invaded. While the West floundered in the depression, even the German proletariat, the Nazis believed, would be content once they shared in the prosperity brought by the new empire and the destruction of "Judeo-bolshevism" in the Soviet Union.

Within three months of the invasion of Poland, the Germans had killed five thousand Jewish civilians and thousands of Poles. Experiments with mobile gassing vans and the building of Auschwitz began in 1940. The efficient killing gas, Zyclon B, was discovered in 1941 by an Austrian firm. The planning of ghettos for Polish Jews probably began in 1938. But as one administrator of the program said in December 1939, the ghettos were temporary: "The final goal must be that we ceaselessly burn out this plague boil." The calls for death to the Jews were neither secret nor rare, and they did not begin with Hitler's famous speech of January 1939. Simply put, no civilized person in a liberal nation could believe it. Only now, with "ethnic cleansing," are we beginning to understand the terrible power of decades of the ideology and politics of hate.

FOUR

The Austrian Empire Through 1918

RACISM AND ANTI-SEMITISM were more intense and widespread among the Germans of the Austrian Empire* than in Germany itself. From 1882 through 1914 demonstrations and riots against Jews and Slavs abounded, and anti-Semitic political parties were supported by millions. In 1911, the last election in the empire, roughly two of three Germans voted for anti-Semitic candidates. By 1935 the authoritarian Catholic government of the Fatherland Front restricted Jewish rights, but the violently extremist Austrian Nazis were the most popular party. When German troops occupied Austria in 1938, widespread looting and physical attacks against Jews occurred with far more popular participation than had ever been experienced in Germany. With the important exception of the Social Democrats, practically all Austrians wanted severe restrictions against the Jews. Proportionately far more Austrians than Germans joined the Nazi party, administered the Holocaust, and worked in the death camps.

Until the mid-nineteenth century, the Austrian Empire was agrarian, semi-feudal, and multi-ethnic, a relic compared to the

---

*The Austrian Empire included Hungary, modern-day Czechoslovakia, Bosnia-Herzegovina, and parts of Serbia, Poland, Romania, and Italy.

centralized, advanced, and unified states of Western Europe. The Austrian Catholic church was more medieval, powerful, and anti-Semitic than elsewhere. The church also regarded as divinely ordained the social order of village, peasant, artisan, and noble under the moral guidance of a church with secular powers. Restrictions against Jews were strong, and the secular humanism of the Enlightenment influenced only the small German and tiny Jewish business communities. True, in 1782 Emperor Joseph II, strongly influenced by the Enlightenment, decreed a variety of reforms including freedom of worship and the end of some restrictions on the Jews, but the reforms failed for lack of support. The vast majority of Slavs remained peasants bound by serfdom; Germans dominated the important positions in all imperial institutions.

The French Revolution threatened the old order with nationalism, executed the king, and deprived the aristocracy of its privileges and the church of its secular powers. Outraged, Austria joined Prussia to invade France, only to be repulsed by the armies of the French republic. Austria was defeated again in 1796 in Italy, and in 1805 when Napoleon's troops occupied Vienna. But defeat did not lead to reform, as in Prussia. Instead in 1809 the Emperor Ferdinand brought Prince Klemens von Metternich to power, commanding him "to rule and change nothing." Both knew that if the revolutionary and liberal nationalism unleashed by 1789 were to inflame the empire's minorities, the empire might be torn apart.

Metternich detested the atheistic Jacobins, bitter enemies of the old social order who had liberated the Jews in 1791. To him the Jews were a race of amoral materialists and the bitter enemies of the Christian social order. Metternich's personal secretary, Friedrich Gentz, hired anti-Semitic publicists and wrote that the Jews were "born representatives of atheism, Jacobinism, and Enlightenment . . . ," responsible for all the "misfortunes of the world" and the "heretical and diseased spirit of 1789." Austrian church publications repeated and intensified such charges and worse throughout the century as threats to their power and traditional social order multiplied.

Gradually the commercial and industrial revolutions began to transform the agrarian empire. Railroads opened markets to manufacturers who expanded and hired industrial workers. Many peasants found new markets for their products and switched from subsistence to cash crops. The predominantly German and Jewish business community grew and supported liberal ideals. Peasants rioted against the bondage of serfdom. Czech, Slovak, and Hungarian intellectuals, reacting against German domination of the empire, revived the language and cultural heritage of their peoples, and demands arose for Slavic equality with the dominating Germans. As revolutions spread throughout Europe in 1848, Viennese students, led by the Jewish Adolf Fischof, joined with industrial workers and bourgeoisie to demand liberal reforms. Czechs, Hungarians, and Italians rose as well, some hoping for independence. The emperor fled Vienna; Metternich fled Europe.

Ignoring overwhelming Christian participation in the Revolutions of 1848, leading Catholic ecclesiastics blamed "Jewish liberalism" and held "arrogant and insolent Jews" responsible for the uprisings. The official church journal called them the "promoters of all that is evil and destructive in modern society." Significantly, outside of Vienna and a few large towns, the sermons of the local priest and columns in the Catholic press were practically the sole source of information and ideas for ~zens. When the revolutions were defeated and their leaders ~ailed, or executed, the government fined the Jewish ~ven though only two hundred Jewish families ~e in Vienna at the time and, though they fa~ ~ rejected revolutionary violence.

~osef, fearful of peasant uprisings, ~hed the ghettos of Vienna in ~wed to purchase landed estates, ~ach, or hold public office. The emperor also signed a concordat giving the Austrian church almost medieval powers, including the control of education. Attacks against Judaism became an integral part of the curriculum. For the next decade, as the common saying went: "the Empire was ruled by a standing army of soldiers, a sitting army of bureaucrats, and a kneeling army of priests."

In 1871 Canon August Rohling, a professor at the University of Prague, published *The Talmud Jew*, claiming that the Talmud commanded Jews to rob, cheat, and murder Christians. The church partially subsidized and distributed the extremely popular book. At a ritual murder trial—there were twelve in the empire from 1870 to 1914—Rohling testified that the Talmud required Jews to use Christian blood in their rituals. When Rabbi Samuel Bloch accused Rohling of perjury and ignorance of Hebrew, Rohling backed down and Bloch, aided by liberals, entered parliament. Although Rohling was fired, his rehash of medieval charges remained extremely popular. The Jesuit *La Civiltà Cattolica* declared in 1881 that all practicing Jews were required to use "the flesh or dried blood of a Christian child." In 1884 a Hasidic Jew was acquitted of ritual murder and riots broke out in Tiszaeszlar, a small town in Hungary. The Liberal party condemned the rioters. Father Sebastian Brunner, editor of the official Austrian Catholic newspaper, responded that "we but defend ourselves against the shameless" and "unbearably destructive activities of Jewish abomination." As a prominent historian of the Habsburg Empire has written: "In Austrian clerical circles, antipathy toward the Jew was relentless, for he belonged to an alien race, an accursed folk, the denier of the Christian Savior, the veritable offspring of th devil."

In the Imperial Parliament established in the 1860s, the (man Liberals, composed of wealthy German and some J businessmen, won the elections of 1867. They had bee ated ever since Pius IX issued his "Syllabus of Errors" condemning liberalism, science, and modern civili giving the papacy unprecedented authoritarian powers over the church. Like many European Catholics, even the pious emperor thought the pope had gone too far. But to his discomfort the German Liberal party legalized civil marriage, secularized education, and granted Jews complete toleration and equality before the law. The Austrian hierarchy immediately condemned this "Parliament of infidels" and crusaded against "Jewish liberalism," the liberal Jewish press, and parliamentary government altogether, supported by vociferous rural priests. Pius IX, notorious enemy of the Jews, declared the legislation "unholy, destructive, abominable, damnable . . . and null and void." Austrian bishops thundered that to obey such laws was to insult God.

These measures and the importance of the Jewish community in the modern sectors of the empire's economy, as well as their support of the German Liberal party, prompted Catholic priests and intellectuals to form a Christian Social Movement. With it they hoped to use anti-Semitism to reverse the trend toward a secular, liberal, and capitalist society. They were inspired by the ideas of Baron Karl von Vogelsang, a leading intellectual and editor of the prestigious daily paper of the Catholic hierarchy, *Das Vaterland*. Its masthead read, "Our Battle Is Against the Spirit of 1789."

Like other European Catholic intellectuals, Vogelsang believed that "Jewish" liberal capitalism destroyed the livelihood of artisans, driving them and displaced peasants into vast factories to produce cheap products under inhumane conditions. It brutalized women and children, hiring workers on the cheap to perform mindless and repetitive tasks on machines that replaced the ancient and personally satisfying skills of artisans. Peasants became discontented industrial workers, torn from the natural limits to cupidity set by nature and deprived of the moral guidance of the village priest. Village kinship ties and generations of face-to-face relationships and the extended family were shattered. Men would become spiritually empty, crammed into vast and ugly industrial cities, either victors or victims in the hedonistic struggle for gain through merciless competition where no man knew his neighbor, life was harsh, and man's moral relationship with God, the church, and his fellow man could not survive. If we do not restrict the Jews, he demanded, our people will become "victims of gin and the Jewish press."

> Jewry is dissolving the Christian order. Workers and craftsmen drift into the factories, landed property and houses into Jewish possession, and the wealth of the people into their pockets. Through their voting laws they dominate elections, politics, parliament, legislation and the ministries: a few years more of such "progress" and Vienna will be called New Jerusalem and old Austria—Palestine.

The Christian Social Movement called for the restoration of the powers of church and guild, and the protection of peasants from "usurious Jews," with state-supplied cheap credit and fair wages for workers. The Jewish liberal press must be banned and parliament replaced by an advisory body of representatives of the guilds, merchants, peasants, landowners, aristocrats, and clergy, each to advise only on matters concerning their own group. Above all the church, the ultimate source of moral authority, must control education so as to lead the fight against the corruption of modern society and the power of the Jews.

Karl Lueger, a lawyer, became the political leader of the Christian Social Movement. His clients were the small businessmen, craftsmen, and displaced peasants who composed the vast majority of Viennese citizens and suffered most from the introduction of free enterprise, the breakdown of the old rural order, and competition from Slavs and Jews arriving in Vienna from the eastern Empire. In the 1870s Lueger led a revolt against the wealthy Germans who dominated the Liberal party and allied himself with a small group of young Liberals, including Jews, who also wanted to help ordinary citizens. But, aware of the power of anti-Semitism among his Viennese constituents, he soon became an outspoken anti-Semite. It was Vogelsang who introduced Lueger to the luminaries of the Christian Social Movement, which included two future cardinals and high-ranking aristocrats. The new movement was inaugurated in a church in 1887, and Lueger was presented later at a meeting to honor Leo XIII; Lueger gave an anti-Semitic speech and toasted the "final victory of Christianity over its enemies."

There is nothing wrong with trying to preserve an older social order, and it is easy to scoff at fantasies of an idyllic past, a dismal future, and the conspiratorial power of a tiny minority. But the power of such ideas among religious fundamentalists should not be underestimated, especially when new values challenge the traditional order and most fundamentalists still live as their ancestors had. The danger results from the fundamentalist insistence on religious explanations for what they define as evil. This attitude led to blaming the Jews for the destruction of the old ways, not only because of ancient religious antagonisms but because of substantial Jewish participation in the modern economic and liberal sectors of society. The relative backwardness that gave strength to the Christian Social Movement also threatened the empire. Even if there had been no Jews in the empire, it would have had to change. The Austrian Empire had to modernize or cease to exist. In the end it would do both.

For economic backwardness and the empire's multi-ethnic antagonisms rapidly weakened the two primary sources of modern state power: industrial might and national loyalty—the means to fight wars and the loyalty of the citizens who must fight them. Defeats by the forces of the French republic and Napoleon first demonstrated Austria's dilemma. Then Franz Josef, to his humiliation, had to ask the tsar for troops to put down the revolutions of his subjects in 1848. In 1859 France and Italy defeated the empire and created a United Kingdom of Italy where Austria had ruled. The decisive blow was the surprisingly swift Prussian victory in 1866, devastating the emperor and allowing the Hungarians, whose leaders had fought for freedom in 1848, to demand and receive partial independence in what was now the Austro-Hungarian Empire.

To industrialize, the empire needed the cooperation of middle-class entrepreneurs and investors, and they demanded liberal economic reforms and constitutional rights. To assure the loyalty of his subjects, the emperor had to make concessions to his discontented Slavs, and the Liberals agreed. Thus the Constitution of 1867 included the rights of man and the citizen, equality before the law, and freedom of press, speech, and assembly, and promised that all ethnic minorities would have the right to preserve their own language and culture. Ethnic voting quotas were passed to pacify the Slavs. But the quotas and high property qualifications were designed to favor the wealthy German and Jewish businessmen (legally classified as Germans) who formed the German Liberal party. The emperor retained the power to select and dismiss prime ministers, summon and dissolve the legislature, and issue emergency decrees.

In the Franco-Prussian War of 1870–1871, Franz Josef hoped for a Prussian defeat so that Austria might again dominate Central Europe. But he was shocked when Austro-Germans celebrated Prussia's victory so wildly that the police had to be called out. Many demonstrators called for unity with Germany—the first strong demand for *Anschluss* (annexation). The war was the first in Europe in which industrial might brought victory. Hence the emperor, as Bismarck had done, allowed the Liberal party to pass legislation limiting guild restrictions in order to give free rein to entrepreneurs, and permitting capital to be invested at limited liability in order to encourage investors to invest in new industries. As in Germany, a burst of uncontrolled and sometimes fraudulent speculation in 1873 brought the first modern depression. Reactionaries and ruined small investors blamed Jewish speculators, the Liberal party, and the Viennese liberal press, almost completely Jewish owned.

As in Germany, the names of a few prominent and fraudulent Jewish speculators were singled out to exaggerate Jewish participation and condemn the immorality of "Jewish capitalism." Demands arose for curbs on all Jewish economic activities as racists ignored the collapse of many Jewish banks, the ruin of thousands of Jewish small investors, and the fraudulent activities of many aristocrats and wealthy Christians. Anti-Semitic agitation reached new heights.

Economic modernization also encouraged ethnic nationalism and separatism. If asked his identity in the eighteenth century, a Slavic peasant would not have said he was Czech, Polish, or Slovenian, he would have identified himself by religion, village, or clan. But industrialism awakened ethnic awareness among those peasants who left the closed world of the village to work in factory and mine. Some became literate and read about their ethnic heritage and culture from the works of those who revived their language, and in industrial towns they all observed that Germans blocked their road to higher positions in imperial institutions and the professions. As resentment grew among the most advanced Slavic groups, they demanded higher ethnic quotas in the Imperial Parliament and local assemblies. In the 1880s Czechs and Slovenes agitated and rioted for equal votes, language rights, and access to all positions. Fearing the empire would be torn apart, Franz Josef made concessions, inevitably at the expense of German predominance. Consistent with their special need for tolerance, Jewish Liberals tended to uphold the emperor.

Georg von Schoenerer led the angry response of German nationalists to these concessions. A former student in Prussia, well acquainted with the racist writing of Wilhelm Marr, he insisted that the Slavs were an inferior race of peasants unfit for equality with the innately superior Germans, and the Jews were bitter enemies of the Germans for supporting concessions. Did not the crash of 1873 demonstrate that the Jews were a dangerous race of economic parasites whose depraved cunning allowed them to exploit and dominate any society foolish enough to permit them entry? Incapable of building a nation of their own, the Jews hoped to use the Slavs in their drive to dominate at German expense. Schoenerer derided Christian anti-Semitism because it had failed to suppress Judaism after centuries of trying, and had allowed Jews to convert and hence corrupt German blood and subvert Germanic institutions anonymously.

Schoenerer's Pan German movement was strong wherever Germans were most threatened by Slavic competition. Because they lived and worked in the major industrialized areas of the empire, Bohemia and Moravia, the Czechs made the most demands; consequently German workers in these areas often supported Schoenerer. University students, the future elite, also flocked to the Pan Germans. Religiously indifferent and identifying with a powerful united Germany rather than with what they saw as a weak mongrel empire, many of them also competed with Jewish students to be lawyers and physicians.

As in Germany, Jews hoped to avoid institutional discrimination through private practice; close to 40 percent were in law and medicine. In 1880 nearly half of Vienna's lawyers and physicians were Jewish; by 1910 they comprised close to 70 percent of its financiers and industrialists, more than 60 percent of its lawyers and physicians, and half its journalists. Correspondingly, the anti-Semitic petition of 1881—so popular among the students of the University of Berlin—and other racist petitions were even more popular in Austria. A decade before German fraternities, Austrian students banned all Jews, including converts to Christianity. They also formed a bodyguard for Schoenerer, cultivated Wagner's cult of racial and cultural superiority, praised the Prussian warrior ethic, and attacked Jewish students. Jews trained in their own dueling fraternities to defend themselves. In the 1880s some 30 percent of Jewish students at the University of Vienna considered themselves Zionists, usually against the will of their assimilated parents.

Schoenerer also gained powerful support from the artisans of Vienna, almost unanimously anti-Semitic by 1880. Not only had "Jewish" liberalism destroyed their traditional monopolies, but Jewish craftsmen from the impoverished eastern empire worked harder for less, no longer limited by guild regulations. Already in 1848 artisans opposed "Jewish free enterprise," and in 1860 the Shoemakers' Guild petitioned the government to keep Jews out of their trade. In giant rallies in the early 1880s, with Schoenerer a featured speaker, thousands of artisans vilified the Jews and overwhelmingly endorsed the racism of blood; after all, even a converted Jewish competitor was a threat. At a mass meeting in 1882, Schoenerer and artisan leaders claimed that the Jews did no honest work. Jewish peddlers, aided by Jewish liberal plutocrats in Parliament, had deliberately set out to destroy honest "Aryan" craftsmen. They proposed higher taxes on Jews, marriage and occupation restrictions, ghettos or expulsion—some justified pogroms. The artisan leaders insisted that Jews had no right to exist; one declared outright that they should be killed.

At the emperor's request, the Rothschilds had organized an international group of investors to finance a railway (the Nordbahn) needed to carry foodstuffs from Budapest to Vienna. When the government began renegotiating the contract in 1884, Schoenerer led large demonstrations to denounce the Rothschilds and Jewish stockholders for exploiting Austrians by charging high prices to benefit their shareholders. Many Liberal and German-Jewish deputies also thought the terms were too high, and Solomon Rothschild was quite willing to negotiate. But such was the strength of anti-Semitism that all issues threatened to become racial issues, regardless of the facts. Schoenerer launched a series of racist petitions and denounced even those journalists and Liberals who supported a moderate compromise as "whores and traitors" bribed by international Jewry. His popularity soared.

In 1884, at the height of artisan agitation, Slavic demands, and the railway agitation, a lowered property qualification gave many artisans and small businessmen the vote. Now they could challenge the Liberal party, whose power rested on a high property qualification that had given only 3 percent of German males the vote. Voters now elected thirteen extreme anti-Semites to the German delegation of the Imperial Parliament, including Franz Schneider, the artisan leader who had called for the murder of the Jews. As Schoenerer entered the Parliament his followers pounded their desks and shouted, "Down with Parliament, down with the Nordbahn Jews, Heil Schoenerer." In the end, Solomon Rothschild voluntarily sacrificed his financial rights to help Franz Josef. It did not help. Racist pamphlets, petitions, and boycotts of Jewish businesses inundated Vienna in the 1880s, and there was a brisk business in anti-Semitic objects and posters. Schoenerer's picture gazed out from countless shop windows and guild establishments; he was the most popular man in Vienna. As the leader of a Catholic movement, Lueger, Schoenerer's main rival, could not adopt outright biological racism and thus deny the redeeming power of baptism. Instead he insisted that centuries of cultural conditioning were needed before a converted Jew could really be German. Nor could Lueger denounce the Slavs as viciously as Schoenerer, for they were Catholics, and the hierarchy, some Slavic, would have none of it.

But Schoenerer lost his parliamentary seat for five years in 1888, punished for leading a violent attack against the editors of a liberal Jewish newspaper he believed had insulted the German kaiser. Lueger swiftly seized his competitor's followers, including Schneider, who became a leading spokesman for the Christian Social Movement. In 1890 the Christian Socials and Pan Germans sponsored joint candidates for the Viennese city council, calling themselves the United Christian Anti-Semites. Their platform declared that Jews should not be allowed in the civil service, the judiciary, teaching, medicine, or law; they must not sell alcohol, be pawnbrokers, own grocery stores, or freely immigrate. Non-Jews "infected by Jewish liberalism" must also be curbed. The coalition won nearly one-third of the seats. Lueger was much in demand at anti-Semitic meetings, often held in churches; racists vied for his support in elections. Franz Josef, fearing ethnic turmoil, asked Pope Leo XIII for a letter condemning Lueger, but the pope refused—he himself sponsored anti-Semitic propaganda. The pope offended the pious emperor by giving Lueger his personal blessing. In 1891 Prince Alois Liechtenstein presented the Christian Social Program to the Imperial Parliament, announcing that it would protect Austrians from Jews who contributed nothing to the Fatherland and accumulated their neighbor's property without honest work. (This from an aristocrat who lived from the labor of his peasants.)

In the parliamentary elections of 1891, Lueger and thirteen other Christian Socials won seats. He celebrated with a speech suggesting that the Jews might be guilty of ritual murder, and thrived in business only because they were unhindered by Christian ethics. Lueger always spoke of rich Jews, though he knew the vast majority of Viennese Jews were poor, not to mention the hundreds of thousands of truly destitute Jews in the eastern empire. He also claimed that Jewish international financiers controlled Austria, though the shareholders of the foreign companies investing in the empire were of many different nationalities. Jews, he insisted, were also the instigators of all revolutions. "Whenever a state has allowed the Jews to become powerful, that state has collapsed." He offered no examples.

In the 1890s racists faced a new enemy in socialism. Led by Victor Adler, the Austrian Social Democrats gained strong support among the three million industrial workers of the empire who worked under miserable conditions. Although there were many Jewish industrialists, the socialist attitude was revealed in the statement:

The struggle between the so-called Aryan and Jewish races leaves us cold. It is all one to us if we are exploited by an Aryan or a Semite. As long as there are a sufficient number of Aryan exploiters, these men have no right to counter protests against exploitation by blaming the Jews.

The Pan Germans pointed out that Victor Adler was a converted Jew. Lueger, heckled by socialists while running for office in 1894, shouted out:

The Jews Marx and Lassalle founded your party. If you keep fighting for them you will not get your precious revolution, you will get the rule of the Jews! They are the real enemies of Christian workers, and it is they who pay the Social Democrats.

German nationalists were furious because socialists recruited Slavic as well as German workers and advocated universal male suffrage. Pan Germans, fearing millions of Slavic voters, denounced this "Jewish" betrayal of German blood.

At practically every school opening and court proceeding, tensions mounted as Czechs boycotted, demonstrated, and rioted for the right to use their own language. Martial law was imposed. Some Czech delegates demanded independence and looked for aid from traditionally friendly republican France or Russia, protector of Slavs and enemy of German influence in the East. The emperor kept trying to placate both Germans and Slavs with alternating concessions, but both groups grew angrier with each concession to the other. German members of the Liberal party began to lose elections or desert the party, but German-Jewish Liberals had little choice. As always, their fate was tied to ethnic and religious tolerance. They had no territories to claim, and as a largely commercial class they could scarcely support Marxists. Nor did sophisticated Viennese Jews relish becoming Zionist pioneers in the deserts of the Ottoman Empire. After Italian Jewry, Viennese Jews had the highest rate of intermarriage and lack of interest in Judaism.

Until 1893 the German Liberal party dominated both the Viennese municipal government and the German delegation to the Imperial Parliament. In 1894 the emperor appointed the Polish count Kasimir Badeni prime minister to try to pacify the Czechs yet again. Badeni ended martial law in Bohemia, freed radical Czechs from prison, and fired the governor of Bohemia, an enemy of Czech agitators. Uproar followed swiftly among Germans, and in 1895 the Christian Socials, campaigning against Liberals, Czechs, and Jews, received a clear majority in elections to the Viennese city council. They promptly voted Lueger mayor while his supporters thronged the streets looking for Jews and Czechs to beat. Four times the emperor, as was his right, refused to confirm Lueger as mayor, even though the pope—pleased to see a Catholic party able to stem the tide of European liberalism—pressured him. Rioting Germans dubbed Franz Josef the "Judenkaiser" and screamed "Death to the Jews."

Both Freud and Herzl observed the crowds chanting, "Lueger shall rule, and the Jews shall be slaughtered." Freud discovered the concept of the Id in 1895; not only the Dreyfus Affair but Lueger's appointment drove Herzl to Zionism in 1897. Many leading Jewish businessmen threatened to leave Vienna, and the grain market moved to Budapest because its employees were constantly harassed. Foreign investors turned away.

In March 1897, with the vote extended to include more lower-middle-class males, the Liberals were crushed 10 to 1 by Christian Socials running under the slogan "Anti-Semites Unite." Excluding the Jewish districts of Vienna, Austrian liberalism was dead. Continuous pandemonium forced Franz Josef to name Lueger mayor in 1897. Now many younger Jews joined the Social Democrats. All other parties had rejected them, and the Liberal party of their fathers was finished. For the first time in Europe, anti-Semites controlled a capital city; not even the Nazis ever won a majority in Berlin. As George

Mosse notes, "Every year tens of thousands of anti-Semitic pamphlets were sent free to all officials of the state and members of the upper ten thousand."

Both Czechs and Germans now rioted as never before, and agitation increased among other Slavic peoples. After Lueger was confirmed as mayor, Badeni tried to balance matters, decreeing that by 1901 all government officials in Bohemia and Moravia had to speak and write Czech as well as German. Nonleftist Germans exploded in protest: how could the language of an inferior peasant people be equated with a great international language? Racist cartoons multiplied. As many as half of all Germans rioted, more than had participated in the Revolutions of 1848. Walkouts, boycotts, fisticuffs, and hurled inkwells, chairs, and cherry bombs paralyzed Parliament. The judicial system stalled, taxes went uncollected. University students rose in fury against the emperor, Slavs, and Jews. Schoenerer's followers raged in Bohemia, especially in the heavily German Sudetenland. In Vienna and Prague, Czechs, Germans, and Jews fought in the streets. Jewish and Czech shops were attacked in Vienna. On the steps of city hall, Lueger started a riot, leading crowds in chanting, "Badeni must go!"

If Badeni remained, martial law would be needed. The emperor fired him. It did not help. Five governments fell in succession trying to appease one side or the other; the emperor was forced to rule by emergency decree. Pan Slav delegates met in Prague in 1898, and Serbs, Russians, and Czechs called for a united front against Germans. Many hoped the recent Franco-Russian alliance would bring war against the Habsburgs. Meanwhile German pamphlets called for "concentrating" Jews and Czechs in camps. Former distinguished German Liberal leaders called for violence against Czechs. In 1899 the Socialist Party Conference called for national equality within a federal state of nationalities, with political and cultural autonomy for all minorities. Outraged extremists demanded that the traitorous Jewish socialists be shot. In 1902 a Christian Social member announced to great applause in the city council, "Yes, we want to annihilate the Jews," and declared that "our program" is the "elimination of Jewry."

As the dialectic of extremes continued, Schoenerer again became the idol of millions. In the elections of 1901 his party drew equal with the Christian Socials, and he entered Parliament to triumphant shouts of "Heil," "Anschluss," and "God save the Hohenzollern Kaiser." But Schoenerer made a fatal mistake. The Pan Germans detested the mongrel Habsburg domains and preferred Prussian nationalistic Protestantism to Catholic internationalism. Schoenerer campaigned to convert Austrians to Lutheranism, the truly Germanic religion of the Prussian warrior elite. He himself preferred paganism. As a Nazi later declared, Christianity was an offshoot of Judaism led by a Jewish coward who counseled meekness—hardly a religion for Aryan warriors. With the help of Lutheran pastors from Germany—followers of Stoecker—Schoenerer gained some seventy thousand converts. But by denouncing both the empire and the religion of over 90 percent of Austro-Germans, Schoenerer was vulnerable. Like his party and the majority of ordinary Austrians, Lueger believed in empire and church. Supported by the papal nuncio, the emperor, and Franz Ferdinand, heir to the throne, Lueger denounced Schoenerer's treason against Catholicism and the empire.

In 1905–1906 the Christian Socials and the Social Democrats mounted demonstrations for universal suffrage. Lueger knew he could gain peasant votes, Adler depended on more Slavic and German worker voters. Franz Josef and his advisers hoped the change might weaken ethnic nationalism by bringing in voters more concerned with their social welfare. They were frightened by the Russian Revolution of 1905 and the huge demonstrations in Austria. Universal suffrage for males was decreed for the elections of 1907. The Pan Germans suffered from Schoenerer's mistakes and almost collapsed, but the Christian Socials and their close allies, the German Clerics, and various

German nationalists—all anti-Semitic—formed the largest single bloc in the new Parliament.

But to the shock of the establishment, the Social Democrats became the single largest party, soaring from eleven to eighty-seven seats and seriously eroding Lueger's Vienna stronghold by winning the new industrial suburbs. Socialism gained from economic progress, and fear drew the remaining establishment to Lueger; the forebears of the Austrian Nazis began to organize in Bohemia. Peasants voted for Lueger, led by Christian Social priests who reinforced their long-standing belief in Jewish usury and mortgage and middleman fraud. Lueger also promised the peasants cheap government credit.

As mayor, Lueger could not pass racist legislation. There were not enough German delegates to control the Imperial Parliament, and only the emperor could approve constitutional changes. Instead Lueger declared that he would fight Jewish socialism and the alleged Jewish financial control of Viennese municipal services. Vienna was the only capital city to have so many basic municipal services owned by foreign stockholders, but the firms involved—British, German, and French—did not have a majority of Jewish stockholders. (Nor does the ethnicity or religion of shareholders determine utility prices.) Lueger lowered utility rates, built schools and hospitals, gave cheap credit to small businessmen, and dispensed more city contracts to local artisans. He built homes for orphans and homeless adults as well, but the Rothschilds had done this before him, and younger Liberals and socialists had long called for most of the reforms. Other mayors in other nations made similar reforms, but only Lueger claimed that his were part of a battle against international Jewry.

As Richard Geehr notes, Lueger partially anticipated the Nazis. Hailed as fuehrer at huge demonstrations, he organized paramilitary auxiliaries that met in semi-mystical ceremonies to solemnly intone their racist ideology. He sponsored a kind of "Lueger Youth" too. A Christian Social Women's League with some twenty thousand members dedicated itself to combating racial mixing, fighting leftist demands for equal rights for women, preventing Jews from teaching, and counseling Christian girls not to work in Jewish households. The party published lists of Jewish merchants to be boycotted; the city distributed anti-Semitic literature to schoolchildren and organized an anti-Semitic Christian teachers association. A city-sponsored cultural association promoted Aryan art and crusaded against the "moral decay" of Gustav Klimt's erotic paintings, the sophisticated decadence of Arthur Schnitzler's stories, Ibsen's theatre of social criticism, Schoenberg's atonal music, and Strindberg's dramas of sexual corruption. Jewish or not, party spokesmen declared, they reflected the Jewish spirit, and Jewish critics had made them famous. The police were even given orders to take special care at Easter to prevent ritual murders.

International anti-Semites made pilgrimages to Lueger and were entertained with his large collection of anti-Semitica. When he died in 1910, the young Hitler attended his elaborate funeral. In the last elections of the empire in 1911, the Christian Socials received 37 percent of the vote, the German Nationals, heirs of Schoenerer, 31 percent: two-thirds of the German electorate had voted for anti-Semitic candidates. The socialists won 32 percent of the vote. The Germans of Austria were now the most divided and the most anti-Semitic people in Western Europe.

Hitler lived in Vienna from 1907 to 1913. Never a reader of anything except the multitude of brutally racist tracts readily available, he learned from experience. He visited the Imperial Parliament and concluded that parliamentary democracy was simply a façade for bitter ethnic conflicts, and that Jews and Slavs were mortal enemies of Germans. Because mainly Jewish districts voted Liberal, he could easily conclude that liberalism was Jewish. Hitler preferred Schoenerer's racism of blood to Lueger's Christian anti-Semitism. Down and out in Vienna, the youthful failure had nothing but his Germanic blood to assure him that he belonged to a superior people. Moreover, as he wrote in *Mein Kampf*, Christians permitted Jews to infiltrate Aryan society with a simple splash of holy water that changed nothing. But he admired Lueger's tactic of gaining power by concentrating on the "single foe"—the Jew. Of socialism he knew only that Jewish names were prominent among its publicists. He made no attempt to counter their arguments; to him, Marxism was simply an attempt at Jewish domination through subversion and the mobilization of Slavs against superior Aryans.

During Hitler's years in Vienna, ethnic conflicts dominated foreign policy. Serbs and Czechs appealed to Russia to help them against the Habsburgs; the German middle classes demanded a final reckoning with the hated Slavs. The popular Christian Social and nationalist press spewed hatred for Serbs, Czechs, and Jews. For tens of thousands of German nationalists, not just Hitler, the confrontation was part of the long racial struggle between inferior Slav and superior Teuton. The Serb terrorists who assassinated the archduke Franz Ferdinand, touching off World War I, hoped to liberate Serbs still in the empire in order to build a greater Serbia. Hitler, like millions, fervently welcomed the war of 1914 as a final swift settling of accounts with arrogant *untermenschen*, a word not invented by the Nazis. Leaflets launched vitriolic attacks against traitorous "Jewish" socialists and Liberals who sought compromise. But Hitler would not fight for a rotting mongrel empire that betrayed German blood. He fled to Munich and, when war came, volunteered for the Bavarian branch of the German army. Ignorant of the large percentage of Social Democrats in the army, Hitler wrote from the front that each soldier had but one thought, to defeat the enemy and then return to destroy the enemy at home, the Jew. He recommended gassing. But it is a dangerous mistake, often made, to believe that Hitler's obsessions were unique. They were shared in varying degrees by hundreds of thousands of Austrians and Germans well before 1914.

As in Germany during the war, though Jews participated in the military in numbers higher than their proportion of the population, the Christian Social journal *Reichspost* and German nationalist publications in Austria claimed they avoided combat duty. They also insisted that the Jewish minister of finance and Jewish black marketers sabotaged the economy. When the Social Democrats called for peace without victory and joined Zionists to support a strike of a million workers in January 1918, talk of a Jewish conspiracy against the war was rife. In early 1918, when Croatians, Poles, Czechs, and Slovaks demanded separate states, German nationalists blamed Jews, Liberals, and socialists because they had long encouraged Slavic rights. Leaflets insisted that Jewry controlled Woodrow Wilson and that Lenin was Jewish.

Racism intensified when tens of thousands of Jewish refugees, ultra-orthodox and Yiddish-speaking, fled to Vienna to avoid furious battles in the East that blasted their villages and killed thousands. Mainly penniless artisans, shopkeepers, or former cattle dealers, many of them were forced to become peddlers in Vienna. Even assimilated Viennese Jews felt the newcomers were superstitious remnants of medieval Poland and a threat to their German identity. The Christian Social party called the refugees usurers, criminals, and profiteers, and falsely claimed that the government intended to seize foodstuffs to feed hundreds of thousands of idle Jews in Vienna. After the war, most returned to the East, and only 25,000 remained in Vienna—as citizens it was their right.

In June 1918 bitter anti-Semitism spewed forth during a "German People's Day" sponsored by Christian Socials, Pan Germans, and German nationalists, together representing more than 60 percent of German Austrians. As in Germany, Jews were blamed for the anticipated military defeat—an attempt to deny that aggressive ethnic nationalism had caused the disastrous war, aggression opposed by Jewish Liberals and Austrian Social Democrats. The mayor of Vienna and leading dignitaries of the Christian Socials and Pan Germans spoke. In the 1918 political campaign, Leopold Kunschak, leader of the Christian Social Workers' Movement, declared: "Nothing is being talked about more in recent years than the decisive hour in which the reckoning with Jews will begin. The Jews know . . . it will be a judgment that will make them shudder." Praising the Christian Middle Ages, Kunschak blamed the Jews for all the traumas of the empire and the war and demanded that refugee Jews be deported or interned in concentration camps. Even Jewish converts, he insisted, were too corrupt to become real Christians. The Christian Social party's foremost publicist also demanded internment or expulsion; another called for a pogrom. The long history of Austrian anti-Semitism would continue without a break after the war, aggravated by the dissolution of the empire, the peace settlements, economic discontent, and the rise of Slavic states where Germans had once ruled.

FIVE

Austria, 1918–1945

THE AUSTRIAN GOVERNMENT ruled by decree until May
1917 because it feared Slavic delegates would declare independence and because the Social Democrats demanded a negotiated
peace once the Serbs had been defeated in 1915. The Christian
Social party and German Nationalists blamed "Jewish" socialists and Liberals because they supported Slavic rights and peace.
When it became obvious in early 1918 that the war was lost
and the empire would be dismantled, Parliament voted unanimously to join with Germany. But the Allies could not allow a
defeated Germany to gain territory from the war. From then on,
as Bruce F. Pauly has written: "With the very important exception of the *Anschluss* question, it is doubtful whether any other
single issue . . . appealed to so large a cross section of the Austrian population as anti-Semitism."

Campaigning for provisional government elections in 1919,
a Christian Social manifesto read: "The corruption and lust for
power which Jewish circles reveal compels the Christian Social
Party to call on the Austrian people to defend themselves as
strenuously as possible against the Jewish peril." In the elec-
ns the Christian Socials won sixty-nine seats; twenty-six
the German Nationalists, and the Social Democrats re-
enty-two. As before 1914, a majority of Austrians
anti-Semites, but the Social Democrats remained
arty. Karl Renner, the socialist leader, became
ristian Social vice chancellor—a formula

for paralysis. Various bills were offered in Parliament to expel Eastern Jews, and some regional governments confiscated their ration cards and forbade them to conduct business, change names, or join the army. The American consul warned the Austrian government that Jewish refugees from the former eastern empire were legally Austrian citizens. Should they be expelled, the food and loans desperately needed would be withheld. Anti-Semites cited the warning as evidence of the Jewish control of America.

Karl Renner led the peace delegation to Paris. As in Germany, a republic with a socialist chancellor bore the suicidal burden of responsibility for a war started by an autocratic empire. The Treaty of Saint-Germain accused Austria of war guilt, demanded reparations (falsely blamed by many on the demands of American Jewish bankers), and limited the army to thirty thousand men. Tiny Austria was an economic disaster, cut off by tariffs from its former raw materials, markets, and capital now owned by the new states formed from former imperial territories—Poland, Czechoslovakia, and Yugoslavia—and other lands awarded to Italy and Romania. Hungary was also completely independent of Austrian power. Czechoslovakia inherited some 80 percent of the industrial equipment of the empire. Thousands of German imperial civil servants had to be laid off. Unemployment soared. International loans were granted only on condition that Austria forget about *Anschluss* and treat its minorities fairly—for many, yet another indication of the power of international Jewry.

Austrians assumed that the millions of ethnic Germans who dwelt in these "successor states" and the former imperial territories they occupied would be awarded to Austria, in accord with Woodrow Wilson's doctrine of national self-determination. But France needed the new states to help ho' Germany in check now that its former ally, Russia, was Bols vik. Consequently the Czechs retained the Sudetenland more than three million Germans; hundreds of thousand remained in other Slavic states and in the new Italian section of the Tyrol. Among the millions of Germans now ruled by Slavs, hatreds were intense and fascist ideas flourished. Hitler was but one of millions of Austrians and Germans who regarded the new Slavic states, including Poland, as artificial and hoped one day that all ethnic Germans would be united in one Reich.

In the elections of 1920 the Christian Social *Reichspost* declared that no true Austrian should vote for any party with a Jewish candidate, and constantly referred to an alleged Jewish world conspiracy. Postwar racism propelled the Christian Socials from sixty-nine to eighty-five seats, while the anti-Semites of the even more extremist Greater German People's party (GDVP), Schoenerer's heirs, gained twenty seats. Roughly the equivalent of the reactionary German DNVP, its supporters were secular racists of some status and education who disliked the priestly influence within the Christian Social party. Since the Social Democrats, with sixty-nine seats, remained the only significant political obstacle to anti-Semitism, Jewish youth began to add to its overwhelmingly proletarian vote. In spite of the large majority of anti-Semites, there was no racist legislation. Austria depended too heavily on the Allies; discrimination remained informal.

The new constitution gave much autonomy to various regions, including Vienna, where socialists dominated the municipal government, led by a high percentage of Jewish leaders. They created Europe's most advanced system of municipal welfare, including much-needed cheap housing for workers in the provocatively named Karl Marx Hof, as well as public baths, hospitals, and kindergartens. Capitalists, industrialists, and landlords, some Jewish, complained bitterly about the strict rent controls and heavy property taxes imposed to pay for the reforms. Ultra-orthodox Jews from the East angered German artisans by working for lower wages and longer hours.

With its Slavic minorities practically gone, Austrian nationalists had only the Jews left to blame for their ills. By 1921 hundreds of thousands of Austrians had joined a variety of anti-Semitic and anti-socialist paramilitary groups. Made up of peasants, artisans, and veterans, and led by the members of the middle and upper classes, the most zealous tended to include those Germans who had fled to Austria after losing power, property, and status to Slavs in the former imperial territories, or who lived near the new borders. All looked forward to the day when they could march on Vienna to clean out the "Jewish reds."

The Heimwehr, or Home Defense Force, was the most influential paramilitary organization. Financed by important landowners and led by former army officers, it was initially organized to defeat invading Yugoslav troops trying to annex the Slovene minority in the province of Carinthia. At its height it boasted some 400,000 members dedicated to fighting the "Judeo-Bolshevik" and Slavic menace. In 1919 Heimwehr leader Dr. Richard Steidle formed an Anti-Semitic League which declared that even one Jewish great-grandparent made one Jewish—more rigid than the Nazis' Nuremberg Laws. The League demanded that Jews be excluded from the civil service, the army, the judiciary, journalism, and teaching, and forbidden to purchase property or trade in cattle or lumber. They would be given only limited access to the professions.

In Styria in 1922, Walter Pfrimer's heavily armed Heimwehr units forced the relatively unarmed socialists to end a general strike—the only weapon available to the left. Grateful industrialists gave the Heimwehr large contributions and hired Heimwehr members as workers. Ernst Roehm, Ludendorff, and agents of the German army supported the Heimwehr, hoping that eventually German and Austrian paramilitaries would combine to overthrow the Austrian and Weimar republics. The Heimwehr regularly distributed pamphlets accusing the Jews of the usual catalog of crimes, including ritual murder.

An Austrian branch of Orgesch, with its 300,000 well-armed paramilitaries, called for the "Germanic race" to "eliminate the international Jewish rabble." Christian Socials and the GDVP supported the Heimwehr, as did many local governments; the fundamentalist peasants of the Alpine regions often formed their own Farmers' Bunds. Organization C, the Munich-based death squad, also operated in Austria. The main veterans' organization, the League of Front Fighters with fifty thousand members, blamed the Jews for the defeat of the empire and hoped to overthrow the republic and rid Austria of Jews, calling for force if necessary.

An Antisemitenbund with fifty thousand members included Engelbert Dollfuss, a leader of Austrian Catholic students and future chancellor, and Walter Riehl, leader of the Austrian Nazis, as well as the omnipresent Kunschak, who constantly called for the expulsion of Jews or their internment in concentration camps. In March 1921 forty thousand attended the Antisemitenbund's International Anti-Semitic Congress in Vienna. The Congress also defined a Jew as anyone with one Jewish grandparent. The bund demanded the expulsion of all Eastern Jews, boycotts of Jewish businesses and professionals, and the exclusion of Jews from law, medicine, teaching, and politics. Local chapters recorded the names and activities of Jews and fought for *Judenrein* schools (free of Jews). Its paper, *Der Eiserne Besen*, like Julius Streicher's notorious *Der Stuermer*, printed lies about Jewish ritual murders, sex crimes, and corruption, and listed Jewish shops for boycotting. The GDVP attacked the Jews as a morally depraved people whose cultural activities insulted German traditional values and were promoted by Jewish critics who dominated the media. The predominantly Jewish ownership of motion picture theatres and the new radical and sexual freedom of films were often cited. The film industry was more open to Jews than most endeavors because, as in the United States, it was new and not already dominated by Gentiles.

Sports, gymnastic, and Alpine clubs, proud of their alleged Aryan physical superiority, despised Jews as a sickly and devious city people who cunningly manipulated and exploited honest Germans. More than fifty thousand Austrians belonged to such clubs, whose action squads fought in the streets against "Judeo-Bolsheviks." Unions of white-collar clerks and public employees, part of Kunschak's Christian Social Movement, idealized medieval Christendom and expressed their Aryan dignity by refusing to strike. Gentile merchants and retailers continued to denounce the alleged dishonest business practices of Jewish merchants. Numerous publications, some read by Hitler, preached the old *voelkisch* illusions: Jews seduce Aryan girls to pollute the race; Jewish international financiers foster economic chaos to help the followers of the Jew Karl Marx foster a revolution whose real purpose is the Jewish conquest of Aryan civilization.

The belief in the secret powers of the Jews was necessary since only about 4 percent of the Austrian population was Jewish, large only by comparison with fewer than 1 percent in Germany and France. Some 200,000 lived in Vienna, the largest concentration of Jewish residents of any major city in Western Europe. (In the election campaign of 1919–1920 the Christian Socials claimed there were 600,000 Viennese Jews.) A sore point among Austrians was the overwhelming presence of Jews in commerce and the professions. Roughly 60 percent were in finance and industry, and about 60 percent of all Viennese lawyers, 47 percent of physicians, and 30 percent of all Viennese university instructors were Jewish. Jews owned a fourth of all Viennese businesses, but most of them were small shops, economically marginal. Forty-five percent of all Viennese Jews were self-employed, usually as pharmacists, shoemakers, tailors, or textile and wine merchants. Ninety percent of all Jews lived in Vienna, not only because it was the commercial center but also because pious rural Austrians, with their almost daily Catholic rituals, were uniquely hostile. As in Lueger's day, rural priests often led racist meetings. The many complaints then and now that there are too many Jews in this or that profession or occupation rests on the assumption that Jews are somehow a bad influence.

Father Ignaz Seipel, professor of theology at the University of Vienna, a former student of Vogelsang and an ally of Lueger, became chancellor in 1922 and dominated politics through most of the decade. He feared that democracy would drive Austria into the hands of Jews and atheistic socialists, and hoped to unify the various groups opposing both. He accepted the church's official position that a converted Jew was a Christian, but he believed that Jews should be restricted by allowing them into the army, judiciary, professions, and politics only in proportion to their percentage of the population. He could not inaugurate an authoritarian regime with anti-Semitic legislation, however, though he hoped it might be possible in the future. Until then Austria's need for Western aid and loans ruled it out. When inflation struck in 1922, Seipel was forced to go from capital to capital begging for loans, again given only on condition that Austria maintain the rights of minorities and drop demands for *Anschluss*. To aggravate matters, the League of Nations, charged with enforcing peace treaties, forced cuts in government expenditures and social welfare programs, demanding too the dismissal of 85,000 civil servants. The old imperial civil service, predominantly German, became the largest single group of unemployed, furious that the victors protected Jews, prevented *Anschluss*, and deprived them of jobs. Lashing out at the League of Nations, international Jewry, and even the Christian Social government, they switched their allegiance to the more extreme racists of the GDVP.

Many Austrians blamed inflation on corrupt Jewish currency speculators, singling out two prominent Jewish criminals but ignoring the involvement of two members of Seipel's cabinet, other Christian Social leaders, and many important non-Jews. They refused to take into account that Jewish Social Democratic leaders first exposed the corruption. In fact those who suffered most were creditors and savers, proportionally many more Jews than Gentiles. Many Viennese banks, mostly Jewish owned, collapsed when outstanding loans were paid back in worthless currency. Small retailers, many Jewish, were also blamed even though they had to pay more to wholesalers than they could charge in prices and often were ruined as a result. Farmers fared best, for they were able to pay off their mortgages in cheap money, wipe out their debts, and profit from rising food prices.

The 1923 elections occurred at the height of postwar anti-Semitism. Chancellor Seipel wanted to end, as he said, Jewish "domination" of the economy, politics, and culture. But he needed the help of Jewish bankers and businessmen to resolve the inflation and feared Allied sanctions if he tried to pass anti-Semitic legislation. Jewish businessmen and orthodox Jews contributed to the Christian Social party because they feared atheistic and anti-capitalist Marxism more than Christian anti-Semitism. Hence during the campaign Seipel attacked only "Jewish bolshevism," a charge that Western politicians did not find objectionable since many said it themselves.

The Austrian Jewish community, excluding the left, trusted Seipel as a moderate, especially because the elections took place amidst rioting and the demands of demagogues that Vienna be seized from the Jews by force while Jews were beaten in streets and cafés. Orthodox Jews supported Seipel because atheistic leftists, many Jewish in origin, openly ridiculed their religion. The nonleftist Jewish community criticized Seipel only for not repudiating his party's insistence that Jews be limited to their percentage of the population in professions and occupations, and the expulsion or even internment of Eastern Jews. They mistook his pragmatic moderation for conviction. In an interview at the end of his life in 1932, unhindered by the responsibilities of office, Seipel revealed his hatred of the Jews. After the crash of 1873, the intensity of anti-Semitism partly hinged on economic well-being, and once Seipel curbed inflation anti-Semitism weakened. But the *Reichspost* continued to attack

Jews in almost every issue for practically every imaginable crime. It is a tragic sign of the intense anti-Semitism of nonleftist Austrians that Jewish voters had such limited choices; there had been no liberal alternative since 1895.

In the 1923 election campaign even the socialists, whose leadership was 80 percent Jewish, tried to fend off the flood of accusations calling them a front for Jewish domination. They pandered to anti-Semites by denouncing wealthy Jewish capitalists and orthodox Jews for supporting, joining, and contributing to Christian Social election funds. They also ridiculed Seipel and his ultra-Catholic party for begging for financial help from rich Jews and votes from orthodox Jews. The attacks were consistent with socialist anti-capitalism and atheism, but some Social Democratic campaign posters and cartoons crudely depicted ugly stereotypes of Jewish capitalists and orthodox rabbis. The socialists did point out that they supported the majority of Jews who were poor and working class. They also attacked the reactionary ethnic nationalists who had demanded war in 1914 and then blamed the Jews when they lost, and pointed out that Clemenceau, not the Jews, had dictated the hated treaty. Nevertheless the use of ethnic stereotypes was extremely offensive, even though the party held to the socialist view that anti-Semitism was a capitalist diversion tactic to evade responsibility for exploitation. Still, as Bruce Pauly notes, the socialists remained "relatively free of anti-Semitic prejudices."

Anti-Semitism helped the Christian Socials win eighty-two seats in the 1923 elections, just one seat short of an absolute majority; the GDVP won ten, the Social Democrats sixty-eight. The Landbund won five by stressing *voelkisch* ideas, and voted with the Christian Social government. Now the anti-Semitic and anti-socialist parties had 70 percent of parliamentary seats. Frightened by the election results and Hitler's *putsch* attempt in November, the Social Democrats never again toyed with anti-Jewish stereotypes. They now formed a Republican Defense League to battle rightist paramilitaries.

In 1926 the platform of the Christian Social party, the only possible choice other than socialism for Jewish voters, condemned "the predominance of the disintegrating Jewish influence." The charge of Jewish socialism seemed more rational in Austria than elsewhere in the West, because after 1918 some 75 percent of Austrian Jews voted socialist. (Of course, more than 90 percent of socialist voters were Gentiles.) There was no non-racist alternative. Even many Jewish small businessmen voted socialist.

Western liberals often wonder why many of the best-educated Germans and Austrians were racist while workers with only an eighth-grade education were far less likely to be, even if unemployed. But as in Germany and Eastern Europe, reactionary and racist views dominated universities and textbooks, and non-Jewish students were either children of the elites or lower-middle-class strivers who competed with Jewish students for professional positions. Hence, as Pauly notes, "No other group in Austria was so racially, passionately, and violently anti-Semitic as students of University age." In 1919 members of the German Student Association, which included the vast majority of undergraduates and was officially recognized by academic authorities, physically attacked Jewish students. Social Democrats condemned student riots, but socialists were rarely students or faculty at universities. Indeed, many professors gave anti-Semitic lectures and supported boycotts of Jewish professors; some did not condemn student violence against Jews. The Academic Senate of the University of Vienna decreed that no student of Jewish origins could register as a German unless he could prove that all four grandparents had been baptized. When the Constitutional Court disallowed this, three days of intense violence followed. In 1931 the New York Times reported that the University of Vienna was like a battlefield. Austrian Nazis, students or not, were invading lecture halls to beat Jewish students. Even as the wounded came streaming out, the government refused to intervene, cynically prating about academic freedom.

The Austrian Nazis originated in the bitter prewar ethnic struggles between Czechs and Germans in Bohemia before 1914, starting as a workers' movement against their Czech competitors and liberal Jews who supported concessions to the Slavs. They were not an electoral force until 1932, however, because of internal divisions, their anti-Catholicism, and above all the presence of so many competitors for the anti-Semitic vote. Nevertheless they formed a far higher proportion of the population than the German Nazis before Hitler's *putsch*. In 1922 the demagogic anti-Semite Dr. Walter Riehl furiously condemned the loss of the Germans' Sudeten homeland to the hated Czechs. The Nazis of the Sudetenland were always more extreme than the German Nazis.

As unemployment soared, the popularity of both fascists and socialists grew. The Austrian government worsened matters by following the usual advice of economic experts and business lobbyists—cutting wages and government benefits while lowering business taxes. The Social Democrats blamed austerity measures for the failing economy; fascists and government spokesmen blamed international Jewry. Fearing a victory of either socialists or fascists, the government amended the constitution in December 1929 to give the chancellor the power to command the army, dissolve Parliament, and issue emergency decrees. On November 9, 1930, the last free elections for the national Parliament left the socialists still the largest party but still outnumbered by the Christian Social coalition. The Austrian Nazis won only 110,000 votes. Frustrated, on Christmas 1930 they painted the Star of David on Jewish-owned stores to encourage boycotts, and bombed and teargassed stores and synagogues. In posters and demonstrations they demanded Jewish blood as they battled leftists and Jewish veterans in the streets.

The new Heimwehr leader, Prince Ernst Starhemberg, opposed the Austrian Nazis because of their anti-Catholicism and feared that *Anschluss* would make them Hitler's favorites. He relied instead on Mussolini to protect Austria from German aggression. In spite of his Catholicism, he did not consider even converted Jews to be Germans or Christians. But he was not extreme enough for the majority of his followers, who began to join or ally themselves with the Nazis. In September 1931 Heimwehr leader Walter Pfrimer joined local Nazis in a *putsch* attempt. The government stopped him and put him on trial. The jury gave him the fascist salute and acquitted him; the government allowed his units to keep their weapons. When the French withdrew crucial loans to prevent a customs union with Germany in 1931, more Austrians, also inspired by Hitler's rise, joined the Nazis. Alfred Frauenfeld, gauleiter of Vienna from 1930 to 1933, organized an SS and imported Nazi speakers from Germany. One commented that the Austrian Nazis were ideologically vague except for their praiseworthy and single-minded hatred of the Jews.

As the German Nazis had done, from 1930 through 1934 the Austrian Nazis absorbed other anti-Semites: supporters of the Heimwehr, the right wing of the Christian Social party, the Landbund, and a variety of small but virulent racist groups. In October 1931, when the German conservative dignitaries of the Harzburg Front allied with Hitler, the German DNVP leader Hugenberg donated funds to the upper-class anti-Semites of the Austrian GDVP; they had won a half-million votes in the Austrian elections of 1930. In 1932 they told their supporters to join the Austrian Nazis because they were the strongest opponents of Jewry. Kunschak's large German Public Employees Movement also moved to the Nazis. The only significant political opposition to racism remained the Social Democrats and the miniscule Communist party.

In April 1932, regional elections in two districts gave the Austrian Nazis 378,000 votes. In Vienna alone their votes rose from 27,500 in 1930 to 201,000, and they gained two to four times their national average in provincial capitals and county seats—and this before Hitler's huge victory of July 1932. The Christian Social Engelbert Dollfuss became chancellor in May 1932, a pious Catholic and avowed enemy of fascists and the "Jewish Marxist spirit." But his coalition with the Heimwehr and the Landbund had only a precarious one-vote majority, and he too lost favor because he was forced to beg for Allied loans, accept a renewal of the ban on *Anschluss*, and fire tens of thousands more civil servants. From 1932 to 1933 Austrian Nazi regional organizations doubled. When Hitler became chancellor, 43,000 more Austrians joined. Local elections in 1933 in Innsbruck, a bastion of rural piety and the Christian Social party, gave the Nazis more than 40 percent. As in Germany, army officers and aristocrats, the most virulent anti-Semites and supporters of *Anschluss*, rushed to join the Nazis. By the end of 1932 about one-third of all Austrians were pro-Nazi, and among Austrians other than the left, anti-Semitism was practically a national consensus.

Many of the most active Nazis were high school or university students; Nazis held an absolute majority in the German Students' Association. Civil servants, employed or unemployed, were heavily pro-Nazi, though threatened with dismissal and loss of pension. Veterans, white-collar workers, small shopkeepers, physicians, lawyers, teachers, pharmacists, architects, engineers, mechanics, railroad and streetcar workers, and artisans joined in great numbers, as did judges and members of the government security services.

There were some 245,000 Protestants in Austria in 1932, mostly the offspring of those whom Schoenerer had persuaded to leave Catholicism for a truly racist Germanic faith. Practically all Protestant clergy were pro-Nazi, and in April 1932 a heavily Protestant town voted the Nazis their first absolute majority. When Hitler gained power, conversions to Protestantism rapidly increased. Until 1932 most peasants and agricultural workers had supported the Christian Social party, the Catholic

Heimwehr, or the Landbund, but farm workers returning from Germany with praise for Hitler and comparatively large savings fostered movement to the Nazis. By 1934 the Carinthia and Styria regions were about 75 percent Nazi, as were many towns elsewhere. By 1933 those who did not support the Nazis were Social Democrats, those who wanted an independent Austria, and some high bureaucrats and nobles who hoped for a return of the Habsburgs. Yet even Archduke Otto, heir to the Habsburg crown, insisted that Austria must take strong anti-Semitic measures.

The Catholic church in Austria remained loyal to the Christian Social party. But by constantly harping on the evils of the Jews it created a climate favorable to the more extreme racism of the Nazis. After all, millions of Austrians looked to the church for moral leadership. Although Austrian bishops warned their followers against Nazi paganism, yet "Catholic journals and newspapers in the First Republic were filled with articles denouncing Jews. . . ." Some clerics even praised the discredited *Protocols of the Elders of Zion,* labeled the Jews a satanic people, or declared they did not possess sufficient redeeming grace to convert in good faith. Christian Social youth activists moved to the Nazis because the party was not hard enough on the Jews. The Bishop of Innsbruck warned the faithful of the Jewish world danger. The Bishop of Linz wrote in 1933 that one could not be a good Catholic and a good Nazi, but then went on to say that the Jews poisoned Christian souls, harmed Austrian culture, morals, economy, medicine, law, and journalism, and were responsible for revolutions, bolshevism, and atheism. He called it the moral duty of faithful Christians to destroy harmful Jewish influences. The Austrian episcopate condemned the letter in December 1933; the Nazis published everything but the objection.

Hoping to seize power, in June 1933 the Nazis launched a campaign of street terror and bombing. Dollfuss immediately outlawed them, and an angry Hitler cut off tourism—crucial to the Austrian economy. In May 1934, fearing the victory of either socialists or Nazis and the end of an independent Austria, Dollfuss and Starhemberg declared a Fatherland Front, banned all political parties, and ended freedom of the press, assembly, and speech. Tens of thousands of Heimwehr members and other groups marched shouting "Heil Dollfuss" under the flag of the Fatherland Front, a crooked cross modeled on the symbol of the medieval Crusades. A concordat gave the church privileges unequaled since the time of Metternich. Amidst calls of "Austria awake!" race, independence, and Catholicism were declared the foundations of the regime. But authoritarian racism only played into the hands of the Austrian Nazis and ultimately of Hitler.

The Austrian Nazis unleashed a wave of bombings against cafés patronized by Jews, government offices, police headquarters, law courts, tourist centers, waterworks, and power plants. Dollfuss purged Nazi sympathizers from state office, imposing martial law and the death penalty against terrorists. Some fifty thousand Nazis were convicted of various offenses, and many pro-Nazi groups were outlawed. In February 1934 Dollfuss also bombarded the socialists in their Viennese stronghold, the Karl Marx Hof, and the left went underground. Open rebellion would have been suicidal, given the armed power of the Heimwehr, the army, the police, and the probable intervention of Hitler. Local socialist units fought the government with guerrilla tactics but were brutally suppressed by Heimwehr and police. The Nazi leader, Theo Habicht, proposed a truce; Dollfuss threw some five thousand Nazis and six hundred socialists into detention camps. Increasingly unpopular, the Dollfuss regime ruled by decree, depending on the support of the army, bureaucrats, and clergy.

Many socialists reluctantly accepted Dollfuss; they knew that neither Hitler nor Mussolini would tolerate a socialist Austria. The Nazis labeled the Fatherland Front a "Jew dictatorship" because many Jewish businessmen, orthodox Jewish leaders, and some Jewish organizations supported the Front, fearing the alternative—the rule of the Austrian Nazis or Hitler. But the regime did not welcome Jewish support or censor anti-Semitic writings. Emmerich Czermak, chairman of the Christian Social party and its spokesman on Jewish affairs, published a book labeling Jews degenerate radicals who should be excluded from politics and otherwise restricted by special laws. But Dollfuss, warned by the Allies and the Americans, allowed anti-Semitic policies to be carried out only by lower-level officials. After the war Starhemberg complained that he and Dollfuss had not been able to defend Austria against the Nazis—German or Austrian—because the Austrian people so willingly believed anti-Semitic fantasies, even about the Fatherland Front. "Although there was not a single Jew in any leadership position . . . the Viennese were telling each other that . . . after all the Nazis were right and that one should clean out the Jews." This from a leading anti-Semite and co-head of the *Judenrein* regime.

In July 1934 Nazis broke into Dollfuss's office and shot and killed him. In a brief conflict the *putschists* were defeated and thousands fled to Germany. Hitler had subsidized Nazi terrorism, but he rebuked the leaders of the *putsch* as premature, telling them he needed time and appeasement to equip his armies and import foodstuffs and war materials. Moreover, he did not wish to antagonize Mussolini, still Austria's protector, and he disliked many Austrian Nazis for refusing to obey him blindly. The Christian Social leader Kurt von Schuschnigg now led the Fatherland Front. Schuschnigg's minister of education said that although Austria could accept orthodox Jews, secular Jews could never be real Germans; Palestine was the place for such dangerous parasites. But like Dollfuss, Schuschnigg could not resolve the contradictions that prevented Austria from being both independent and anti-Nazi. By now most Austrians wanted him to compromise with the Austrian Nazis and Hitler.

Attempting to outbid the Nazis, Schuschnigg allowed the revival of the Antisemitenbund, the Front Fighters League, and the Pan Germans (now called the Pan Aryan Union). Dollfuss had banned them for distributing Nazi literature when the party was outlawed. Kunschak declared that "Either one solves [the Jewish question] in a timely way, inspired by reason and humaneness, or it will be solved in the way an unreasoning animal attacks his prey, with enraged, wild instincts." The government planned to segregate Jewish pupils and have them taught only by Jewish teachers, but the lack of sufficient Jewish teachers prevented it. As a result of earlier discrimination, only 180 of 5,000 teachers in Vienna were Jewish. The government also encouraged the Union of Christian German Physicians to fight the "degenerate" influence of the Jews, and the Society of German Lawyers to boycott international conferences if Jewish lawyers attended. Leading officials, including the mayor of Vienna, reviled the Jews; Kunschak insisted that "the guilt of a Jew is that he is born a Jew." Thus the logic of the death camps.

The government fired Jewish physicians from city hospitals, the civil service, municipal jobs, and state firms. By 1937 only 154 of Vienna's thousands of city employees were Jewish. The Fatherland Front and the *Reichspost* demanded boycotts of Jewish businesses and for convenience published the names of Jewish firms, something the Nazis had been doing since the late 1920s. When the liberal and famous Jewish-owned *Neue Freie Presse* got into debt, the government made certain it ended in Catholic hands. Jewish journalists were fired or allowed to cover only sports or cultural events. The popular Austrian Gymnastic Association instructed its members to stay away from Jews or writing that contained "Jewish" ideas. Schuschnigg allowed the Nazis to resume publishing, but only if they attacked the Jews and not his government.

Schuschnigg's actions only encouraged the Nazis and their popularity. His supporters and more Heimwehr and Christian Social party members rapidly moved to the Nazis, desiring stronger anti-Semitic measures and *Anschluss* with a newly powerful Germany. In October 1936 Schuschnigg organized his own paramilitary unit, fired Starhemberg, and outlawed all other paramilitaries. By then the Fatherland Front had very little popular support. The military, meanwhile, wanted *Anschluss*. In June 1936 Mussolini, in return for Hitler's support for his Ethiopian campaign, insisted that Schuschnigg compromise with Hitler. In April 1937 Hitler promised Mussolini once again that he had no interest in the South Tyrol with its large ethnic German population, angering many Austrian Nazis. Only socialists, Catholics who feared Nazi paganism, and pro-Habsburg aristocrats now opposed *Anschluss*. The left still resisted anti-Semitism but made no strong point of it, aware that many workers were anti-Semites. Universities became too dangerous for Jewish students.

The church dropped its opposition to the Nazis. In 1937 the Austrian bishop Alois Hudal dedicated a book to Adolf Hitler, calling him the "the Siegfried of German hope and Greatness," and claiming that racism was compatible with Christianity. During the Third Reich, Bishop Hudal was the Nazi representative to the Vatican; after the war he helped Nazi war criminals escape to Latin America. Schuschnigg, Archbishop Theodor Cardinal Innitzer, and all but a few of the most determined Christian Social members favored cooperation with the Nazis. As Lueger had done, the mayor of Vienna often gave anti-Semitic speeches.

By 1936 tens of thousands of Jews lived on charity. Austrian Nazis seized Jewish property, called for death to the Jews, and beat them with impunity. The largest number of Jews that ever turned out for the elections to the Jewish Community organization that year voted 70 percent Zionist. Ernst Kaltenbrunner, the notorious mass murderer later hanged at Nuremberg, left the Heimwehr to become head of the Austrian Nazi SS, persuading the Austrian Adolf Eichmann to leave his own vicious paramilitary group and join him. With Hitler's approval, Austrian Nazis joined the Fatherland Front. Josef Leopold, Nazi

leader from 1933 through 1938, demanded that the Front pro-
hibit all Jewish activities and ally itself militarily with the Reich.
Austrians and foreign observers expected the imminent arrival
of the German army in 1937. Even the international press knew
that the Austrian Nazis would win an absolute majority if elections were held.

By November 1937 Hitler knew that no nation would fight
for Austria because of their fear of war and the Austrian public's strong support for *Anschluss*. On February 12, 1938,
Hitler summoned Schuschnigg to Berchtesgaden and gave his
ultimatum: release the remaining interned Nazis, appoint the
pro-Nazi Artur Seyss-Inquart minister of interior and a Nazi
minister of economics, and merge the two economies. In desper-
ation Schuschnigg planned a plebiscite for March 14 calling for
an independent and Christian Austria with equal rights for all
those who "declare for race and Fatherland." Hitler demanded
he postpone it, Mussolini refused to help, and Schuschnigg's advisers told him the army and the police would not resist the
Germans. Schuschnigg capitulated and appointed Seyss-Inquart
chancellor; Hitler chose his cabinet ministers.

German troops occupied Austria in March 1938; the League
of Nations did not even meet to discuss it. Half a million
Austrians greeted Hitler in the Heldenplatz in Vienna—it was
and remains the largest gathering of Austrians ever. Hitler's
plebiscite received overwhelming support, though known anti-
Nazis, socialists, and Communists could not vote. Cardinal Innitzer and his bishops warmly welcomed Hitler and ordered
church bells to ring; Pius XI summoned Innitzer to the Vatican
to reproach him for his pro-Nazi statements. The Nazis held a
massive anti-Catholic rally culminating in an attack on the cardinal's palace. When Innitzer objected, Hitler forbade some 150
priests to teach, established compulsory civil marriage, liberal-
ized divorce laws, and seized church property.

Before German troops arrived, Austrian Nazis occupied
public buildings and, aided by numerous civilians and the po-

lice, looted Jewish property and grossly humiliated and physically attacked Jews. They also plundered some thirty thousand Jewish businesses before the new government could do it. Pastor Johannes Iverson, head of the Swedish mission, wrote that the Austrians seemed to believe the Jews "must be fumigated like lice." An international outcry occurred when the *Reader's Digest* published William L. Shirer's description of the "orgy of sadism" against Jews by Austrians, declaring it worse than anything he had ever seen in Berlin. The German SS journal reported that the SS had no need to organize anti-Jewish actions; the Austrians had done it themselves overnight. Racist laws were applied more vigorously than in Germany. Austrians competed to become *Judenrein*: some beat Jews to death, others drove them out of towns and districts or forced them across the eastern borders. *Kristallnacht* in Vienna was worse than in Berlin, and more civilians participated. Jews were harassed out of public and private employment. Sixteen thousand Jewish children were expelled from schools, and anti-Semitic films were regularly shown to schoolchildren.

The Germans fined the Jewish community and sent its leaders to Dachau; they also stole the Habsburg crown jewels. Jews owned more than eighty banks in Vienna; all but eight were immediately taken over. In fourteen months all Jewish businesses were gone, and Jews had been evicted from flats, placed on curfew, and forbidden to purchase groceries except in the afternoon when most stores were empty of scarce necessities. Hundreds of Jews committed suicide. Fifty thousand Jews registered in Vienna for emigration. Tragically, seventeen thousand Austrian Jews found refuge in nations later occupied by Germany. In the spring of 1941 the German army killed many thousands of Austrian Jews in Serbia.

One in ten Austrians, compared to one in fifteen Germans, joined the Nazi party—one of every four adult males in Austria. About 8.5 percent of the population of greater Germany was Austrian, but Austrians made up close to 15 percent of the SS.

Roughly 70 percent of Eichmann's staff was Austrian. Euthanasia was first committed by gassing at Hartheim Castle in Austria. Unlike German bishops, the Austrian episcopate did not protest, probably because there was no public outcry as in Germany. An Austrian firm constructed the first mobile gassing vans and gas chamber. Forty percent of concentration camp staff were Austrian. Odilo Globocnik, supervisor of Treblinka, Sobibor, and Belzec, was Austrian, as was most of his staff; under them 1.6 million Jews died.

More deliberate killing took place at Mauthausen in Austria than in any camp in Germany. Of the 5.1 million Jews who died, Simon Wiesenthal estimated that Austrians were responsible for roughly half. The deportation of Jews to the East was much more rapid than in Germany, public approval more common. Austrian Jews discovered they were better off in Berlin than in Vienna. Far more German than Austrian Jews survived the war. Of 67,601 Austrian Jews sent to concentration camps or ghettos, 2,142 were alive at war's end. Slovenes and Austrian Communists backed by the Soviet government did most of the resistance fighting. Some Austrians aided Stauffenberg's attempt to assassinate Hitler, but Austrians were more willing than Germans to betray the resistance and Jews. The time to consider Austria Hitler's victim has long since passed.

The denazification of Austria that ended in 1949 was a farce. The reconstituted Christian Social party, renamed the Austrian People's party, allowed Leopold Kunschak, still one of its leaders, to continue his virulent anti-Semitic speeches. The Communists, briefly strong because of the Soviet occupation, tracked down some Nazi war criminals. But the Social Democratic party did not welcome former Jewish leaders from exile or attempt to pursue Nazi war criminals, unlike the German Social Democrats. Like the Austrian People's party, it competed for the ex-Nazi vote. The socialists insisted, undoubtedly correctly, that hunting war criminals would cost them hundreds of thousands of votes. Former Nazis, highly respected, assumed important public roles even though the constitution, essentially written by the Allies, forbade it. Spectators cheered when ex-Nazi killers were acquitted in the few trials that did occur. Franz Novak, Eichmann's former transportation chief, played a leading role in the postwar SS veterans' organization. He was tried in 1960 because international outcries embarrassed the government. He received eight years for "public violence." The judge, a former Nazi prosecutor, set aside the verdict. In 1966, when the Germans finally took steps against some of their most notorious mass murderers, Simon Wiesenthal sent a document listing Austrian war crimes to the government. He received no response.

Until recently, the period from 1918 until 1945 was ignored in Austrian high school textbooks, and Mauthausen was a forbidden topic. To speak disparagingly of the Nazis in the early 1950s often aroused instant anger, as the author knows from personal experience. Hans Mikoletzky, director of the National Archives, wrote the leading book on contemporary Austrian history in 1957 and won the highest Austrian prize. Of the four hundred pages, fewer than four dealt with the Holocaust—and in them Germany was held solely responsible. The Austrian Parliament ignored all claims for reparations. A poll taken in 1984 indicated that 85 percent of the population still showed some degree of anti-Semitism; 20 percent said that Auschwitz had its positive aspects. It is no surprise that the Jewish population in Austria declined from 11,000 in 1954 to 6,000 in 1986—out of 7.6 million Austrians. A minor point perhaps, but Vienna, once the center of European culture, became a cultural backwater without its Jewish community. It must be said, however, that over the last few years the Austrian government has encouraged a reevaluation of the Austrian role in the Holocaust. The Holocaust is now studied in the schools, and many, especially the young, have spoken out against the terrors of the past and Austria's participation in them.

SIX

France Before 1914

MANY BELIEVE that anti-Semitism was just as dangerous in France as in Germany, because in the nineteenth and early twentieth centuries the amount of hate literature in France was immense and anti-Semites numbered in the millions. But these factors are not the only measure of racism's power to do serious damage. As Germany showed, anti-Semitism must be strong among the political elites and the electorate. But if the power of the ideas and groups that oppose racism is strong enough, it will deny success to racists. In France the followers of the eighteenth-century Enlightenment—the *philosophes*—created an intellectual force that seriously weakened both Christian and racist anti-Semitism. With the Revolution of 1789 began the struggle to create a liberal democratic society in France, one that would support religious toleration, encourage the assimilation of the Jewish community, and drastically curtail the political power of anti-Semitism.

Sir Isaac Newton's great work of 1687, the *Principia Mathematica*, and John Locke's philosophy inspired the *philosophes*. Newton revealed a universe of matter in motion, powered by the law of gravity and understood through mathematics. His work reinforced what Spinoza and others had argued: God was not the miracle-working God of Scripture but a Great Engineer or Supreme Mathematician who created the laws of the universe and the moral sensibilities innate to mankind, both accessible to reason and comprising a rational religion or "deism."

The particular dogmas of the historical religions were simply useful myths for the moral instruction of the uneducated masses. They should be free to believe them, but the state should forbid religious persecution based merely on competing ancient delusions.

Extending the work of Locke, the *philosophes* held that all ideas came from our sensations and experience, not divine revelation. Society, family, class, and education formed the opinions, abilities, and moral character of mankind. One was not born with the innate traits of a peasant, merchant, or noble; the environment shaped us, and society limited or encouraged social mobility. Consequently, although the *philosophes* considered the petty commerce and moneylending of the Jews detestable, they believed these activities were not innate Jewish traits but the consequences of Christian oppression. End discrimination and the Jews would gradually assimilate into all occupations and perhaps eventually adopt deism. Even Voltaire, the one anti-Semite among the *philosophes*, opposed the persecution of the Jews. Diderot found Judaism absurd but denounced Christianity as even more absurd, the worst of all religions because of its history of bloody oppression. Montesquieu was positively pro-Jewish. D'Alembert thought Christian dogmas unbelievable. Rousseau insisted that Jews be allowed freely to debate their differences with Christians—a truly explosive idea even now, for it means publicly denying the divinity of Christ. The *philosophes* eagerly supported David Hume's demonstration that there could be no rational proof of the existence of God or of miracles. Robespierre thought all religions corrupt and saw no reason to single out the Jews. He hoped to replace them all with a religion of reason that stressed only civic virtue.

The *philosophes* also sought the natural laws of society created by the "Great Author of Nature." Adam Smith had argued that just as the law of gravity kept the universe moving harmoniously, so too the invisible hand of economic law, if left alone by government, guilds, or business monopolies, would establish natural levels for prices, wages, and interest. He did not say so, but if interest rates followed the law of supply and demand, usury was a misnomer. Thus it was nonsense to single out the Jews for economic corruption. The ideas of the Enlightenment destroyed the medieval image of the Jews as heretics and parasitic usurers. And two centuries of bloody wars of religion brought many—like Thomas Hobbes, a closet atheist—to demand that princes use force to end religious persecution and conflict.

In France the new ideas were powerful weapons against the secular powers and vast wealth of the Catholic church and the privileges of a decadent, state-subsidized aristocracy. Enlightenment attitudes were also popular among the commercial and professional classes of Holland, England, Scotland, the American colonies, and Scandinavia. Secular but not atheist, riding the wave of expanding commercial activity from the wealth of overseas empires, the newly confident and independent Western bourgeoisie believed that science and reason provided an irrefutable basis for their own ideas, values, and interests. Neither democrats nor revolutionaries, the *philosophes* distrusted the illiterate masses and hoped enlightened princes would make the necessary reforms. But the kings of France could hardly abandon the very beliefs that sanctioned their power. It took the revolutionaries of 1789 to pass the desired laws: freedom of speech and assembly, equality before the law, inviolability of private property, and freedom of religion. Workmen's guilds were outlawed in the name of free enterprise. Priests became paid civil servants required to swear a loyalty oath to the revolutionary state. The church was stripped of its secular powers, its vast landholdings nationalized and auctioned off. In 1791 France became the first country in Europe to liberate the Jews from all civic disabilities.

Legal liberation did not, of course, end anti-Semitism or informal discrimination, but it opened the way to toleration and assimilation. Unfortunately Jews were expected to give extraordinary proof of patriotism, and the crimes of a Jew were often condemned as that of "the Jews." Jews were also expected to move swiftly into other occupations. Few people understood how difficult it is for different ethnic and religious groups to assimilate after centuries in restricted roles and still subject to discrimination. Jewish intellectuals, painfully aware of the difference between theoretical acceptance and actual discrimination, were condemned for their irony and skepticism by defenders of the status quo. Nevertheless France became home to one of the most assimilated Jewish communities in Europe. Napoleon also upheld religious and civil freedom, though he pandered to anti-Semites when it suited his political purposes. Unlike German elites, however, the political leaders of France never adopted the idea that they belonged to a superior race.

The Revolution and later the reign of Napoleon created a new France. In the 1790s nobles and bishops, bereft of offices and property, became emigrés in Austria and Prussia, organizing counterrevolution. From the middle classes emerged a new class of wealthy landowners who bought at auction the immense landed wealth of church and nobles. Peasants no longer owed fees or free services to their lords. Universal male suffrage was part of the Constitution of 1793, though Robespierre, embattled by civil war, foreign invasion, and the radical Parisian left, never carried it out. After his fall, France became a republic dominated by wealthy property owners, many with lucrative government contracts, who wanted votes only for the wealthy. Napoleon distributed national properties and titles to reward his favorites; many were regicides who feared the return of monarchy and the aristocratic emigrés hoping to regain their lands and high offices. Above all, the upper middle classes wanted social stability and economic freedom.

When Louis XVIII returned in 1814 he feared another revolution and decreed a Charter of Rights, including an elected Chamber of Deputies, ministers responsible to the king, some freedom of the press, and taxation only with consent. Catholicism remained the official religion of France, but all religions were tolerated. Louis did not reverse the sale of nationalized church and aristocratic property or cancel titles conferred by Napoleon, and he declared that no one was to be punished for previous opinions or votes. But the ultra-royalist aristocratic and clerical emigrés, angered by the king's concessions, were determined to regain their lands, power, and wealth. The king's brother and heir to the throne, the Count d'Artois, was their leader, a thickheaded reactionary and anti-Semite, incapable of compromise. In 1789 he opposed any concessions by Louis XVI. In 1792, invading France at the head of a small army of emigrés along with Austria and Prussia, he was routed by peasant guerrillas. In 1815 Louis XVIII appeased the ultras, placing some 6,000 into the army; Napoleon's soldiers despised them as traitors. In the elections of 1815 only 90,000 out of 32 million Frenchmen were eligible to vote, and only 15,000 of the wealthiest allowed to run for office. Hence the vast majority of deputies were government officials, aristocrats, or bishops. It was the most reactionary Chamber in the history of France.

The ultras refused to admit that massive dissatisfaction with the Old Regime had helped cause the Revolution. Their most influential intellectual, Count Joseph de Maistre, literally believed that God determined the course of history. Man could not even create an insect, let alone a constitution superior to the divinely established social order. The Revolution was God's plan to purge those who followed the Enlightenment and assumed they could rule without him. Hence the atheistic Jacobins who murdered the king, overthrew the aristocracy, and plunged Europe into slaughter in the name of the alleged Rights of Man. Naturally they also destroyed the Christian guilds and liberated the Jews, greedy parasites and mortal enemies of Christ. Let the Revolution run its bloody course, de Maistre wrote from exile, for only then would men learn from "God's demons," Robespierre and Napoleon, the horrors that result

from godless rule. The masses would beg for the return of
crown and altar; princes and nobles would lament the consequences of toying with reform; the clergy would put away their
Voltaire and their worldly cynicism. Church powers would be
restored. The Jews would be driven back into the ghetto where
they belonged, suspended in time until the remnant accepted
Christ in the Final Days.

The Viscount de Bonald, political leader of the ultras, demanded full restoration of the lands and powers of church, nobility, and guilds. Free enterprise, he declared, favored only
Jews whose wealth and immorality allowed them to exploit
honest workers. The self-sufficient rural villagers would become
anonymous workers in factory towns, bereft of their ancient
skills. They would lose their close-knit village ties and awareness of the limits that nature imposed on man's appetites.
Above all, their respect for priest and church and Christian
morality would be eroded. And if the Jews remained liberated,
Bonald warned, the unbridled cunning and materialism of a
race that had murdered its own Messiah would ruin France.

De Maistre and Bonald were the first important Catholic intellectuals to attack capitalism and liberalism and insist that
Jews were the primary cause and beneficiaries of both. They reinforced Christian anti-Semitism among those Catholic royalists who detested the Revolution of 1789 and sought religious
explanations for the social upheavals threatening their interests
and powers. A century later the Vichy regime republished the
writings of both de Maistre and Bonald to justify their reactionary values and anti-Semitism.

The ultras failed to restore their powers and privileges. But,
as de Maistre predicted, clerics and aristocrats became more
reactionary, church attendance rose dramatically, a variety of
ultra-conservative Catholic lay organizations sprang up, and
hundreds of thousands of Frenchmen attended religious ceremonies to purge the sins of the Revolution and swear allegiance
to king and pope. A white terror took murderous revenge on

local revolutionaries, including Jews who had not been involved. Artois and the ultras pressured the king to dissolve the Chamber in 1816, but new elections gave the moderate king's ministers a working majority. The ultras, still strongest in the Chamber, regained some of their land, and the army was purged of liberal officers. Artois headed the National Guard and enrolled only reliable reactionaries. Government subsidies helped train new priests—the most reactionary in living memory—and the clergy regained control of secondary education.

When Louis XVIII died in 1824, Artois became King Charles X. A fan of de Maistre, he detested Jews, Protestants, and the bourgeoisie. Moderate conservatives, crushed in the elections of 1824, watched in fury as Charles X rewarded his loyal emigré supporters, some seventy thousand nobles and clergy, with a one-billion-franc indemnity for their confiscated lands. Bonald pushed the measure easily through the Chamber because three hundred deputies profited from the legislation. Charles X also used state funds to save the indebted estates of loyal nobles. But the moderate landowners who had benefited from the revolutionary and Napoleonic land settlements were incensed because they paid the bulk of the taxes. Bonald severely censored the press to silence them, declaring that France needed no plague of false doctrines because the king had eighty thousand loyal landowners to advise him. Anti-clericalism, deeply ingrained since the Revolution, rekindled in reaction to laws that called for the terrible mutilation and execution of any who profaned sacred objects or questioned the divine right of kings. Bonald declared it merciful to send blasphemers to God; de Maistre had long insisted that the executioner was the ultimate guarantor of social stability.

Moderate monarchists and wealthy landowners joined in the elections of 1827 and crushed the ultras. As befits a king by divine right, Charles X ignored the results and appointed as his chief minister Prince Jules de Polignac, former favorite of Marie Antoinette, ex-prisoner of Napoleon, and one who claimed to receive political advice from the Virgin Mary. Courvoisier, a former white terrorist and now minister of justice, boasted that he took his advice from the Book of the Apocalypse. Ultras were favored in all government appointments, and former emigré Jesuits advised Charles X. Paris students marched against the king, who planned a coup to end parliamentary rule altogether, and wealthy opposition leaders organized against him under the conservative liberal Adolphe Thiers.

In 1830 the king dissolved the hostile Chamber and called for new elections. Royalists and bishops declared it criminal heresy to vote against the king, but the ultras lost almost two to one. Charles X then decreed his famous July Ordinances, ending freedom of the press, dissolving the Chamber, and denying the vote to all except the most reactionary among the already tiny electorate. Huge riots in Paris left eighteen hundred dead. To forestall Parisian radicals, moderate deputies declared a provisional government and offered the throne to the Duke of Orleans, Louis Philippe, anathema to the ultras. Although of royal birth, his father had supported the initial phase of 1789 and voted to execute Louis XVI. Similar in outlook to the wealthy landowners, financiers, and bankers who selected him, Louis Philippe ignored divine right and deemed himself a citizen king. He had good relationships with the Jewish community. Unable to rally forces of support, Charles X abdicated and fled the country. The emigré nobles and bishops of the ultras foundered on the opposition of those who had benefited from the Revolution and Napoleon. The ultras, the only significant political force that intended harm to the Jews, retreated to their chateaux, politically impotent. In his old age a despairing de Maistre declared that the pope, not kings, should rule Europe.

Many historians still believe that before the 1880s anti-Semitism in France came mainly from the left. They refer to the so-called "utopian Socialists," Charles Fourier and Pierre-Joseph Proudhon, and also Alphonse Toussenal—all extreme anti-Semites. But "left" is an inaccurate label for these men.

Fourier hated modern commercial society, identified it with Jews, and hoped to replace it with small, self-sufficient rural collectives of farmers and artisans. If he must be classified, he ought to be called a utopian reactionary, except for his famous call for free sex, ignored by his followers. Indeed, the ideal of rural communes was popular among German anti-Semites who also hated urban and industrial society and wanted a rural breeding community for the racially pure; the young Himmler belonged to one. Leftists, however, believed artisans and peasants were doomed to disappear under capitalism, and welcomed the change as a prelude to socialism. As we know, they also believed that anti-Semitism was a reactionary tactic intended to divert the attention of industrial workers from their real enemy, capitalism.

Toussenal, author of *The Jews: Kings of Our Epoch* (1845), denounced Jewish international finance and also idealized rural life. He wrote for the conservative press and attacked the Jews for denying Christ, hardly a leftist concern. Proudhon, famous for the phrase he later regretted, "Property is Theft," also wished to preserve traditional France, and believed Jewish international financiers and predatory Protestant merchants to be its chief enemies. He condemned trade unions, hated democracy, defended slavery, and even called for the extermination of the Jews. He had no influence among socialists but was a favorite of the most important ultra-royalist and anti-Semitic organization of modern France, the Action Française; his works were revived by the Vichy regime. Otherwise neither Fourier nor Proudhon found significant political support in France. In Central and Eastern Europe artisans and peasants avidly supported anti-Semitic movements, but French guilds, outlawed in 1791, were politically impotent. French peasants were satisfied because of the protection and subsidies they received from republican governments. In fact, political anti-Semitism in nineteenth-century France, far from being leftist, remained royalist and Catholic.

In the 1840s a surge of idealistic liberal and romantic nationalism culminated in the Revolution of 1848, whose leaders welcomed Jewish participation. They condemned Louis Philippe's rule as a corrupt plutocracy that ignored the fate of the average Frenchman. Royalists, the clergy, and the old aristocracy did not support him, and after riots in Paris the National Guard deserted the king. In a time of idealism, a regime that stood for nothing but wealth and property collapsed. Louis abdicated and fled, unlamented. Liberals, led by the romantic and idealistic poet Alphonse de Lamartine, formed a provisional government and demanded universal suffrage and freedom of religion. Meanwhile all Europe erupted in liberal and nationalist revolutions, accompanied by demands for parliamentary assemblies and religious freedom.

But in the first elections ever held under universal suffrage in France, the peasants followed the lead of local notables and priests and voted against "Red Paris." Of the 900 elected to the Chamber of Deputies, half were monarchists, divided between 300 followers of Louis Philippe's grandson and 150 followers of the grandson of Charles X. General Louis Cavaignac harshly suppressed thousands of frustrated, half-starved, and violent Parisians in May 1849; everywhere in Europe liberals faced defeat. But Cavaignac wanted a republic. Monarchs, emperors, and military leaders seemed unnecessary now that universal male suffrage had proven a bulwark of conservative order. Accordingly he and his advisers planned an elected chamber with legislative power balanced by a president with executive power.

The nephew of the great Napoleon ran for and won the presidency as the candidate of order, calculated to appeal to all moderate and wealthy conservative proprietors, who gained two-thirds of the votes for the Chamber. They proceeded to purge leftists and radicals from the government and deprive millions of them of the right to vote. Napoleon III curried favor by protesting the decision. But he also appeased the church by restoring educational powers to the clergy and regaining Rome for Pius IX, driven out by revolutionaries. In 1851, unable to run for a second term, Napoleon III seized power by force. The oligarchy preferred him to either the discredited monarchy or a radical republic, though some 100,000 fought briefly against him. He dissolved the Assembly, arrested extremists of left and right, and declared himself emperor.

To remain popular, Napoleon III needed a prosperous France; republicans and radicals were still agitating in Paris and many cities, and monarchists still hoped for a restoration. The followers of Saint-Simon had laid the ideological basis for prosperity in the 1830s. Unlike Fourier and Proudhon, they embraced industrial and commercial progress and rejected anti-Semitism. Under their influence, Napoleon III founded new banks to extend credit for public works, including the massive reconstruction of Paris, and subsidized industries. Neither he nor the bulk of his supporters had any interest in reversing the civic gains of the Jewish community, which they regarded as a force for economic progress. Napoleon III encouraged their economic activities. Napoleon consistently received more than 80 percent of the vote. He won liberal support when he helped Italy fight Austrian imperialism, then lost it when he prevented Italians from forcing the Papal States into the new Italy. To regain their support, he promised a "Liberal Empire." But by now many wealthy landowners and professionals believed that parliamentary government was preferable, after all. They dominated the Assembly and hated the taxes they paid to support the emperor's industrial policies and concessions to the church. In elections in 1869, Napoleon's candidates did poorly. He offered a more democratic constitution but recklessly declared war against Prussia over a minor diplomatic rebuff. Bismarck's victory led to a revival of autocracy and anti-Semitism in Germany. Napoleon's defeat led to the Third Republic.

A Provisional Government of National Defense, led by Léon Gambetta, an ardent republican, raised an army to fight on after the emperor surrendered, while in Paris the famous and radical Jacobin commune fought against a Prussian siege. Prussia prevailed over both, and in January 1871 the Chamber sued for peace; Gambetta resigned. In the elections for a constitutional assembly, those who had never supported political anti-Semitism, republicans and former supporters of Louis Philippe, won a total of 442 seats, while the Legitimists, who favored a return of the Bourbons and enjoyed ultra support, won only 182. Taken together the monarchists were a majority, but they could not cooperate. The republicans, who received the most votes of the three groups, chose Thiers, the popular conservative republican, to hold temporary executive power. His government tried to disarm the Paris commune and collect back rents left unpaid by starved and blasted Parisians. The commune resisted, and with much bloodshed the government defeated them. There would be no radical republic, and monarchy seemed more irrelevant than ever, as did the Bourbons and the ultras. After all, the last of the Bourbon kings, Charles X, had left no fond memories.

The incorporation of Alsace-Lorraine into the new German Empire weakened another strong source of French anti-Semitism. Alsatian Jews were mostly Yiddish-speaking, orthodox, and German in origin, many of them moneylenders hated by the peasants. Even the revolutionary deputies from Alsace in 1789 were anti-Semitic, and Napoleon I had passed discriminatory restrictions against Jewish creditors to please Alsatians. But after 1871 two-thirds of the sixty thousand Jews of France lived in Paris and the rest mainly in other towns. Unlike the situation in Germany, there were very few rural Jewish middlemen to arouse peasant wrath during times of agrarian depression.

A republic seemed the only alternative to discredited monarchies and a defeated empire. The defeat of France and German unification brought great prestige to the Prussian autocracy and their values in Germany, including anti-Semitism. But in France by 1877, led by Gambetta, a republican and left-republican majority of some two-thirds of the electorate dominated the

French Assembly. Social order and property seemed safe after the defeat of the commune, and the all-important French peasant vote, pro-monarchist in 1871, had moved to the republicans. By contrast, in Germany small peasant landowners almost always supported aristocratic or populist reactionaries and racists.

By 1880 the Third Republic was a true parliamentary government. The majority political parties and therefore the electorate selected the prime minister, something that did not happen in Germany until the Weimar Republic of 1919, and then only by the insistence of the victorious Allies. French liberals and radical socialists (left-wing liberals in contemporary American usage) almost always dominated the Third Republic and local governments; it was the ultimate triumph of the Enlightenment, the Revolution of 1789, and liberal values. French rabbinical authorities even feared that Judaism would disappear through assimilation. But most Jewish leaders believed that Judaic ethics reinforced the republican values of liberty, equality, and fraternity and thought of themselves as Frenchmen of Jewish origins. Where the Weimar Republic was a product of defeat, French republicanism was associated with patriotic nationalism and resistance to the reactionaries of Prussia and Austria, from 1789 and Napoleon I through the Paris commune of 1871.

Consequently French leaders, unlike those of Prussia, found anti-Semitism politically irrelevant. French Catholic royalists, priests, and Catholic intellectuals, including religious orders and their publishing houses, remained the major producers of anti-Semitic literature. One cannot overestimate the vileness of some of these writings, notably those of *La Croix*, an official publication of the church much loved by Pope Leo XIII. As in Germany, Austria, and the East, the future of the Jewish community depended on the power of liberal values, and in France they predominated. But the consolidation of the power of the republicans in the early 1880s led to a revival of anti-Semitism.

The revival culminated with the publication in 1886 of the royalist Edouard Drumont's sensational best-seller *La France Juive* (Jewish France). A massive two-volume work filled with practically every anti-Semitic fiction, it sold more than a million copies. Sensationalist and vitriolic, it reflected the hatred of the republic by monarchists and clerics, who blamed Jews, Protestants, and Freemasons for its victory. Drumont mixed medieval superstition with modern racist nonsense: rabbis kidnapped innocent Christian infants to drain their blood in a blood ritual; they knew that Christian blood was pure and Jewish blood infected with nervous and sexual diseases, including homosexuality. Bereft of all idealism, the Jews obeyed the Talmud's alleged command to destroy Christianity; everywhere they subverted traditional Christian society. Like the popes of the Counter-Reformation, Drumont insisted that Jews had inspired Protestantism and hoped to destroy Catholic moral values. Had not a Jewish deputy introduced a bill to legalize divorce? Naturally Drumont despised Jews as bloodsuckers who avoided productive labor.

Replete with lurid gossip, scandalous rumors, and distortions "supported" by anonymous sources and lies, Drumont's book claimed to reveal the alleged corruption of the Jews and their bribery and mastery over Republican leaders who had desecrated the France of the Old Regime. During the Old Regime, he declared, France had been animated by the high moral vision of the church, the firm and just hand of the monarchy, and the sturdy buttress of peasants, artisans, and rural priests—a Golden Age destroyed by the Enlightenment and the Revolution. Drumont also charged that Jewish merchants deliberately ruined French retailers by cutting prices, false advertising, ruthless cunning, and sharp dealing in the new Jewish-owned department stores. Small retailers who could not adapt to the new techniques of modern retailing—advertising, bulk purchasing, low profit rates, and swift turnover—remained fans of Drumont and anti-Semitism down through the 1940s, when the Vichy government revived his writings.

Like all extreme anti-Semites, Drumont claimed that the enemies of France were either Jews or their dupes, avoiding the inconvenient fact that Gentiles were overwhelmingly responsible for the events that racists hated. Thus Drumont insisted the *philosophes* were either Jews or their tools—including Voltaire. Robespierre and Napoleon, he insisted, were either Jewish or controlled by them; Gambetta was certainly Jewish. (He wasn't.) In his popular journal *La Libre Parole*, Drumont declared that the Revolution of 1789 benefited only Jews, and like so many anti-Semites he insisted that Jewish nihilists, led by Karl Marx, had invented socialism to destroy France and Europe so their race could gain mastery. Drumont also attacked the Freemasons as a Jewish-dominated conspiracy, another common theme of French anti-Semites because of the Freemasons' faith in the Enlightenment and their secular humanism—for Drumont simply another Jewish attack against the one true faith.

Like most anti-Semites, Drumont detested the assimilated and progressive Jews who were most zealous in their support of the republic. If millions of Gentiles voted for the republic it was because Frenchmen were becoming "Judaized." Such circular reasoning is a consistent and necessary feature of anti-Semitism. Like de Maistre and Bonald, Drumont could not admit that although there were a few Jewish participants in the Revolution of 1789, it was, of course, overwhelmingly the work of non-Jewish Frenchmen who were disgusted with Drumont's beloved Old Regime. A bitter Drumont wrote that the huge demonstrations of 1889 celebrating the centenary of the Revolution were really commemorating the victory of the Jews.

In Germany the best-selling and vicious anti-Semites of the 1880s and 1890s, Paul de Lagarde and Julius Langbehn, who anticipated the Nazis in every way, were read by the ruling elites. But Drumont's dogmatic egomania antagonized every possible ally except rural priests, diehard royalists, and small businessmen. His near pornographic anti-Semitism and sensationalist gossip could create an immense best-seller but could not sway the ruling elites or the electorate. Frustrated, Drumont blasted away at nearly all groups. The upper classes, he complained, denounced anarchists but happily stole the property of church and nobility in the Revolution of 1789. Paid by Jewish gold, the police and the judiciary covered for the corrupt politicians of the Jewish republic—a phrase that German reactionaries later used to denounce the Weimar Republic. The aristocracy pretended to despise Jews but socialized with them and married their sons to their rich daughters. We should not be surprised at this behavior, he noted, for when the peasants of southwest France rose against the Revolution in the 1790s, aristocrats fled to Vienna and Berlin rather than risk their lives. Worst of all, he fumed, the army accepted and promoted Jewish officers, unlike the Germans who wisely allowed no Jews in their permanent officer corps. When the pope recommended that Catholics make their peace with the republic in 1892, Drumont denounced bishops who did so as betrayers of Christ.

Drumont wanted a traveling exhibition built to illustrate the supposed ugly physical and moral characteristics of the Jews, as the Nazis and Vichy did later. Close Jewish stores and seize their profits, Drumont demanded, and hand them over to the small businessmen, artisans, and peasants whom the republic robs. Confiscate all Jewish wealth and, like the medieval monarchs, drive them from France. Otherwise they would make France a Jewish state. A strong leader was needed, willing to rid France of its Jews even if it meant pillage and murder.

In 1889 Drumont briefly supported General Boulanger, minister of war, who seemed to be the popular strongman who could bring down the republic and avenge the defeat of 1870. Overwhelmingly elected to the Chamber of Deputies in 1889, Boulanger was at first supported by the nationalist and anti-

Semitic street toughs, the "League of Patriots" led by Paul Deroulède. But Drumont was enraged when the general repudiated anti-Semitism. In the end Boulanger, convicted of treason, fled France. In 1889 enemies of the republic were again decisively defeated in the elections. Frustrated and bitter, Drumont predicted that ultimately his forces would have to kill the Jews; they deserved it, for did they not plot the death of France?

As in Austria, an anti-Semitic Catholic party, the Christian Democrats, was formed to defeat the Third Republic and restore the church to its former power. The aristocrats who led it, Count Albert du Mun and La Tour du Pin, wished to restore the traditional society of monarch, village, guild, and peasant—ruined, they claimed, by "Jewish" secular liberalism and capitalism. But they never gained significant electoral support, even when the pope instructed them to drop their demand to restore the monarchy and work within the Chamber. Millions of ordinary Frenchmen had done relatively well under the republic. Simple folk wisdom recalled how harsh the rule of the Old Regime had been for them. To most Frenchmen, royalists and clerics seemed simply bent on regaining their old privileges at the expense of the majority. In 1889 Drumont and other anti-Semites ran for the City Council of Paris; all were soundly defeated. In 1893 about a fourth of the German electorate voted for reactionary anti-Semites; in the same year French republicans again won handily in the Chamber—anti-Semitism was not even an issue.

But there were still millions of French anti-Semites, and the Dreyfus Affair brought them to the fore in an uproar that still leads many to believe that anti-Semitism was potentially as destructive in France as in Germany. Yet in the end the affair transformed a conservative republican government into one dominated by radical liberals and anti-clerics.

The apparent discovery that Alfred Dreyfus, a Jewish officer on the General Staff, was a German spy seemed a godsend to anti-Semites. They and many army officers, heavily influenced by Jesuits and royalists, believed Jewish officers prone to treason. Nevertheless there were eight Jewish generals and hundreds of Jewish officers in the French army. (There could be no Dreyfus case in Germany because no Jew would be permitted to become, like Dreyfus, an intern on the General Staff.)

In 1894 a court martial declared Dreyfus guilty. Almost no one thought him innocent. The evidence seemed damning, and the Jewish community felt only shame. Exultant cries of Jewish treason rose from Drumont and the Catholic press, especially the official *La Croix*, which denounced Dreyfus and the Jews as a deicidal and treasonous race. (In 1998 the editors of *La Croix* finally apologized for their many vicious anti-Semitic articles during the Dreyfus Affair.) Anti-Semitism was also intensified because thousands of Jews fleeing Russian pogroms ultimately arrived in France. Many were orthodox, Zionist, or leftist, in stark contrast to the well-assimilated Jewish community, and hence easier targets for racists.

Yet in spite of Dreyfus's conviction, in 1895 the French elected a government of liberals, radical liberals, progressives, and socialists at a time when anti-Semitism raged in Austria and Germany. Even when the Chamber of Deputies voted unanimously to send Dreyfus to Devil's Island, only a handful of deputies attacked "the Jews" as such. The heroic efforts of Dreyfus's brother Mathieu soon raised doubts about Dreyfus's guilt, and in 1896 Colonel Georges Picquart reviewed the evidence and voiced his suspicions. He was silenced and banished to a remote post. High-ranking army officers, aware that Dreyfus was the wrong man, forged documents and withheld evidence of Dreyfus's innocence and the guilt of another. Army intelligence falsely claimed it had damning secret evidence against Dreyfus, evidence that if revealed would weaken national security and start a war with Germany before France was prepared. Drumont and army officers concocted a tale of an international Jewish conspiracy out to destroy the French army. With the aid of the Russian secret police, anti-Semites forged the infamous *Protocols of the Elders of Zion,* which maintained, among other nonsense, that "Liberty, Equality, Fraternity" was in reality a slogan used by the Jews to conquer the world. Picquart's revelations, supported by a small group of intellectuals, led to Émile Zola's famous article denouncing the cover-up, *J'accuse.* Journalists demanded a new investigation; deputies raised questions in the Chamber. Army leaders and politicians who had forged evidence or supported those who did knew their careers were finished should neutral judges review the case. To divert attention, the culprits insisted that the army itself was under attack. Soon the affair was more than a question of Dreyfus's guilt or innocence, it was a political confrontation between the republic and its enemies among army, church, and royalists, many of whom had found sanctuary from the hated republic as army officers. Vituperation flooded a divided France. Maurice Barrès, a deputy in 1898 and at the time the most famous French intellectual, wrote: "I assume Dreyfus is guilty because of his race." He later preached a French version of the Nazi slogan of blood and soil, but his reputation failed to outlast the true horror of blood and death in the mud of the trenches in 1914–1918.

Extensive anti-Semitic rioting occurred in many French cities in the wake of the Dreyfus Affair; cries of "Death to the Jews" were common. In Algiers, where rightist colonialists detested both Jews and Arabs, severe outbursts brought martial law. Drumont's paper, the Augustinian Fathers of the Assumption, and *La Croix* insisted that reopening the Dreyfus case would benefit only what they saw as the international Jewish syndicate. Royalists and church leaders, including one archbishop, founded anti-Semitic societies, among them the Jeunesse Antisémitique, the Patrie Française, and, as mentioned earlier, the Action Française led by Charles Maurras, later a prominent supporter of the Vichy government. Army officers risked their careers if they did not defend the verdict, and many joined in street demonstrations against Dreyfus and the Jews. In the east and south of France, traditional home of anti-Semites and enemies of the Revolution, large crowds joined the assault. At the height of the agitation in 1899, French Algerian colonialists elected Drumont to the Chamber of Deputies, where he joined eighteen other extreme anti-Semites.

The turmoil gave the illusion that France was the most anti-Semitic European nation, except to those who were aware of events in Vienna. Theodor Herzl, who as a journalist had witnessed the Viennese mobs calling for death to the Jews during Lueger's rise in the 1890s, also covered Drumont's earlier libel trial for accusing the president of France of accepting Jewish bribes. With the Dreyfus Affair, Herzl despaired. If Frenchmen, heirs of the revolutionary tradition, could be so anti-Semitic, there seemed to be no safe future for European Jewry. In 1897, ironically inspired by attending one of Wagner's operas, Herzl wrote his famous call for a Jewish home in Palestine and planned the first international meeting of Zionists.

Socialists won some forty seats in the French elections of 1893, led by Jean Jaurès, who believed in a peaceful and democratic path to socialism. By 1898 Jaurès, an early supporter of Dreyfus, convinced his followers that the attack on Dreyfus was an attack on the republic and the left, and they became the first party to issue a signed manifesto in favor of Dreyfus. Yet even the leading Conservative party in France, the Union Républicain Democratique, found anti-Semitism irrelevant, and most peasants remained loyal to the republic, always solicitous of their needs. Anti-Semitism among university students and the professional and white-collar classes, though present, was far weaker than among their counterparts in Germany. In the elections of May 1898, the supporters of the Republic again won overwhelmingly, and Dreyfus gained a review of the verdict. Rightist militants demonstrated against him, but republican and socialist demonstrators far outnumbered them. Lt. Col. Hubert Henry, one of the forgers, publicly exposed the lies of the army, and huge demonstrations of workers, students, and ordinary citizens marched in Paris chanting "Long Live the Republic." In February 1899 the nationalist Deroulède tried but failed to persuade a regiment to lead a military coup.

By now most of the public and the Chamber had had enough of the anti-Semitic uproar. A military court tried to protect the culprits by declaring Dreyfus guilty "with extenuating circumstances." But in 1899 Prime Minister Waldeck-Rousseau pardoned Dreyfus, who was later cleared of all charges. Supported by the Chamber of Deputies, Waldeck-Rousseau set out to destroy the enemies of the republic. The government arrested Jules Guérin, head of the Anti-Semitic League. Waldeck-Rousseau appointed a republican general minister of war to purge the army and also severely restricted church powers over public education. Soon state schoolchildren far outnumbered those in church schools—the culmination of attempts since 1789 to offer free and secular education. Much to the annoyance of local priests and nobles, the average teacher was usually an advocate of the secular humanism of the Enlightenment, and many favored socialism. At the same time German teachers were denouncing the Social Democrats as Jewish traitors, playing leading roles in anti-Semitic organizations, and glorifying Prussian autocratic militarism and war.

In the election of 1902 a republican victory, led by their left wing, sanctioned Waldeck-Rousseau's actions. Jaurès's socialists, who defended the republic and rejected revolutionary rhetoric, outvoted their orthodox Marxist rivals. German Social Democrats were much stronger, but without a republic to support, many of their leaders still spoke of revolution even as they pursued peaceful reform. There had been some fifty or so anti-Semites in the French Chamber since 1899, including Drumont, but in 1902 all lost their seats. The number of subscribers to Drumont's journal rapidly declined. Emile Combes, prime minister in 1902, enjoyed a large majority and led the first republican government supported by socialists. More royalists and

Catholics were purged from the army and the civil service; Jews and republicans in both institutions faced less discrimination. More than one hundred church schools and many religious orders were closed—monks left France en masse. In 1904–1905 the government broke diplomatic relations with the Vatican, and tens of thousands of congratulatory messages arrived from all regions and municipalities. Drumont, *La Croix*, and provincial religious publications still disseminated their poison, but they seemed politically extinct. In 1905 Clemenceau appointed Colonel Picquart minister of war; in 1906 radical liberals won again. In 1914 the Chamber chose a moderate socialist as premier—René Viviani. When France seemed finally ready to confront the new challenges generated by industrialism, the country was tragically plunged into war. Its aftermath would show that reaction and anti-Semitism were far from dead.

SEVEN

France, 1914–1945

THE FRENCH REPUBLIC began the war under a government of National Union led by a moderate socialist premier. Even in the darkest days of 1917 there was no resort to military dictatorship or an outburst of anti-Semitism, as in Germany. Selected premier in 1917, Clemenceau, a radical republican, governed harshly but did not violate the constitution. In Germany, defeat brought the despised Weimar Republic; in France, victory enhanced the prestige of the Third Republic. But France was debt-ridden, her northeast territories devastated, and her people traumatized by the loss of more than 10 percent of the male population.

Naturally the French longed for peace, even as hundreds of thousands of reactionary nationalists in Germany sought revenge and blamed the Jews, not the autocratic elites actually responsible, for the defeat. Clemenceau, determined to enforce a harsh treaty, won the elections of November 1919 and ruled with a like-minded Chamber of Deputies composed mainly of war veterans who wanted their benefits and pensions protected. In general the French public thought Clemenceau was not severe enough on the Germans, and in 1923 Raymond Poincaré, a conservative republican, replaced him. When he invaded the Ruhr because of a minor violation of the Versailles Treaty, he infuriated the German public, provoked even more support for German paramilitaries, and emboldened Hitler to attempt his *putsch*.

In 1924 a coalition of the left gained power in France. In reaction veterans, partly inspired by Mussolini, organized the Faisceau and the Jeunesses Patriotes. Like the Italian dictator, they despised democratic politics as a dirty bourgeois game, hated socialism, wanted an authoritarian government, and were not anti-Semitic. Business interests who feared leftist legislation subsidized them. But the two organizations had nowhere near the power, numbers, or popularity of German paramilitaries. Without serious public dissatisfaction with the republic to exploit, the Faisceau rapidly collapsed, and both organizations lost most of their business subsidies. Republicans continued to dominate politics as they had since the late 1870s. In 1927 the center right, again led by Poincaré, defeated the leftist coalition.

The only significant anti-Semitic organization remained the Action Française. Founded during the Dreyfus Affair by Catholic royalists hoping to "purify" France by throwing out all aliens, restoring monarchy, and reversing the Revolution of 1789, the AF had some 60,000 members and a paper with a circulation of 100,000. Many French officers, including Marshal Philippe Pétain, hero of the war, admired the Action Française, but the army was not an instrument of reaction as in Germany. The German High Command recruited only rightists, whereas the French army included soldiers of all political opinions. A French officer would damage his career if he openly opposed the republic, and no secret military funds or arms were given to fascist organizations as they were in Germany. To the vast majority of Frenchmen, the Action Française was irrelevant. More or less satisfied with modern commercial and industrial society, they had no desire for authoritarianism or pleasant memories of a monarchy that had ended with the reactionary stupidities of Charles X and the plutocratic indifference of Louis Philippe. Moreover, Pope Pius XI briefly excommunicated the Action Française in 1926, partly because its arrogant leader, Charles Maurras, habitually made such statements as: "I see no reason to believe the Gospels according to four obscure Jews."

The postwar inflation in France did not intensify racism as in Germany. The French inflation was much less severe, but, more important, French reactionaries had never successfully persuaded large sections of the public to hold the Jews responsible for economic catastrophes as racists had in Germany, Austria, and Eastern Europe. The political elites of France, business oriented unlike Prussian aristocrats, naturally approved of commerce, and Jews were not as overrepresented in the modern sectors of the economy as in Central and Eastern Europe. When the French invaded the Ruhr at the height of the German inflation, close to 30 percent of the German electorate voted for anti-Semitic candidates. In France a left republican coalition won, and anti-Semitism was politically insignificant. In addition, republicanism was strong in French rural districts while in Germany anti-Semitism and bitter contempt for Weimar thrived among landowners large and small.

The early 1930s brought a marked resurgence of fascism in France, prompted mainly by an influx of German Jewish refugees. The republic had accepted more German Jewish refugees than any other nation. American visas were shamefully scarce because the U.S. State Department, the Congress, and most of the public did not want refugee Jews. In 1921 France already had more immigrants as a percentage of the population than the vaunted land of immigrants, the United States. From 1930 to 1940 the Jewish population of France rose from 180,000 to 350,000. Impoverished Jewish refugees accepted lower pay if they found jobs, as many did in the textile trades. French textile workers responded by demanding quotas as they had in the nineteenth century. Physicians and lawyers also wanted restrictions against Jewish refugee competition. In 1932 the republic placed quotas on Jews and all foreign physicians and lawyers; left republicans, socialists, and Communists protested, though unemployment was high among their voters.

Some conservative newspapers demanded that Jewish refugees find work on farms or in mines, like the Poles and Italians who had worked in France for generations. But unemployment had already forced about a quarter of a million of these immigrants to return home, and Jews, with few exceptions, had no safe home to go to. Strong objections also were raised against orthodox Jews who fled to France to escape the postwar years of fighting and terror in the East that had cost thousands of their coreligionists their lives. Even many French Jews were hostile toward a people they regarded as living remnants of Polish ghetto superstitions and a threat to their own acceptance as patriotic Frenchmen of Jewish faith. With Hitler's selection as chancellor in Germany, some twenty thousand more German Jewish refugees fled to France. Many were leftists who wrote anti-fascist literature and demanded boycotts against Germany. Most Frenchmen, right and left, resented attempts by a guest people to drag France nearer to war simply to help Jews and leftists against Nazi oppression. Yet in spite of renewed public antagonism toward Jews, in the year of Hitler's greatest electoral victory, 1932, the republican left and socialists gained control of the French Chamber.

With the depression, tensions accelerated. Six different governments rose and fell from 1932 to 1934, and unemployment quadrupled, reviving fascist movements on a much larger scale than in the 1920s. By 1934 France had more than 400,000 fascists. The most important organizations were the Solidarité Française with some 150,000 members, La Rocque's Cross of Fire with 100,000, and the Jeunesses Patriotes with 80,000. Nevertheless French fascists did not blame the Jews for the depression, as did the Nazis. The man who would become the most important fascist leader, Col. François de La Rocque, attributed the depression to greed, easy credit, and a lack of idealism, and held that Jews could be good Frenchmen unless they were Marxists, Freemasons, or atheists. Nor did French fascists identify liberalism and Marxism with the Jews, as fascists in Central and Eastern Europe had done for decades. This was because the majority of Frenchmen supported the liberal Third

Republic, and because Jews did not find it necessary to support socialism as they did in Austria and the East where all other major parties were anti-Semitic. The older assimilated French Jewish community remained conservative republicans, as one would expect from a business and commercial class. La Rocque, like Mussolini, accepted Jewish recruits and declared that the French and Germans were mixed races and that biological racism was absurd.

In February 1934 riots against the government led many to believe a fascist coup was imminent. In January officials had revealed that a Russian Jewish immigrant, Serge Stavisky, had bribed police, judges, and politicians to cover up widespread financial fraud. Led by the Action Française, rightists accused the government of being rotten to the core and made much of the Jewish origins of Stavisky in hopes that public anger would bring down the republic. The government of Edouard Daladier further enraged reactionaries by appointing a socialist minister of the interior and firing the Paris police chief, who habitually encouraged his men to attack leftist demonstrators and go easy on demonstrating fascist leagues.

The riots culminated in attacks on the Chamber of Deputies, but it was not an attempted fascist coup. Of approximately fifty thousand rioters, some four thousand were Communists and ten thousand were veterans, there mainly to protect their benefits from austerity cuts. The million members of the National Union of War Veterans, unlike the German Stahlhelm, did not wish to overthrow the republic or get rid of the Jews. Many demonstrators acted out of anger at corruption or to find relief from various economic ills. Nevertheless most of the rioters belonged to the fascist Blueshirts of the Jeunesses Patriotes and La Rocque's Cross of Fire, yet they refused to attack the police, something Nazi observers found ridiculous. La Rocque and other fascist leaders, taken by surprise, stayed away. More to the point, conservative republicans, their press, and the French public disapproved of the riots—whereas Hitler's *putsch* was admired by most of the citizens of Munich, the German Conservative party, and millions of Germans and Austrians. Had the threat in France been extreme, the army would have stopped the rioters; the German High Command, however, had already made it clear in 1919 that it would defend the Weimar Republic only against revolutionaries of the left. The only notable political consequence in France was the resignation of Daladier and the installation of a new conservative government that swiftly restored order.

Even those French fascists and conservatives who applauded the Nazis' dismantling of the German left were appalled by the savagery of Hitler's murder of hundreds of his SA leaders in June 1934. The German army and the German conservatives of the DNVP, as we know, supported the killings of those who had hoped to replace them in army, government, and corporation. In response to the rioting fascist leagues, moreover, unlike the German left, French socialists and Communists united and joined millions of radical workers in a massive general strike to defend the republic. German and Austrian paramilitaries had been heavily armed, but the French government strictly limited the weapons and hence the power of the fascist leagues.

Even so, massive demonstrations and leftist unity brought the Cross of Fire some 228,000 new members by 1935, making it the largest fascist organization. Still, La Rocque insisted he was no fan of Hitler, and publicly rejected not only biological racism but also Hitler's racist excesses and fantasies and his persecution of the Jews. In 1936 La Rocque participated in joint memorial services for the Jewish war dead in the synagogue of the chief rabbi of France, and boasted to the International League Against Anti-Semitism that Jewish war veterans were an important part of the Cross of Fire. The Solidarité Française announced that it did not oppose all Jews, only Jewish leftists and recent immigrants who took jobs from Frenchmen. Perhaps these denunciations and protestations were insincere, but politicians gain support by what they say and do, not by private beliefs they do not mention or act upon.

Not all La Rocque's disciples followed his lead. In Algeria and Alsace, which like Germany had long histories of anti-Semitism, many Cross of Fire leaders were avowed racists. In 1937 when La Rocque spoke in Algeria, his audience shouted out "Down with the Jews," but he countered that it was not a question of religion. Algerian Jews had gained citizenship in 1870 and voted overwhelmingly liberal or left. The French Algerian colonialists had driven indigenous Arabs off the land and supported Drumont and now La Rocque because they hated Jews for heeding Arab grievances and voting socialist. Furious in 1936 when the leftist coalition led by the Jewish socialist Léon Blum extended citizenship to some 27,000 Muslims, Algerian members of the Cross of Fire called for a *Judenrein* Algeria. La Rocque supported their economic boycotts but not their call for pogroms and expulsion. The long history of anti-Semitism in Alsace helped make it a stronghold of the Cross of Fire, and its leaders—educated upper- and middle-class engineers, business people, and shopkeepers—were far more racist than French fascists in general.

Excluding Alsace and Algeria, however, French fascist ideology did not begin to compare with the murderous Nazi belief in blood, race, and soil. French hostility toward refugee Jews competing for jobs and professions, anger at militant Jewish refugee leftists, and contempt for ultra-orthodox Jewish immigrants did not lead to denunciations of all Jews as racially contaminated, and the older Jewish community was not targeted. Artisans, so prominent in anti-Semitic movements in Austria and Germany, had not been politically strong in France since the outlawing of the guilds in 1791, and peasants tended to support the republic because it attended to their needs and protected them from Marxist extremists within the government who would ignore them. The leaders of protest movements of taxi drivers, civil servants, and war widows in France, when bitter about government taxation and regulation, lobbied the republican government for changes in legislation. In Germany similar groups denounced the immensely unpopular "Jewish" republic altogether and ultimately joined the Nazis to get rid of it.

Biological and racist nationalism contradicted the Enlightenment-based secular nationalism and reformist egalitarianism of the revolutionary tradition of 1789, 1848, and the Third Republic. La Rocque reviled democratic liberalism and those politicians who refused to suppress the left and the republican beliefs of the vast majority of French public school teachers—but he did not single out the Jews. He did claim that fascism was the last barrier against the enemies of Christian civilization, but he insisted that he respected Judaism and concentrated on socialists and Freemasons—the most radical followers of the Enlightenment—as the chief enemies. French history, in short, worked against anti-Semitism with as much force as German and Austrian history favored the ethnic hatreds and religious intolerance of the radical right. Even in 1937, when La Rocque's movement reached its peak of about a million members, opposing workers, middle-class groups, and the left mobilized far more for street demonstrations than did the fascist leagues.

The depression helped Hitler win votes; in France it helped the left. As unemployment increased and factories closed, French conservatives, like conservatives elsewhere, demanded lower business taxes, less government spending, and a budget balanced by cuts in social programs, arguing that such measures would increase investment and revive the economy. Left republicans and socialists pointed out that without customers, businessmen would not be able to increase their production with gains from reduced taxes. Liberals and leftists wanted, therefore, to increase business taxes, use deficit spending for public works, and raise wages to increase purchasing power, production, and employment.

In Germany in 1930 Hindenburg had used his emergency powers to remove the Social Democratic government and give chancellors with no parliamentary support the power to carry out the harsh austerity measures demanded by the reactionaries of the DNVP. The German left could not stop Hindenburg; they knew that the army would have easily destroyed them, with popular and paramilitary support. The army had been illegally training SA units for just such a contingency since 1930. But in France, when the conservative republican government gave a onetime special-decree law to Premier Pierre Laval to cut wages and raise taxes, more than a thousand riots and demonstrations protested both the radical right and the government.

As the cost of living rose and purchasing power declined, factories closed and workers were discharged, but some took over factories in sit-in strikes in what seemed a preview of Marxist predictions of the eventual proletarian ownership of the means of production. On July 14, 1935, Bastille Day, when 30,000 of La Rocque's men marched in Paris, 300,000 leftist demonstrators dwarfed his effort. Hitler and Mussolini's destruction of the left taught French socialists and Communists to work together. Unlike German leftists, however, they were defending a popular republic and had no reactionary army or armed paramilitaries to fear. In the summer of 1935 more than a million protesters hit the streets. In the winter of 1936 more pay cuts brought more strikes and demonstrations by both public employees and the kinds of middle-class taxpayers' federations and peasant organizations that in 1932 had supported the Nazis.

The most striking contrast with Germany, however, occurred in the elections of May 1936, when French voters reacted to the depression and fascism by electing the famous Popular Front of socialists, Communists, and left republicans. The socialists gained the most votes in the coalition, and their leader, Léon Blum, headed the new government. Although the popular vote was close, the Popular Front won 380 seats to the

222 of the republican conservative National Front. The National Front wanted authoritarian policies to enforce austerity and weaken the left; they had no love for radical Jewish immigrants but did not campaign against Jews or the republic. Many state employees and lower-middle-class groups voted for the Popular Front, while by 1932 their German counterparts voted heavily Nazi.

The old enemies of the republic—the church, the aristocracy, and the Action Française—bitterly denounced the Popular Front and blamed it on radical Jews. Many in high social circles, furious that a Jewish socialist now headed the government, uttered the famous phrase "Better Hitler than Blum." They would have their wish. But monarchism and racism remained politically irrelevant to the vast majority of voters. Although La Rocque had threatened coups at various times, in 1937 he admitted to his followers that they would be crushed if they tried.

Léon Blum was an early supporter of Dreyfus and had been a democratic socialist since 1899. His victory was greeted by a wave of strikes, and frightened employers met with union leaders under Blum's auspices to negotiate the famous Matignon Accords. The Accords raised wages 12 percent on average, granted collective bargaining rights, established the forty-hour week and eight-hour day, and provided for annual two-week paid vacations. Blum's government also aided farmers by increasing prices for their products and extending easier credit. It raised the compulsory schooling age to fourteen and nationalized the Bank of France and the arms industry. In 1936 Blum's government declared paramilitary organizations illegal. La Rocque was fined and his organization banned. He promptly renamed it the Parti Social Français (PSF) and declared it a normal electoral party.

The victory of the Popular Front brought new supporters and funds to a fascist backlash. La Rocque's PSF reached an astounding 700,000 to 1.2 million members during the Popular Front, more than double Nazi membership in Germany when

Hitler was given power by Hindenburg. In 1936 Jacques Doriot, a former leftist, founded the fascist PPF with 50,000 members, largely lower middle class. He turned out to be a vicious anti-Semite, but until Vichy he had to claim to oppose anti-Semitism and support the republic to avoid being banned.

In 1934 Henri Dorgères founded a Peasant Front, the "Greenshirts," with about 120,000 landowners. Like fascists elsewhere, Dorgères idealized rural peasant life and lamented the rise of a rootless socialist proletariat and the "moral decay" of urban life. Although personally hostile to Jews, he did not single them out as the major enemies of the peasants, as the Nazis had done. With so few Jewish rural middlemen, Dorgères held Republican politicians, the Popular Front, bureaucrats, and farm trusts responsible for the agrarian depression. He called for legislation to protect the prices of farm products, cut the cost of fertilizer and farm machinery, placed higher tariffs on imported foodstuffs, and ended farm foreclosures—all issues that the Nazis converted into reasons for racial persecution. Correspondingly, Dorgères's peasant landowners feared not Jews but radical landless peasants who demanded land reform and supported the Popular Front. Nonetheless Dorgères's supporters in Alsace, where Jews were often rural middlemen, regularly blamed Jews for rural suffering, as did his followers among the farming colonialists of Algeria. But the Greenshirts never received millions of rural votes, as the Nazis did, because, unlike German governments, republican governments of the left or right routinely aided French peasants, regarding them as the backbone of France. Dorgères even denounced fascists as unpatriotic supporters of foreign ideologies.

Paradoxically the major source of French fascist strength revealed its weakness. Before Hitler's electoral breakthrough in 1930, the Nazis had financed their movement with membership dues, donations, and special membership assessments. French fascists showed no such sacrificial ideological conviction. The perfume tycoon François Coty financed the Solidarité Française

(SF) and paid large salaries to its middle-class leaders. In 1934 Coty went bankrupt and his Solidarité Française, then the largest fascist organization, practically collapsed. The leader of the SF, Jean Renaud, bereft of Coty's wealth, had only enough business funds to hire about five thousand activists. Coty had been a convinced anti-Semite, and Renaud attacked immigrant and leftist Jews and the "moral decay" allegedly caused by the Jewish corruption of French culture with pornography and anarchistic literature, art, and film. The SF also used fake statistics to question the war effort of the Jews and blamed them for bolshevism and the Popular Front.

Significantly, the attempt to imitate the Nazi concentration on the Jews attracted few new members or votes in France, but fascist groups did receive support from business leaders. Pierre Taittinger, the champagne magnate, subsidized the Jeunesses Patriotes. Doriot's PPF received payments from the Steel Trust, heavy industry, and commercial interests, including three major Jewish banks, until he revealed his anti-Semitism in 1938. He also paid his street fighters, organized by a former member of the Action Française, Joseph Darnand, who later helped the Gestapo round up Jews for the death camps.

La Rocque had been a well-connected company executive and received large subsidies from the Rothschild and Dreyfus banks as well as from metal, coal, electricity, railroad, steel, and oil interests. Funds also came from some of the most prestigious and wealthy aristocrats and landowners of France, families that had supported radical right and anti-Semitic causes since the Revolution of 1789. The conservative minister of the interior in 1930–1932 and briefly premier, André Tardieu, illegally contributed secret government funds; the Bank of France, the Action Française, and Mussolini also contributed. Five million francs entered fascist coffers in 1937–1938, and another 15 million went to finance the 1940 elections that would have occurred if the Germans had not invaded. Employers also arranged to hire La Rocque's followers when jobs were scarce. French fascist organizers, staff members, and activists were always well paid, unlike their Nazi counterparts before Hitler gained power.

Corporate motives were simplicity itself. La Rocque and Doriot wholeheartedly endorsed private property and lower business taxes, and condemned Blum's wage increases and land reform proposals. They hoped to destroy the Popular Front, militant trade unions, and socialism. La Rocque's corporate supporters wanted a return to the days before the Popular Front, when they had practically dictated republican economic policies. La Rocque said nothing about the hypocrisy of capitalists who demanded lower taxes with the excuse that they lacked the resources to revive the French economy even as they invested huge sums abroad. He continued to blame the depression on greed—not corporate greed, of course, but the higher wages negotiated for workers by the Popular Front.

Other than corporate contributions, French fascists never enjoyed the support of a wide range of powerful elites or a significant portion of the voters. Many members of the church hierarchy and the aristocracy still detested the Jews and endorsed La Rocque, but the Dreyfus fiasco had cost all of them credibility. The army General Staff, their old allies, stayed aloof; they disliked the republic and Blum, but the victory of 1918 had amply restored the prestige they had lost in the Franco-Prussian War and the Dreyfus Affair. More decisively perhaps, the Popular Front had increased the military budget more than any government since 1918, out of fear of German rearmament. Many students of the military academies and the prestigious École Polytechnique, headed for high positions in the bureaucracy, supported La Rocque, but their numbers do not compare to those German university students who supported Hitler before he was handed power. The Blueshirts of the Jeunesses Patriotes, the Solidarité Française, and the Cross of Fire had close ties to the Republican Federation, the conservative party of France, but it possessed neither the power nor the racism of the German right.

Although French conservatives detested radical Jews and the left in general, they were quite comfortable with the older conservative Jewish community, among whom they had many allies. Some famous Parisian intellectuals were anti-Semites, but German intellectuals such as Lagarde and Langbehn were profoundly more vicious and much more influential by far among powerful German elites. La Rocque could not match Hitler's 400,000-man armed SA or his strong support among army officers, and Blum easily outlawed his unarmed paramilitaries. In Germany even regional Social Democratic governments had great difficulties trying to curb the paramilitaries.

The Popular Front was not brought down by elite intervention and fascist votes, as was the less militant left in Germany in 1930. In just over a year the normal processes of parliamentary democracy ended Blum's rule. He alienated his Communist allies when, fearing civil strife in a divided France, he refused to help the legally elected Spanish Republic against Franco's fascist-supported counterrevolution. To resolve the economic crisis, Blum increased taxes on the wealthy, but they evaded them by the various means available to the rich. Blum could not prevent such economic sabotage with new legislation without driving the Radical Republicans from his coalition. Moreover, increased taxes and government borrowing to pay for social reforms caused international currency speculators to sell French francs cheaply, effectively sabotaging the reforms. French exports became correspondingly cheaper, but international tariffs increasingly shrank foreign markets as governments protected their internal markets for their own manufacturers. The consequent inflation and soaring national debt caused Blum's defeat after the business-dominated Senate refused him the power to issue decree laws, as it had done for Laval so that he could cut wages in 1935. The Radical Republicans also received large subsidies to persuade them to desert Blum. Their leader, Daladier, broke with the Popular Front and formed a new center-right government in April 1937. The Popular Front had lasted from May 1936 to April 1937. The corporations and banks that had supported the fascists with generous funds ceased to do so once the Popular Front was gone and they could again dictate the economic policies of the republic. The Nazis had not depended on corporate funding and received important corporate contributions only after they received 18 percent of the vote in 1930, and they were never willing to be mere puppets for corporate interests.

With the left out of power and the republic's obvious subservience to corporate interests, La Rocque's PSF had little impact on voters. It attracted roughly the same kinds of voters as the Nazis: lower-middle-class merchants, artisans, retail shopkeepers, office workers, civil servants, journalists, lawyers, and physicians, but not the industrial proletariat. Yet La Rocque never gained enough individuals from these groups to do more than elect twelve deputies and a few mayors and municipal councillors in 1938. There simply was not enough popular antagonism toward the republic or the left.

Blum's government had not resolved the problems of the depression. Only Sweden, where the dominant Social Democrats passed far-reaching social reforms, and Germany, where Hitler subsidized heavy industry with huge sums for rearmament, did so. Even so, under the Popular Front the French economy improved. By 1938 unemployment was down, industrial production and exports were up, and the income of farmers and workers had increased. Fascist appeals to farmers and retail shopkeepers had little impact. Unlike German socialists, the Popular Front, excluding the minority Communists, regarded the neighborhood small retailer and the peasant as essential to the French way of life. Consequently, unlike German politicians, both French republicans and socialists voted overwhelmingly for aid to small farmers and restrictions on the spread of large retail outlets.

Like all fascist movements, French fascists appealed to the sacred warrior traditions of the nation, organized themselves in military hierarchies, and held solemn rituals for the war dead and comrades killed in street battles with the left. But, as we know, the most successful military tradition in France was that of the revolutionary Republic of 1791 and the enlightened tyranny of Napoleon. Even the republican icon Gambetta had kept his troops fighting after the defeat of Napoleon III and the surrender of the royalists. Above all, the Third Republic had won the most destructive war in history. All German chancellors, not just Hitler, hoped one day to tear up the Versailles Treaty and restore previous German territory and power, but the Third Republic had no pressing foreign policy need except for allies to help keep Germany weak. Even the militancy of French fascists was a façade; they had no desire to fight a war against Germany to benefit, as they believed, only German Jews and socialists, and in this they shared the view of a large majority of Frenchmen. Fascist warmongering thrived only in defeated nations, where millions hated the peace settlements of 1918–1919. In fact French fascists demonstrated for peace during the Munich crisis and denounced "Jewish Communists" for trying to drive France into war. But their demonstrations could not further La Rocque's cause.

The French public itself overwhelmingly approved the Munich Agreement, by which the European powers appeased Hitler, permitting immediate German occupation of the Sudetenland. So did Western leaders, including not only Chamberlain but also Daladier and Roosevelt. Given the trauma of 1914–1918 and the fear of massive air bombardments, a war to prevent Hitler from seizing the Sudetenland was extremely unpopular throughout the West. In France only the Communists and two other deputies voted against the Munich agreement—

seventy-five votes of some six hundred. And when Stalin signed the Nazi-Soviet Pact, even the servile French Communists ceased to oppose Nazi Germany, though German Communists died in Gestapo torture chambers and Stalin delivered many to Hitler and death.

In late 1938 Doriot revealed his racism when his paper insisted that Jewish blood was corrupt, and demanded special taxes against them and their exclusion from all business activities. Jewish socialists, Doriot claimed, pretended to be democratic but were really Bolsheviks and a front for establishing their universal domination. His openness reflected the fact that his movement depended mainly on his Algerian supporters. With only five thousand members, Doriot's PPF had no real influence in metropolitan France.

By 1939 nearly half of all Jews in France had been born elsewhere—about 325,000. The French popular press, always conservative, denounced Jewish immigrants but also the savagery of *Kristallnacht*. Even *La Croix*, which had attacked the Jews so brutally during the Dreyfus Affair, urged help during the Evian Conference of 1938 for a people that faced "complete extermination." French anger at refugee Jews was defused when the republic itself betrayed its values in 1938–1939. Although discrimination because of race or religion was illegal, Daladier and the Chamber restricted the activities of all immigrants. As war loomed they also interned refugees, mostly Jewish, in camps and under terrible conditions.

German armored columns stormed into France in 1940. The French showed little enthusiasm for war; some towns declared neutrality even as French soldiers died in battle. President Paul Reynaud resigned, and on June 17, 1940, Pétain was chosen to rally a humiliated France, lead a provisional government, and ask for armistice terms. Pierre Laval lobbied intensively to give Pétain's government full powers, promising that a constitution would eventually be promulgated. The assembled senators and deputies—minus forty who were in prison or had fled to continue the war from overseas—voted overwhelmingly for the bill. But the French electorate never voted for the new government located in Vichy, and Pétain violated his mandate by banning all political parties, refusing to call the National Assembly into session or offer a new constitution. Instead he decreed an "emergency dictatorship."

Pétain had opposed Dreyfus and supported the Action Française and La Rocque during the Popular Front. His rule was quite consistent with the Catholic traditionalism, authoritarianism, and anti-Semitism of the Action Française. The Vichy government revived Drumont's writings and those of other famous anti-Semites. Annoyed at the failure of the French to understand the "crimes" of the Jews, Vichy organized a traveling exhibition replete with crude physical stereotypes. Such exhibitions were very popular in Germany and Austria; the French public showed little interest.

As Michael Marrus and Robert Paxton point out in their definitive study, Vichy adopted anti-Semitic measures before German pressure required them to do so. Located in southern France outside the German occupation zone, the Vichy government was relatively independent in its first year or so. The anti-Semite Xavier Vallat was appointed to head the agencies governing the Jews, and he recruited many of his personnel from the fascist leagues and the Action Française. In the fall of 1940 Vichy excluded Jews from important positions in the civil service, the army, and the media and placed quotas on Jews in the professions. Jewish property was seized and Jewish shops boycotted. Selling books by Jewish authors was prohibited, and some Jews were sent to the colonies as forced labor. Vichy set up special camps in 1940 and interned some 28,000 Jewish refugees from unoccupied France, although Pétain excluded prominent Jews and Jewish veterans. Camp conditions were far worse than under the republic. The highest civil servants approved actions against the Jews; many had long been anti-

Semites and were pleased to be liberated from the restraints of republican tolerance.

When the armistice was declared in 1940, Doriot's thugs rioted, smashed the windows of Jewish shops, and beat Jews in the streets. Doriot denounced the government of 1936–1940 as a coalition of Jewish plutocrats and Bolsheviks. By 1942 the anti-Semitism of his PPF was no different from that of the Nazis. As for La Rocque, he heartily approved Vichy's authoritarianism and denounced the de-Christianization of France by Jews and especially Freemasons, though he still excluded Jewish war veterans, religious Jews, and Jewish opponents of Marxism from his tirades. Through 1941, while no strong public opinion for or against anti-Semitic measures was evident, there were objections to the corrupt extortion of Jewish properties by Vichy officials. When the truth about camp conditions was revealed in 1941, foreign opinion and significant numbers of Frenchmen were appalled. By 1942 some three thousand had died in the camps, mostly Jews.

Deprived of property and jobs, Jewish refugees were forced to work the black market to survive, giving Vichy an excuse to punish them. Jews were forced to flee to towns in unoccupied France and compete with non-Jews for jobs, housing, and food, increasing hostility against them. Many Jews, especially German Jews, formed resistance groups. Pétain and Laval believed the Germans would give France more autonomy or even allow them to become partners in "the new Order" in Europe if they sacrificed Jewish refugees. Vichy officials later claimed that they did not know the Germans were killing Jews by the tens of thousands, but by the summer of 1941 they must have known. The British government had communicated the horror by radio more than once during the early summer. The Catholic clergy, generally Vichy supporters, knew already in 1940 from their Polish priests that the Germans were killing thousands of Jews and Poles.

In late 1941 the Germans began registering French Jews for deportation to the East and ordered the arrest of all Jews in Paris, announcing as well that foreign Jews would be deported from the occupied zone. They asked the Vichy regime to segregate Jews and adopt harsher measures. Vichy complied. Jews were banned from theatres, parks, museums, campgrounds, libraries, and concerts; shopping for food was made extremely difficult for them. In 1942 the Germans sought 250,000 French volunteers to work in Germany; in February 1943 they made it obligatory and forced Vichy to agree. Ultimately 730,000 workers were sent—the largest contingent of foreign workers in Germany. The deportations caused more public outcry than the measures against foreign Jews, and may have turned the majority of the French public against Vichy.

In February 1942 the first convoys left France for Auschwitz. Amidst horrifying scenes, Jewish children, held behind in stadiums open to public view after their parents had been deported, wandered about, hungry, sick, and forced to fend for themselves. Disgust with Vichy increased. Laval had offered the Germans the children of Jewish refugees if the Gestapo would spare French-born Jewish citizens. He said he was happy to see foreign Jews deported, and he must have known what fate awaited them. A shocked public witnessed more sickening scenes as children without parents were driven into freight cars. Some Catholic leaders protested, including the papal nuncio—a strong contrast with the silent German bishops and the papal nuncio in Germany, but French Catholic leaders kept their protests private, partly because the Vichy government was committed to Catholicism and its interpretation of traditional "family values" and morality. Even *La Croix* protested. Some close advisers to Pétain were upset; many war veterans returned their medals.

In November 1942 the Germans occupied the south of France and began to round up all Jews. With some hesitation the Vichy government agreed to stamp all Jewish personal papers "Jew," helping the Germans enormously. The Germans wanted a more brutal anti-Semite to direct Vichy's Jewish policy. Louis Darquier de Pellepoix was duly appointed in May 1942; he had used Nazi subsidies in the 1930s to found an anti-Semitic organization. Like the Germans, he wanted no exceptions, but Pétain still hoped to exclude Jewish war veterans, as Hindenburg had in 1933. Hitler had waited until Hindenburg died in 1934, but he had no need to placate Pétain and did not. By now there was much evidence of public disgust with the deportations and with forcing Jews to wear the yellow star.

Many Jews fled or joined the Resistance. Sometimes the French police helped Jews escape to Spain or ignored laws against them. By contrast, the first Nazi Gestapo members were willing volunteers from the German police. Some French Gentiles wore the yellow star in protest, and the Germans finally abandoned the policy in the unoccupied zone. The Germans had difficulty getting all the Jews they wanted; many thousands escaped. The occupiers needed French cooperation to carry out Jewish policies, and at times the Vichy regime refused. Had Vichy refused cooperation more often and more vigorously, thousands of lives could have been saved. July 1943 was evidently the only time Pétain complained to the Germans about the suffering of French Jews, but by then his regime was distinctly unpopular with the majority of the French and without influence on the Nazis.

German arrests of French Jews were denounced as violations of French autonomy by some government officials when it became clear that the Germans were losing the war. Even La Rocque and some members of the Vichy government wanted Pétain to make secret arrangements with the Allies. In July 1943 Vichy withdrew the cooperation of the French police with the Germans and replaced Pellepoix by one who would not cooperate with the killers. Over Pétain's objections, Joseph Darnand, an Algerian member of Doriot's PPF, formed a brutal militia with hundreds of fascist volunteers to help the SS hunt down Jews for the death camps. Some French aristocrats formed a volunteer French SS division and were sent to the East to help battle the Bolsheviks. They soon became cynical when they realized that they were to advance in order to cover the retreat of German units.

Of the roughly 350,000 Jews in France in 1940, 70,000 were eventually sent east. The Germans murdered 97 percent of the adults and all 10,000 children. Some 9,000 children and a much greater number of adults were kept safe from the Germans and their French helpers. Many French citizens, including church officials, helped save Jews. Protestants, historically coupled with Jews as enemies of France by reactionaries, were more outspoken and helped more than Catholics in proportion to their numbers. The Resistance saved many Jews as well. But clandestine Jewish resistance groups saved the most Jews, taking enormous risks. Pétain, consistent with prewar French fascist attitudes and his affinity for the Action Française, did not protest the forced deportation of refugee Jews but was reluctant to turn over members of the assimilated Jewish community.

Vichy would not have killed Jews on its own, but Pétain and his officials knew that death awaited the tens of thousands of Jews they helped deport. Such guilt can never be forgotten or forgiven, but it does not fall on France or all Frenchmen. After the defeat of the Germans, some 74 percent of the public voted for a republic in the 1945 elections. The guilt falls not on the entire nation but on those Frenchmen who had tried to harm the Jews since 1789 and cooperated with or approved German and Vichy racist policies.

EIGHT

Anti-Semitism in Poland to 1918

In MUCH OF Eastern Europe during the modern era, the force of ethnic nationalism, religious fundamentalism, and reactionary politics, combined with the extreme weakness of liberal and social democratic parties, made anti-Semitism far more damaging than in the West. Yet before the modern era many different ethnic and religious groups often lived side by side in relative peace. The authorities of the Ottoman and Habsburg empires—but not the Russian tsars—who dominated the area often permitted their subjects to follow their own customs and religion undisturbed as long as they paid their taxes and provided soldiers.

Before the nineteenth century, the vast peasant majority in the East would have been more likely to identify themselves by religion, village, or clan rather than ethnicity. Influenced by Western liberal nationalism at the start of the nineteenth century, however, intellectuals began to cultivate the history, literature, customs, religion, and unique "racial" character of their particular ethnic group. Over time, demands for ethnic political autonomy arose, demands forcefully resisted by imperial authorities and met by counterresistance and calls for independence. Given the confusing mixture of different peoples in the same territories, rising nationalists also struggled against other ethnic and religious groups over competing historical claims to those territories. Those who gained their independence from the Eastern empires usually discriminated against and often tried to force assimilation upon minorities within their borders. In turn, minorities fought back, hoping to merge their peoples and lands with ethnic brothers in the new nations that emerged before and after World War I, when the three empires were defeated.

By the later nineteenth century, Czechs, Serbs, and Slovenes struggled to break free from the Austrian Empire; Poles fought to throw off Russian and Prussian control; and in 1912–1913 several Balkan nations fought the Ottoman Empire and then one another for the territories they conquered. Serbia initiated the outbreak of World War I by trying to liberate Serbs still within the Austrian Empire. In the peace settlements of 1919, Czechs gained millions of unwilling German and Slovak subjects, and soon Ukrainians and Poles fought each other and the Soviet Union for the same land. Germans battled to hold on to the Baltic States and part of Poland. Hungarians invaded Romania to restore territories lost by the peace treaties. Austrians fought invading Slovenes trying to annex fellow Slovenes. Croatians and Serbs struggled for domination of the newly formed Kingdom of Serbs and Croats, known today as the former Yugoslavia. Greeks and Turks battled with unbelievable ruthlessness for control of Asia Minor. The history of nations is written in blood, and the children of its victims do not forget.

In the East, Jews made up roughly 10 percent of the population, compared to 1 percent in the West. Extreme ethnic hostility made the situation of the Jews uniquely precarious. Without territory to claim, and already despised for their religion, they were increasingly seen as a large and unwanted foreign presence. Because such a high percentage of Jews were in commerce, industry, or the professions, racial stereotyping and envy were intense, especially among those who were or hoped to be in the modern sectors of the economy. Moreover, the peasants of Eastern Europe—the overwhelming majority of the population—were more backward and fundamentalist in religion than in the West, and where it was strong, the Catholic church constantly reviled the Jews as it had done since the fourth century. As ethnic tensions multiplied in the nineteenth century, many Jews turned to Zionism to escape the dangers of ethnic hatreds in the East in the hope of building a Jewish state in the Middle East. Others became socialists, joining those who hoped to create a society that rejected ethnic hatreds in favor of working-class solidarity and progressive reform. Often non-Jews, unversed in the ways that social oppression and historical experience guide or force choices, believed that Jews innately preferred commerce and usury so as to exploit honest producers. Or they were seen as unpatriotic Zionists or subversive leftists. Ethnic tensions were magnified because the groups that opposed racism—secular humanists, pluralistic liberals, and democratic socialists—were dramatically weaker than in the West, where the Enlightenment had done its work. Those few Jews who did assimilate had to surrender their religious and cultural heritage and usually break their family ties. Even then they would rarely be allowed to forget their Jewish origins or escape harm.

The history of Poland exemplifies all these factors. Consequently, along with the Ukraine and Romania, Poland became more anti-Semitic than any Western nation, including Germany and Austria. Yet historically Poland had been a relatively tolerant land of many different ethnic and religious groups, including, among others, Lithuanians, White Russians, Ukrainians, Germans, and the largest Jewish community in Europe. For centuries each group lived according to its own religious and secular customs; the kings of Poland did not enforce their Catholic religion on minorities or join the Crusades, and Poland did not suffer the bloody decades of religious warfare that devastated the West. The Jews enjoyed most civic rights, including owning land and bearing arms. Indeed, from the fourteenth century on, Polish monarchs welcomed thousands of Jews fleeing persecution in Western Europe.

Many Polish Jews were peasants. About one-third were artisans—tailors, metal workers, furriers, masons, carpenters, jewelers, and others—with their own craft guilds. Many were government administrators and tax and toll collectors for monarchs or nobles, and Jews often battled side by side with Poles against foreign invaders or helped conquer territory and establish settlements in the Ukraine. Some wealthy converted Jews even became nobles. Thus Polish Jews did not fit the medieval Western stereotype of moneylenders and dealers in petty commerce, except in parts of Poland and after modern discrimination had done its work.

Jews maintained a wide variety of institutions ruled by rabbinical authorities and community councils in accordance with Jewish law. For economic reasons, Polish kings protected Jews and their religious freedom with various edicts and charters. By the mid-seventeenth century the Jews, about 5 percent of the population, led Poland's agrarian and commercial advance, deriving advantage from their experience in commerce and contacts with the products, languages, and needs of the advanced civilizations of the East. As exporters, Jewish merchants were the major force behind the change from the self-sufficient feudal manor to capitalist export agriculture. Their connections throughout the Diaspora gave them information about local prices and economic needs. Often they were financial agents and estate managers for the Polish nobility, supervising peasant labor and the production and distribution of farm products, collecting taxes, and managing the landlord's inns. The sixteenth century is usually seen as the Golden Age of Polish Jewry.

Nevertheless anti-Semitism grew apace. The church, the only authoritative source of moral judgment in a society of mainly illiterate peasants, indoctrinated them with a barrage of fantasies, including ritual murder and the desecration of the eucharistic bread. Many Poles complained bitterly about noblemen and monarchs using and protecting their Jewish money managers. The introduction of modern economic techniques by Jewish entrepreneurs infuriated Christian guild members by threatening their monopolies, and angered competing Polish businessmen. Merchants tried to force Jews out of business and replace them as collectors of tolls and taxes. Sometimes they succeeded in persuading city councils to place special taxes on Jews or force them outside the city gates. Polish physicians denounced the nobility's preference for Jewish physicians. Peasants blamed Jewish estate managers who, following the orders of absentee Polish landlords, squeezed them for every last bit of profit.

Drunkenness was a widespread vice among the peasants by the seventeenth century, and although distilling was a noble monopoly, Jews leased or managed the inns where drink was sold. Landlords forced peasants to drink only at their inns and to buy vodka from them on feast and wedding days. Yet peasant contact was with the Jews, not with the nobles who gained the most profit from the trade. Hence it became a popular charge in fiction and folklore that villainous Jews corrupted and bankrupted the Polish people with drink (a charge repeated by Cardinal Glemp as late as the 1980s). The church also insisted that the trade in drink was part of the Jewish battle against Christianity, though vodka was often sold on church lands and two-thirds of innkeepers were Catholics.

The Counter-Reformation of the sixteenth century, led by Pope Paul IV—who blamed Jewish influence for the Reformation—brought an intense reaction against Jews as well as Protestants. In Poland, theology students and urban mobs often led pogroms against the "Christ-killers." The papal nuncio tried to put an end to the printing of the Talmud and the building of synagogues; Polish Jesuits used their extensive educational network to malign both Protestantism and Judaism. The extremely popular Jesuit Piotr Skarga, a raving anti-Semite, court preacher to King Sigismund III in the early seventeenth century, warned that if the Jews remained in Poland, the country would become prey to foreign powers. Poles hailed him as a prophet for his apparent prediction of the eighteenth-century partition of Poland, though the Jews had nothing to do with it. The church demanded that Jews be required to wear yellow symbols and live in ghettos; some wanted them driven out of Poland. As in medieval Europe, passion plays held in cathedral squares depicted the old fiction of Jews as tormenters of Christ and tools of Satan. In the 1630s the popular layman Syzmon Starowolski and many others wrote tracts demanding the repression of all non-Catholics as heretics and exploiters. There were pogroms, of course, and Catholics massacred the Protestants of the town of Auschwitz.

Some towns passed anti-Jewish legislation; monarchs often refused to enforce such laws but were too weak to reverse them. Western princes tamed their nobility and increased their power with taxes paid by the new wealth of the bourgeoisie, but there were too few wealthy bourgeois to enable Polish monarchs to weaken their magnates by fielding expensive standing armies to end their power. The nobles, some 10 percent of the population, elected the kings, and to win, potential candidates had to surrender land and power. In the famous Librum Veto of 1589, even one Polish magnate could veto royal legislation. Consequently, as the power of centralized states increased in the West, the vast Kingdom of Poland-Lithuania, as it was then called, grew disastrously weak and tempting to foreign powers.

In 1648 catastrophe struck. Cossacks led Ukrainian peasants in a revolution against Polish landlords and their Jewish agents. Violence escalated with the simultaneous invasion of Russians, Swedes, and Prussians. The Cossacks took no prisoners, and Ukrainian peasants slaughtered Jews with glee. As many as 130,000 of 480,000 Jews may have died. Even so, by 1750 some 800,000 Jews lived in Poland, one-third of all the

Jews in the world. About 80 percent lived in the famous *shtetls*, small-town retail and artisan centers for the countryside. Anti-Semitism continued to rise as more Poles competed with Jews as artisans, salt traders, mining entrepreneurs, and commercial competitors. Jews who traveled as salesmen or artisans often found their lives in danger; many moved to the relative safety of *shtetls*, though they were no haven against pogroms. In synods and sermons the Catholic church attacked Judaism as an offense to God. Many who simply wished to end Jewish economic competition hid their greed behind the sanction of the church.

There were enlightened Poles, of course, but there was no Polish Enlightenment. Given Polish hostility, Jews had to become Catholics if they wanted any chance of acceptance. In the latter half of the eighteenth century, thousands did so, led by the "Messiah" Jacob Frank—just as Western Jews began supporting Enlightenment ideas. But tens of thousands of rural Polish Jews preferred the opposite; they joined the Hasidic revival of Baal Shem Tov, who valued the ecstatic experience of the divine presence and joyous worship over traditional rabbinical learning and doctrine. The Hasidic movement separated Polish Jews even more markedly from Polish Catholics as well as from Western assimilated Jewry—as it still does.

In 1772 Poland's lack of a strong central power brought the first of three partitions by the predatory despots of Prussia, Russia, and Austria. The partitions and the influence of the French Revolution of 1789 touched off a revolt of the lesser nobility, whose constitution abolished the Librum Veto. Furious, the upper nobility invited Russians and Prussians to suppress the new parliament, resulting in a second partition in 1793. In 1794 the workers of Warsaw supported a revolution led by Tadeusz Kosciuszko. The first and most influential of many Polish liberal and idealist nationalists, Kosciuszko fought in the American Revolution before leading a Polish army, and Polish Jews fought with him. His defeat led to the third and final partition of Poland in 1795.

When Napoleon defeated Prussia in 1807 he created the Duchy of Warsaw out of Prussian Poland, but Poles received no real power. Without an indigenous and progressive middle class, Napoleon needed the cooperation of the upper nobility against Russia; thus he did not impose reforms as in Germany and Italy. Serfs still owed forced labor and other obligations to their lords; the church retained all its revenues and remained the state religion. Bowing to the power of Polish anti-Semitism, Napoleon did nothing for the Jews. But Polish liberal nationalists, admirers of 1789, still believed Napoleon would grant Poland independence and allow liberal reforms, including Jewish liberation, if he defeated Russia with their help. One hundred thousand Poles invaded Russia with him; twenty thousand returned. Napoleon gone, the Congress of Vienna, under Prince Metternich of Austria, established Congress Poland and gave it to Tsar Alexander, now king of Poland and one who despised both Poles and Jews.

Poland was gone, but the ideal of a free Poland lived on. Intellectuals celebrated the language, culture, and history of Poland in epic poetry and dramas. Polish secret societies formed, inspired by the fiery and influential liberal nationalism of the poet Adam Mickiewicz, who was arrested and deported by the Russians in 1823. From exile he called for a reunited and free Poland and an alliance between Poles, the "Christ of Nations," and their suffering "older brothers," the Jews, to fight for "our freedom and yours."

In 1830, when the French overthrew Charles X, the tsar threatened to move Russian troops through Congress Poland to crush the revolution. In November Polish nationalists declared the tsar deposed and Polish Jews joined them, welcomed as Polish patriots. The chief rabbi of Warsaw blessed the revolution, and the rebels called for independence and the emancipation of serfs and Jews. But in 1832 they were easily defeated. Tsar Nicholas executed 254 rebels and brutally forced 80,000 to Siberia; 10,000 liberal Poles fled into exile. A huge army of occupation was established at Polish expense, and all civil rights and institutions of higher education were abolished. A papal encyclical of 1832 condemned Polish liberals and praised the tsar, and the Vatican chastised Polish priests who had joined the struggle for Poland. Pope Gregory XVI excommunicated the Polish insurgents; his predecessor had done the same to Kosciuszko. The Vatican preferred despots to those who stood for freedom of religion.

Poles and Polish Jews fought in the liberal revolutions of 1848. When the revolutions failed, secret societies continued to work for a free and democratic Poland with freedom of religion. But ethnic nationalism and liberalism were at best irrelevant to the masses of overburdened peasants. Nevertheless in January 1863 Polish liberals rose again, often with the blessings of both rabbis and priests. Cossacks descended on peaceful church meetings, killed protesters, and deported thousands in a wave of preventive arrests. Guerrilla war broke out. Some 200,000 Poles fought Russia to a standstill for sixteen months, but no help arrived, and again Russian brutality repressed the uprising. In 1865 the leaders of the revolution were hanged, and one thousand Polish priests were exiled to Siberia. The very name of Poland was formally abolished. An entire generation of Poles lost their careers; thousands were sent to Siberia, most never to return. Many Poles were furious because the Vatican did not object to Russian atrocities. Pope Pius IX, although ultra-reactionary, nevertheless apologized in an encyclical of April 1864 titled: "Woe to Me That I Kept Silent." (Pius XII could not bring himself to do even that when the Nazis later murdered hundreds of Polish priests and millions of Poles, not to mention the Jews.)

The tsars used force to try to convert Jews and Poles in the Pale of Settlement, Russia's large share of partitioned Poland. The pious tsar hated the Jews and hoped to erase Polish identity as well. To speak Polish or practice Catholicism was treason; Poles and Jews must become orthodox Christians or suffer.

Poles had to reject their origins to join the civil service. Censor-
ship was extreme. There could be no Poland, in part because it
would bar the Russian army from marching westward against
outbreaks of revolutionary and liberal nationalism. Secret
agents and provocateurs infiltrated Polish groups. Poles served
in the army, but no Polish regiments were allowed. Children
were forced to study Russian history and language in the
schools, but their parents and grandparents kept the dream of a
free Poland alive.

In Prussian Poland, meanwhile, Polish names were removed
from streets and schools, and bonuses were offered to German
officials and teachers who would work there. The Polish language was banned. Teachers were forbidden to join Polish or
Catholic societies; priests and students had to pass exams in
German culture. During the Polish Revolution of 1863, Bismarck declared he would join Russia if needed to prevent an independent Poland, and "if we want to exist, we would have no
choice but to exterminate them." When Polish delegates to the
Prussian parliament protested the partitions in 1869, Bismarck,
then minister-president, replied that Poles were incapable of
self-rule and lucky to be ruled by Prussians. "No one plunders
you now," he declared, "but the usurious Jew." In 1885 some
thirty thousand Poles were expelled on suspicion of political activities. In 1894 a wealthy and powerful German lobbying organization, the German Society for the Eastern Borders, spoke of
Lebensraum and, like many Nazis later, compared themselves
to the Teutonic Knights, the religious order that in medieval
times had slaughtered vast numbers of Slavs and resettled Germans on their lands. Most Germans regarded Poles as inferior
and the notion of a Polish state ridiculous—as they would in
Nazi times. Through subsidies and oppression, the Prussian
government attempted to colonize Polish areas with Germans.

The harsh policies of Russia and Prussia strengthened a
fierce Polish nationalist reaction and ended liberal idealism.
Many Poles adopted a belief in a unique and superior biological

Polishness, and ruled out assimilation and equality for minorities in any future Poland. In contrast, in the Austrian partition area, Galicia, the idea of Polish independence receded when Franz Josef began to favor Polish aristocrats to counterbalance obstreperous Hungarians and Germans, and granted equality to the Polish language and institutions. Consequently Polish leaders in the Austrian partition attained high cultural and political standing and were relatively content to remain in the empire until the 1914–1918 war.

The brutal suppression of liberal nationalism brought calls among the Poles for the use of force to gain ethnically mixed territory, justified by alleged racial superiority. Now Poles spoke of "Poland for the Poles," excluded the Jews, and expressed contempt for the Ukrainians, Lithuanians, and White Russians who inhabited former Polish territories. Minority leaders replied in kind, claiming superiority and full right to their territories. As liberal attitudes died, all nationalities began to view the Jews as an alien and disruptive community. Polish Jews were no longer thought capable of being truly Polish. A pogrom in Warsaw in 1881 predated the tsar's famous decree of the anti-Semitic "May Laws" in 1882 and the infamous Russian pogroms that followed.

Josef Pilsudski, who would become Poland's preeminent leader in the early twentieth century, retained a tolerant attitude toward minorities. Born a Pole in Lithuania, his grandmother, mother, and wife all worked secretly against the tsars, and he cooperated with Polish Jews and other minorities, believing they would be patriotic Poles if treated fairly. He was not religious and did not believe a true Pole must be Catholic, especially given the Vatican's support of Russian tyranny. In his simple, soldierly way, he thought anti-Semitism unworthy of Poles.

A student in the 1880s, Pilsudski joined the Polish Socialist party (PPS) because he believed in social justice and because it supported Polish independence. Like other parties, the PPS wished to include all former Polish territories—Lithuania, the Ukraine, and White Russia—but supported equal rights and cultural and religious autonomy for minorities. Orthodox Polish Marxists, led by the brilliant Rosa Luxemburg, despised Polish nationalism. Like Karl Marx, they believed "the proletariat has no Fatherland." But Pilsudski believed that class conflict, like ethnic hostility, would only divide and weaken Poles, and preferred the PPS partly because—given Poland's retarded economic development—it included small craftsmen and landless farm workers as well as the industrial proletariat.

Pilsudski had learned from tsarist oppression that only force could defeat the Russians. Like Lenin, he was sent to Siberia for allegedly plotting against the life of the tsar; like Stalin, he led terrorist raids on Russian banks. These activities and his daring rescues of Polish prisoners made him the leader of the nationalist wing of Polish socialism, and he became editor of their clandestine paper, *The Worker*.

By the 1890s reactionary ethnic nationalism with no concessions to minority autonomy was the most popular attitude in Eastern Europe. Notwithstanding Pilsudski, most Poles felt the same. Russian and Prussian oppression had left no room for a belief in the idea of a universal humanity encouraged by the Enlightenment. Serbs, Hungarians, Croatians, Albanians, Romanians, and Poles wrote epics, histories, and poems about the bloody sacrifices for national freedom of their peoples and claimed racial superiority dating back to tribal days, just as those Germans who prefigured the Nazis were doing. Paradoxically, the allegedly unique traits were similar among different peoples. Each seemed to be the inheritors of the noble warrior aristocracy and productive, sturdy peasants, superior to their oppressors and the minorities among them. The roles associated with Jews—commerce, banking, moneylending, and middleman activities—were denounced as the racial traits of the sly, unproductive, and immoral people whose cunning enabled them to exploit the otherwise superior indigenous ethnic group.

Roman Dmowski, Pilsudski's political competitor, led those Poles who preferred a racist path to a greater Poland. Founding the National Democrats, or Endek, in 1897, he preached the superiority of Polish character and blood, ignoring the interbreeding of Europeans over centuries that made nonsense of notions of racial purity. Dmowski and Endek dismissed Ukrainians and White Russians as simple peasants, unable to rise above their humble positions. But Dmowski feared the Jews as an immoral and insidious race of urban parasites who killed their own Messiah, despised hard work on the land, and regarded Poles as uncivilized peasants. When old Polish families went bankrupt, he asked, was there not always a Jew lurking about, eager to purchase their homes and possessions on the cheap? Dmowski especially hated those Jews in the higher levels of commerce, banking, and industry—actually very few. Nevertheless he insisted that they controlled Poland's economy and if not stopped or driven out would end up dominating politics as well. Poland would become "Judeo-Polonia." In 1914 Dmowski wrote, "On the Banks of the Vistula there is no room for two Nationalities." Endek led frequent boycotts of Jewish stores; the masthead of its newspaper read: "Patronize your own." The church joined in: the future Pius XI, papal diplomat in Poland in World War I, wrote to the Vatican that "Of the most evil and strongest influences that are felt here, perhaps the strongest and most evil is that of the Jews."

In the 1890s the Polish Jews of the Russian Pale of Settlement were terrorized by the "Black Hundreds," reactionary racists aided by the tsarist government. Hundreds of thousands of Jews fled into Polish territories. Dmowski praised the Russians for justly punishing the unwanted Jews. Most of the refugees were old and poor orthodox artisans, cobblers, hat makers, and small shopkeepers who spoke Yiddish and led a miserable existence in crowded cities. Meanwhile hundreds of thousands of Polish Jews were leaving their villages for the cities to take advantage of new opportunities in commerce, banking, and industry, especially textiles, the historical pump primer for the industrial revolution. Jews had pioneered in these sectors of the economy, and Gentiles were hard put to compete with those whose skills had been honed for decades and who tended to hire their coreligionists, already experienced in petty retail businesses.

By 1897 the Jews of Warsaw comprised 34 percent of the city's population. (In 1914 Vienna the figure was 10 percent, and in Berlin that year 4 percent.) Endek despised Warsaw as a Jewish city, a complaint supported by dispossessed peasants who had moved to Warsaw to compete with Jews for lower-middle-class positions. Endek also did well among those Poles competing against Jews in commerce, retail, and artisan work, as well as those who were or hoped to become physicians or lawyers—where Jews flocked to seek private practice and avoid institutional oppression. Envy and anger were more extreme than in Germany, because the German middle classes could compete on equal terms, and proportionally far more Polish Jews were predominant in the modern sectors of the Polish economy. Consequently Dmowski and Endek demanded that Poles replace Jews in commerce, banking, industry, the crafts, and the professions, even if Jews had to be forced out of these positions and out of Poland as well.

Dmowski's most fervent supporters came from the German section of partitioned Poland, which was heavily Polish, unlike the eastern territories which contained a large proportion of minorities. He hoped to ally with Russia to win Polish freedom from the Germans and be rewarded with autonomy for Poles in the Russian Empire. Pilsudski seemed even more unrealistic. He believed Poland could eventually be liberated from both Russia and Germany. Consequently he rejected the Marxist notion of class conflict as well as reactionary Polish nationalism because both divided and weakened Poles. Raised among Lithuanians, he knew how extreme Polish nationalism created a counterreaction among minorities. Indeed, Ukrainians, White Russians,

Germans, and Lithuanians, angered by Polish nationalists' claim to gain control over these former Polish territories, had already countered with demands for independence. They wanted to be rid of both Poles and Jews.

In 1892 in Galicia, a priest cofounded what would soon become the most important peasant party, Piast. Piast demanded that Jews leave Poland or end their demands for autonomy and convert. Small landowning peasants supported Piast, led by a prosperous farmer, Wincenty Witos, who hoped to remove Jewish influence from the villages and the local economy, peacefully if possible. In the *shtetls*, orthodox and Yiddish-speaking refugees from Russia owned small stores, traded in horses and cattle, and were craftsmen and moneylenders. Although the Jews were practically as poor as Polish villagers, Piast called them wealthy parasites who bought livestock on the cheap, overpriced their wares, and gave credit at usurious rates. But regular banks would rarely lend to peasants because of the great risk of default, and Jews also knew that local law enforcement would usually support Polish debtors who defaulted.

The lesser clergy shared the reactionary attitudes of Endek and Piast, not those of the religiously indifferent and tolerant Pilsudski. For the first time Polish nationalism was acceptable to the Vatican because Endek was devoutly Catholic and without trace of the liberal and revolutionary nationalism that had been destroyed in 1863. The clergy constantly agitated against the Jews, especially among peasants and artisans, as did the Christian Democratic Party of Labor, composed mainly of guildsmen. Popular literature and schoolbooks distributed among peasant children told tales of the evil Jews who killed Christ, exploited Poles, and poisoned them with alcohol.

Unable to assimilate in the face of such hostility, and because of their attachment to their own culture and religion, Jews wanted to hold on to their semi-autonomy. But by 1900 most Poles resented Jewish communal autonomy; a new Poland must be ethnically and religiously one. Endek and Piast scorned the few Jews who had assimilated, mostly wealthy merchants. Even conversion, as secular racists insisted throughout Europe, could not remove the "evil" traits of the Jews. Nothing could satisfy Polish racists except their disappearance.

Endek's ethnic nationalism necessarily meant the suppression or forced assimilation of minorities, for no Polish leader wished to surrender the eastern "historic territories," even though the majority of the population there consisted of minorities, not ethnic Poles. In response, many Jews became members of a variety of Zionist organizations. White Russians, Ukrainians, and Lithuanians had their own territory to defend, and Germans looked to the protection of Germany. But the Jews had neither territory nor powerful allies, and Jewish nationalism took the form of Zionism. It was more than nationalism, for many Zionists wanted a Jewish nation to end the skewed social development that found so many Jews in commerce, trade, banking, and moneylending. In a Jewish nation, all occupations and vocations would be Jewish; one could be judged on one's merits and defend oneself against enemies. But few established and seemingly safe Western Jews were interested in a hard life as agrarian pioneers in the harsh deserts of the Ottoman Empire among Arabs who did not welcome them. The older generation of deeply orthodox Jews formed Agudat Israel to protect their faith, which at the time did not permit attempts to establish a Jewish state.

A Jewish Labor Bund, founded in 1897, attracted many from the large numbers of Jewish proletarians, in hopes that socialism would eventually end ethnic hatreds and nationalist extremism. The Jewish Bund often cooperated with Polish socialists, and they jointly struck both Jewish- and Polish-owned factories. Jews employed almost half of all Polish workers, in stark contrast to the West, and hence anti-Semitism among Polish workers, socialists included, was not uncommon. Although the Polish Socialist party officially opposed anti-Semitism, it kept Jews out of important positions because it feared too close an identification with them. For the Polish middle classes, Zionism, Hasidism, and the Bund clearly demonstrated that Jews were either unpatriotic, religious enemies, or subversive revolutionaries. Regardless of political allegiance, the Jews of Poland had to defend Jewish autonomy if only because most Poles refused to accept them simply as citizens of Jewish faith.

As war threatened between tsarist Russia and Austria-Hungary over control of the Balkans, Austria allowed Pilsudski to organize and train a division of Poles to help fight the Russians. Consequently Austria became a haven for Polish nationalists, including many Polish Jews. In 1914–1918 Poles fought in all European armies, but only Pilsudski's ten thousand fought directly to free Poland, increasing his prestige. Because Poland was one of the two major battlegrounds of the war, to win Polish support the Russian Parliament (Duma), the kaiser, the British, the French, and later the Bolsheviks all promised Poland independence. President Woodrow Wilson made it one of his fourteen points for a peace settlement and included access to the sea. In reality the Germans, the tsar, and the Bolsheviks did not want a free Poland. If Russia won, the tsar had no intention of surrendering its share of the partitions, and the Bolsheviks wanted to hold on to all tsarist territories, including the former Polish eastern territories with their numerous White Russians and Ukrainians.

When the Bolsheviks surrendered, Ludendorff and the German High Command began to build an empire in Poland and western Russia to be populated by German settlers at the expense of Poles, Jews, and other inhabitants. To do so they offered Pilsudski the chance to act as a front man in a puppet government. He refused to betray Poland and was jailed, adding immensely to his prestige among his fellow countrymen. Only Wilson and the French were sincere in desiring an independent Poland. Wilson was partly motivated by his ideal of national independence, but he and the Allies—especially the French—wanted a strong barrier in the east against Germans and Bolsheviks.

Pilsudski hoped that Germany would defeat Russia and then the Allies would defeat Germany, opening the way to the liberation of Poland. Incredibly, all three empires lost, and in 1918 Poland was suddenly free, though not by its own efforts, as generations of revolutionaries had hoped. Nevertheless Pilsudski returned in triumph with his troops. In 1918 he was hailed as Poland's national hero, one who had stood against both Russia and Germany. He was named head of state and commander-in-chief of the Polish army. He could easily have been dictator but preferred a democratic Poland. In either case his task would not be easy. In the battles between Germany and Russia on Polish soil, some 12 percent of Poles died, and her industry and agriculture were devastated. Jewish civilians also suffered terrible losses of life and property at the hands of marauding armies of Russians, Germans, and Ukrainians.

At the Paris Peace Conference in 1919, the Allies received delegations from the various nationalities of the former empires. Dmowski headed the Polish delegation because he had supported the Allied cause whereas Pilsudski's forces had fought with Austria. But Dmowski demanded that a new Poland include the pre-partition eastern territories. The Allies had assumed a new Poland would include only the much smaller area inhabited mainly by ethnic Poles. Lloyd George denounced Dmowski's "small power imperialism" while he and the French were busy swallowing up the Middle East. Poland was awarded German territory—the famous Polish Corridor—as well as economic rights over the former German city of Danzig, a port on the Baltic Sea. The Allies thought this both fair and practical, because East Prussia, the center of German militarism and autocracy, was thus separated from Germany. Millions of ethnic Germans remained in the new Poland, in Czechoslovakia, and in other new Eastern European nations.

During the Holocaust, ethnic Germans in the East would play a particularly murderous role and seize much Jewish and Polish property.

In spite of a plebiscite won by the Germans after World War I, Poland annexed the rich mining area of German Upper Silesia by force, creating more German antagonism. The French signed treaties of alliance with Poland and the new Eastern European states, establishing Poland firmly in the Allied camp. But Poland's position was still precarious. One-third of her citizens were minorities, and the Ukrainians and White Russians among them wanted independence. Ominously, Poland contained 750,000 Germans who looked to the Fatherland to save them from the despised Poles, and the Soviets coveted the eastern areas of Poland that had belonged to tsarist Russia.

It would be a goal of any German statesman, not just Hitler, to restore German territories and treat Poland as a satellite. Accordingly, a free Poland would depend on the continued weakness of Germany and the USSR and the firm military support of France, with whom Poland signed a secret military agreement in 1921. By herself Poland could not hope to withstand the two potentially great powers, should they revive. And as the postwar period would show, the power of anti-Semitism in the new Poland was such that the fate of the Jews of Poland was at risk whether Poland was defeated or not.

NINE

Poland, 1919–1947

THE LIBERATION of Poland after more than a century of oppression brought wild rejoicing—and pogroms. In 1919–1920 boycotts or violence erupted against Jews in more than a hundred towns—violence ignored or sometimes aided by the police, even though the Jewish community had also rejoiced at Poland's liberation. The Polish press published a constant stream of anti-Semitic diatribes. Jewish students were practically excluded from Polish universities. The Christian Democratic Party of Labor, mainly artisans and anti-Semitic since the 1890s, demanded that all Jews who had not converted to Christianity before 1918 be driven out of Poland—in short, almost all of them.

The Allies, alarmed by this violence, insisted that the Polish Constitution of 1921 guarantee minority rights and that Jews suffer no discrimination because of their religion. Spurred by the Endek press, popular opinion in Poland was infuriated. Why should Poles be required to give special guarantees to Jews when Western states did not? (But of course there were no pogroms in the West.) When Jewish groups in the United States opposed loans to Poland until the pogroms had ended, the government, now led by the anti-Semites of Endek and Piast, cited this as proof of an international Jewish conspiracy against Poland and ignored the minority-rights clause. Piast's program of 1921 railed against the Jews and other minorities and insisted they wanted to dominate Poland. Enforcing minority ethnic rights on a sovereign nation, as we know today, is extremely difficult, but the Allies did not try; they needed a crucial ally against Germany and bolshevism.

The government declared Jewish autonomy inconsistent with the new Poland and pointed to the proliferation of Jewish newspapers, political parties, hospitals, credit unions, cooperatives, publishing houses, and sport clubs. These institutions, and the high proportion of Polish Jewry in commerce, banking, and industry, reinforced the old charge that the Jews formed a state within a state. Even antagonists of Polish anti-Semitism have said that anti-Semitism had a more objective basis in Poland than when it was directed against the assimilated and tiny Jewish communities of the West. But to be accepted by large numbers of the educated and influential, all racial myths need some appearance of reality, however slight. Jewish attempts to preserve autonomy throughout Eastern Europe were necessary if Jewish culture and religion were to survive a hostile environment where assimilation was unwelcome and required that one break all ties to one's religion, community, and probably family. The myths of the anti-Semites in Eastern Europe were not more objective than in the West, just easier for the uneducated to believe.

In January 1919 the first elections in an independent Poland gave Endek a spectacular 34 percent of the vote; it would remain the largest single party in Poland. The most important peasant party, Piast, led by Witos, won 12 percent of the vote and joined with Endek and a smaller anti-Semitic party to dominate the governments of the early 1920s. All told, more than half the electorate voted for anti-Semitic measures while in postwar Germany the governing parties until 1932 opposed racism or thought it politically irrelevant.

Some opposition was active in Poland. The Populist-Liberation party won 16 percent of the vote and demanded land reform at the expense of the great landowners; its left wing believed anti-Semitism a tactic of landowners to divert attention from their exploitation of the peasantry. The Polish Socialists, who opposed anti-Semitism, won 10 percent of the vote. (In Germany the Social Democrats were the largest single party in the Weimar Republic until 1932.)

From 1919 through 1921, Poland fought against Ukrainians, Germans, Lithuanians, and Czechs for territories that were once part of pre-partition Poland. But Pilsudski's war against the Soviet Union was the most significant. He hoped to seize former Polish territories in the Ukraine and White Russia and form a federation with all minorities' rights protected by a benevolent and democratic leadership. Endek, however, wanted to annex these lands and suppress the "racially inferior" minorities. The Red Army advanced to the gates of Warsaw, but Pilsudski defeated them and conquered much of Poland's former territories. Pilsudski's already immense prestige soared among ordinary Poles.

Millions of Poles viewed the conflict with the Soviets as a battle against "Judeo-bolshevism." The myth that bolshevism was a Jewish conspiracy was widespread throughout Europe and the United States, especially among Christian fundamentalists and political reactionaries. In Poland the attitude was reinforced by the actions of the Red Army as it moved toward Warsaw, setting up governing and security committees that most Poles believed (without proof) were predominantly Jewish. The government even interned Polish-Jewish military officers as security risks. When international protests arose, the government accused international Jewry of slandering Poland, and Prime Minister Witos and the Piast press grossly exaggerated Jewish cooperation with the Red Army. In fact the vast majority of politically aware Polish Jews supported Zionism, orthodoxy, or the anti-Communist Jewish Labor Bund. Those Jews who supported the Soviets were either Marxists or reacting against Polish anti-Semitism. Lenin had actively campaigned against anti-Semitism because it was supported by Bolshevik enemies—the tsarist Whites and the Greens, Ukrainian nationalists. Even radical leftist Russian Jews had supported democratic socialism and joined Lenin only when the choice was either Lenin or the virulently anti-Semitic forces of the Whites. Campaigning for elections in 1922, Endek and Piast claimed yet again that the Jews wished to dominate Poland economically and politically. Endek, supported by some allied Christian anti-Semitic parties, received 40 percent of the vote, Piast 18 percent. Other smaller parties also campaigned against the Jews. To protect their interests, Ukrainians, White Russians, and Jews formed a Bloc of Nationalities; the thirty-five Jewish delegates received the majority of the minority votes and led the bloc. Whenever the major parties were closely divided over issues, the bloc could be decisive.

To weaken President Pilsudski, the government wrote a constitution preventing him from heading the army and allowing the parliament to veto his appointments for prime minister and his cabinet. Insulted, Pilsudski refused to run for president in the new elections. A deadlock over other candidates gave the Bloc of Nationalities the opportunity to select as president Pilsudski's close friend Gabriel Narutowicz, a democrat and Christian who opposed racism. In his inaugural address he declared equality for all minorities, touching off a furious campaign by nationalists and church leaders against this "President of the Jews." Endek refused to support a president imposed by Jewry and routinely drowned out Jewish delegates with insults. In a few days Narutowicz was assassinated by a reactionary anti-Semite. Some churches held thanksgiving masses; many parishioners refused to believe Narutowicz was Catholic and labeled him the King of the Jews. The reactionary press glorified the murderer and threatened a coup, but the furious Pilsudski, still army chief of staff, warned Endek that he would use troops against them. From then on Pilsudski detested parliament because its blind partisanship, racism, and corruption—the sale of import and export licenses—mocked his battles for a free and moral Poland.

In 1923 Polish socialists and Jewish Bundists agreed to work together against fascism and racism. Although socialist leaders officially condemned anti-Semitism, they did not appoint Jews to important positions because they feared that the anti-Semitism of many workers employed by Jews would drive them to Endek. The miniscule Democratic party and the Communists also opposed anti-Semitism, but the Communists had enraged Poles by belittling Polish independence and opposing the war against the Bolsheviks. Declared illegal, they were forced underground. Jews formed 20 percent of the tiny Communist party, giving the illusion of Jewish bolshevism more credence than in the West. Although communists were atheists and despised Jewish culture, to racists a Jew is a Jew by blood, regardless of behavior or attitudes.

The government insisted that a true Pole must be ethnically Polish and religiously Catholic. More than ever the Jews were considered outsiders, and assimilation was out of the question. Out of necessity as well as commitment, therefore, Jews had to protect their autonomous religious and secular culture, and all major Jewish groups did so, including the Zionists, the orthodox Jews of Agudat Israel, and the Jewish Labor Bund. Consequently all were thought by a majority of Poles to be obstacles to a truly Polish state. In 1925 the government signed a concordat that declared Roman Catholicism the state religion, gave priests government salaries, protected the vast lands of the church from taxes and land reform, and made religious instruction compulsory. In no other European nation did the church have such power. The majority of the clergy supported Endek, and the church conducted unbelievably malevolent anti-Semitic campaigns down to World War II.

Jews comprised 10 percent of the Polish population, and nearly half lived in towns larger than twenty thousand. Sixty percent were in commerce, and half of all physicians and one-third of all lawyers were Jewish, arousing extreme resentment among Poles who worked in the modern sectors of the economy or hoped to. But Polish Jews had far fewer career choices than Polish Catholics. It was dangerous to own land among hostile Catholic peasants, though there were Jewish farmers. The government restricted Jewish artisans, made it extremely difficult for Jews to study at university, and kept Jews out of the civil service. Jews joined the Polish army, but most Polish officers despised them as disloyal cowards. The religious rules of orthodox Jews closed many occupations to them; the government and private enterprises made no concessions. Hence the two communities, trading accusations of anti-Semitism and anti-Polonism, grew ever more dangerously apart with each passing year. In Western nations Jews were so few that anti-Semites had to create fantastic conspiracy theories about Jewish wealth and power, whereas such illusions came easier to Poles because of the large number of Jews and their numerous autonomous Jewish institutions. But Jews were actually less numerous among the truly wealthy and powerful than their proportion of the population. The vast majority, artisans and small shopkeepers, were poor.

Poverty increases ethnic tensions. Seventy-five percent of rural Poles lived at or near starvation levels, foraging for a living because millions of acres of forests and land had been devastated by warring armies. Of fifteen million rural dwellers, five million were superfluous; thus Poland had to import food. Desperate for land, peasants paid too much for it and lacked the capital needed for agrarian technology. The custom of dividing the land among sons created unprofitable dwarf holdings. Embittered peasants survived only by ceaseless drudgery. Because there were far more peasants in Poland than in the West, their votes were crucial, and many still looked upon the Jews as literally satanic enemies of Christianity, a view encouraged by many clergy. The Endek press, supported by landowners fearing land reform, insisted, as the Nazis did, that Jewish middlemen caused rural misery by buying farm products cheap, selling fertilizer and machinery at unreasonable prices, and lending money at usurious rates. But landless agricultural laborers often held the great landowners responsible for their misery, supported land reform, and sometimes voted left.

In truth all ordinary Poles, Jewish or not, were trapped in economic circumstances they could not control. When land reform finally came, peasants were too poor to purchase the six million acres the government bought from large landowners to sell to them. Amidst the misery of rural life, drunkenness flourished. As before 1914, the clergy blamed Jewish innkeepers, and Endek told peasants to patronize only Christian taverns, as if that would make a difference. Industrial workers—just under a million—were little better off than rural folk and too few to enable Polish socialists to threaten the right. During the war Germans and Russians had destroyed the railways and dismantled huge textile works, shipping the machinery home. Poland lost 35 percent of its already meager prewar industrial production and most of its old markets. In 1919 unemployment was an astounding 85 percent. Drive the Jews out of the economy, Endek insisted, and Poland will prosper. As it was, all professions placed obstacles against the entry of Jews.

In 1923 inflation destroyed Polish currency. As prices soared, ordinary customers, untutored in the complexities of economic crises, blamed "gouging Jews." But as elsewhere, retailers, Jewish or not, were themselves victims, forced to purchase goods at ever-higher prices and unable to sell at a profit to ever-fewer and poorer customers. Many government employees were fired, making matters worse. Half of Poland's exports went to Germany, but the German government refused to buy Polish coal from the former German territory, now Polish, of Upper Silesia. International credit was unavailable. With two-thirds of the population living in misery, ethnic and religious hatreds flourished. Ukrainians and White Russians hated Poles and Jews; ethnic Germans detested them all and looked for the Fatherland eventually to rescue them from such *untermenschen*.

In the early 1920s violent demonstrations and thousands of

strikes rocked Poland. In 1926 Pilsudski, furious that corrupt politicians prospered while ordinary Poles suffered, decided to move against his enemy, Prime Minister Witos. Pilsudski took Warsaw by force in a short struggle. A simple military man, he planned no sweeping reforms but had vague notions of a Poland morally renewed and transcending all ideological, religious, and ethnic divisions. His authoritarian regime prospered when a strike by British coal miners gave Poland a surplus of exports over imports, and half a million peasants found work in France and Germany and sent money home. Foreign financiers began to invest and offer loans. New employment opportunities in textiles, mining, and metalworking brought a decline of some 15 percent in the rural population. In the late 1920s Poland was better off than ever before.

Pilsudski was neither religious nor racist, and had no objection to Judaism or the Jewish role in the economy. Consequently he repealed many of the anti-Jewish laws still existing from tsarist days or passed by the previous government. He recognized Jewish self-governing institutions and restored subsidies to Jewish schools taken away by the previous regime in violation of the constitution. In 1928 he repressed violent anti-Semitic activities inspired by Endek. Calling his movement Sanacja (moral cleansing), Pilsudski formed a nonpartisan bloc, and intimidated parliamentarians granted him extensive emergency powers. Thereupon he arrested opponents, illegally used government funds for his movement, and confiscated Endek newspapers. In the 1928 elections his popular prestige, a leftist peasant party of agricultural workers, and the National Minorities Bloc helped Pilsudski win 29 percent of the vote; Endek's vote declined precipitously. But the socialists also won 29 percent and joined with moderate leftists to elect their own prime minister and investigate Pilsudski's misuse of government funds. Pilsudski forced new elections for November 1930, seized three thousand leaders of the opposition, both left and right, and suppressed Endek publications while his campaign workers stole votes. Attempts to arouse the people against him failed against the force of his previous achievements and economic improvement.

The depression of 1929 intensified economic competition and racial tension between Poles, Jews, and all minorities. As elsewhere, the government worsened matters by trying to balance the budget through cuts in civil service pay and the firing of thousands. The misery of the peasants was unimaginable. Money ceased to circulate among them, and returning immigrants fired from jobs abroad added to their burdens. Peasant anti-Semitism intensified. Industrial employment fell 40 percent, consumption of necessities by half. Agudat Israel joined Pilsudski's government, and the Minorities Bloc cooperated with him, counting on his tolerance. Most Jewish groups supported Pilsudski, enabling Endek and other reactionaries to insist that international Jewry caused the economic collapse and that Jews dominated the regime. But for the Jewish community, with Hitler in power and the virulence of anti-Semitism in Poland, Pilsudski seemed the only hope against a fascist Poland.

Many believed—and it may have been true—that Pilsudski secretly tried to persuade the French to join with Poland in a preventive war against Germany before Hitler could rearm. Moreover, Pilsudski forced Witos into exile, declared several openly fascistic groups illegal, and imprisoned their leaders. Among them was the National Radical Camp (ONR). Renaming itself Falanga, it formed assault groups and fought Jewish students. Pilsudski also banned Endek, but it too returned, even more extremist under another name.

Pilsudski died in May 1935, sending a chill through the Jewish community. Sanacja ruled until the war, now simply another corrupt Eastern European military regime exploiting anti-Semitism to gain popular support. Its new leader was Marshall Edward Smigly-Rydz, and his government declared emigration the only solution to the "Jewish problem." The minister of education authorized ghetto benches—special seats in the back rows—for Jewish students and allowed them to be beaten. Some faculty resigned in protest, but the prestigious Polish Union of Academic Corporations demanded that Jews be driven out altogether. Most university students supported Endek or Falanga, which wanted Jews thrown out of the army, forbidden to participate in Polish enterprises or to employ or work for Poles. Their leaders insisted that "a radical elimination of the Jews from Poland is the ultimate solution of the Polish problem."

Jewish student defense groups fought violent militants trying to establish "Jewless days," and some died. Nationalist intellectuals denounced Jewish cultural influence for allegedly subverting Polish Christian morality. In 1936 the Radical Peasant party declared that Zionist Jews did not intend to resettle in the arid deserts of Palestine but wanted to seize control of Polish trade, banking, industry, and land in order to create a Judeo-Poland. Pogroms broke out that year, though the government disapproved. Its later actions showed that it preferred measures that would resolve the "Jewish problem" legally and finally, as did Hitler himself. After Pilsudski's death, in short, all but the PPS, the tiny Democratic party, and the discredited Communists wished to rid Poland of its Jews.

With Pilsudski gone, the government allied itself closely with the church. In 1936 Cardinal Hlond, head of the Catholic church in Poland, issued a pastoral letter to be read in all churches. In it he accused Jews of being atheistic Bolsheviks, even though he knew that about one-third of Polish Jews were orthodox and that there were immensely more Zionists, socialists, and other Jews than had ever joined the miniscule Polish Communist party. Hlond also accused Jews of being white slavers, swindlers, usurers, and pornographers. "There will be a Jewish problem as long as the Jews remain," he declared. He added that some Jews were righteous and that Poles should reject violence—qualifications that must have struck the average Pole as humanitarian gestures necessary to a cardinal, especially because Hlond also promoted the government's call for economic boycotts regardless of the righteousness of "some" Jews. In 1937 a synod of bishops demanded that Jewish schoolchildren be segregated and that no Jew be allowed to teach Catholics. Throughout the 1920s and 1930s clerics taught the evils of the Jews to schoolchildren. The Catholic press harped on the *Protocols of the Elders of Zion* long after it had been proved a forgery, thus morally sanctioning the belief that Jews, regardless of differences in social position, were secretly united in a centuries-old international conspiracy against Gentiles. Hitler said the same.

The government now placed schools, the civil service, some markets, and public transport off limits to Jews. The regime also nationalized sectors of the economy in which Jewish firms were important, depriving tens of thousands of Jews of jobs selling tobacco, salt, alcohol, and matches. Saturday work was made compulsory, forcing out religious Jews; others were simply fired from state-owned industries. Banks and tax officials discriminated against Jews. The government supported placards announcing "This is a Christian store." Placards exhorting the public "Do not buy at Jewish stores" were abundant at Christmastime and at Easter, including one declaring "A Poland Free from Jews Is a Free Poland." A law obliged shopkeepers to post their names in store windows to make discrimination easier for consumers. Photos of Poles patronizing Jewish stores were circulated to reveal "traitors." "Jewish-free" market days were established, and Jews were prevented from buying land. The government encouraged organizations of physicians, lawyers, and engineers to exclude Jews. Local officials discriminated even more. The government encouraged Jews to go to Palestine or anywhere. Anti-Semites, of course, often approved of Zionism.

When Polish artisans lobbied for restrictions on Jewish craftsmen, the government obliged by requiring stiff written exams in Polish, even for Jewish workers who had already demonstrated the necessary skills but had difficulties reading Polish. In 1937 the government supported the General Congress of Christian Merchants by giving cheap credit to Polish shopkeepers to enable them to outcompete Jewish merchants. Yet the Jewish merchants survived, and Polish merchants asked the government to subsidize German merchants as well to help drive out Jewish shop owners. It was a dangerous game. The German minority, openly pro-Nazi, detested both Poles and Jews and waited for Hitler, who had declared he would one day bring Polish ethnic Germans into the Reich.

In 1937 the government decreed ritual slaughter illegal, both attacking Judaism and ruining Jewish butchers. Endek encouraged peasants to seize Jewish shops. The Falanga and other fascist groups once banned by Pilsudski assaulted Jews as the police stood by; "Beat the Jews" became a popular slogan. But hundreds of thousands of Jewish workers went on strike, and Jewish shopkeepers, businessmen, and factory owners closed down to attend protest demonstrations supported by many Polish leftists and democrats. The Bund and Zionists, aided by some Polish socialists, formed self-defense units to resist. Greatly outnumbered, their efforts increased retaliation.

In 1937 the Polish Socialist party condemned reaction and anti-Semitism at its party congress and collaborated with the Jewish Bund in demonstrations and elections, joined by the tiny Democratic party. Surprisingly, those political parties that represented Polish peasants, including Piast, began to draw back from their previous singling out of the Jews as the main enemy of the peasant. Even Piast began to see that anti-Semitism was a tool of the government and Endek to divert attention from the exploitation of peasants by landholding gentry. But one must doubt that such a last-minute modification could change the minds of supporters nurtured on anti-Semitism since the 1890s, and their hope to be able to replace rural Jewish middlemen in Poland.

In 1937 the government issued millions of copies of a declaration denouncing the Jews in the name of Polish racial purity and economic well-being, and sponsored huge rallies demanding that Poland be governed by a single national will focused on Catholicism, the military, and anti-Semitism. The government also organized a Camp of National Unity (OZON) led by an extreme anti-Semite, Col. Adam Koc, who called for an end to Jewish cultural and political influence and the mass emigration of the Jews. OZON attracted some two million members. Although claiming to base its principles on Catholicism, OZON did not regard a converted Jew as a true Christian. Even so, Endek's radical wing accused OZON of being too easy on the Jews, demanding that Jews be driven from Poland by force.

In 1938 the Evian Conference met to persuade nations to accept German Jewish refugees, but the Polish, Hungarian, and Romanian governments requested that their Jews be taken as well. As the conference proved, mass emigration, forced or voluntary, was impossible; no government would accept a significant number of assimilated German Jews, let alone millions of impoverished Polish Jews. Poland then requested that the international community provide it with colonies for its Jews!

In the elections of 1938 the drumbeat of anti-Semitic measures brought the government 77 percent of all deputies and practically all Senate seats, seats held by representatives of the Polish elites. The Nazis never came close to such a resounding victory. In September 1938 Hitler told the Polish ambassador, Jan Lipski, that he intended to drive the Jews out of Europe and that Poland could help. Lipski replied that if Hitler succeeded, the Poles would erect a statue in his honor in Warsaw. Endek claimed that Freemasons and Jews had instigated German designs on Poland, and because Hitler had crushed them Germany was no longer dangerous. Proposals for a variety of new restrictions and plans for forced emigration appeared in parliament and in numerous articles and pamphlets just before the war.

On the eve of the German invasion, the Polish government devoted less time to the German threat than to discussing ways of getting rid of its Jews. If it had succeeded, Poland's economy, the employment of non-Jews, and government income would have been seriously damaged. Jews paid more than one-third of all taxes and employed millions of Poles. Even Hitler postponed driving the last Jewish businesses out of existence until 1938 because of the economic costs to his preparations for war. As the conflict loomed, the Polish government asked England for help against Germany, yet even then the Polish ambassador was instructed to ask the British also to help the Poles with their "Jewish problem." We cannot know what measures the Polish government would have taken against the Jews had it not been for the German invasion. As we have learned, however, government-encouraged "ethnic cleansing," with popular support, has few limits.

The frenzy of Polish anti-Semitism led most Jews except the ultra-orthodox to consider emigration or resistance. Half of all German Jews left their country before the outbreak of war, as well as some 400,000 Polish Jews. But Britain limited emigration to Palestine in 1939, and only France accepted a significant number of Jewish refugees in the 1930s. Other nations accepted a few wealthy Jews, but the Polish government severely restricted the amount of money Jews could take with them. Zionists and Bundists knew that a mass migration of Polish Jews was impossible. But until the Germans marched in, Polish Jews could not know what awaited them. The most extreme Zionists, followers of the militant Vladimir Jabotinsky, suspected it, and he had a significant Polish following, though many Jews believed that he aggravated an already perilous situation.

The Poles were also unaware of Nazi plans for them. No German government had ever reconciled itself to the Versailles Treaty provisions giving Poland former German territory. The Nazis did not think there should even be a Poland. Hitler intended to murder tens of millions and enslave the remainder.

In 1935 the French had proposed a mutual assistance pact with the Soviets and Czechs such that Russia would aid the

Czechs if France did. But in order to aid the Czechs, the Red Army would have to go through Poland—and no Polish government could allow that. At the very least, Stalin would seize Poland's eastern territories and murder those he assumed were enemies of the Bolsheviks. When the Germans violated the Munich Agreement by dismantling Czechoslovakia, appeasement ended as the British guaranteed to aid Poland if its independence were threatened. On April 6, 1939, Hitler issued secret military instructions to prepare to invade Poland—his killing squads were already in training. A week later Soviet foreign minister Maxim Litvinov offered a Soviet, British, and French alliance to aid any nation attacked by Germany, including a guarantee of safety for Romania, Latvia, Poland, Estonia, and Finland—in effect bringing all under Soviet domination. But the British government could hardly give Stalin what it refused Hitler, and in any event most British leaders believed the Nazis preferable to the Bolsheviks—at least Hitler believed in private property.

Goering and Ribbentrop now suggested that Poland revise the Versailles Treaty provisions in Germany's favor and ally itself with Germany. In January 1939 Hitler told Polish foreign minister Jozef Beck that together they could destroy bolshevism. Beck refused. With Czechoslovakia torn asunder in March 1939, Poland was practically surrounded by German troops. In August 1939 the Nazi-Soviet Pact gave Hitler a free hand to invade. The Polish government did not know that the British military had informed Prime Minister Chamberlain that it would be unable to aid Poland directly. The French crouched defensively in the Maginot Line; there would be no strong offensive to divert German troops from Poland. Without swift Allied support, Poland was certain to become a victim of either Germany or the Soviet Union—or both, as it turned out.

Allied governments and their military experts were unaware of the potential of the German blitzkrieg, the use of independently operating armored columns driving through enemy lines in swift pincer movements to cut off and demoralize enemy troops. The Polish military believed they could hold off the Germans for the few months needed for the Allies to fight their way into Germany. They were wrong, but there was no other way to save Poland. On September 1, 1939, Hitler invaded; on the 3rd, the English and French declared war. In the end, the Poles performed better in 1939 than the French and British did in 1940. The Allies did not even mount a bombing raid to help the Poles.

As German troops advanced they murdered thousands of Jewish and Polish noncombatant civilians. Some Poles also killed Jews and often barred them from bomb shelters. Poland surrendered on October 5. In the next weeks more than a million Poles and Jews were forced from their homes into eastern Poland, where most of the killing would occur. The occupiers gave much Jewish and Polish property to ethnic Germans, who looted or killed Jews with sadistic pleasure. German bureaucrats began planning to resettle millions of "Aryans" in the East.

The Soviets invaded eastern Poland on September 17, 1939. Soviet security forces killed those who resisted and rounded up "class enemies" and possible Resistance leaders: socialists, military officers, clergy, aristocrats, and wealthy merchants. About one-third of their victims were Jewish. Many were sent to the Gulag and died of starvation, disease, or murder. In 1940 the Soviets shot some fifteen thousand Polish officers. They also killed those Polish Communists suspected of being too independent of the Soviets. Ukrainian and White Russian peasants joined the Soviets to attack their Polish landlords, but the Soviets did not allow them to assault Jews. The Soviets claimed to be liberators of poor Jewish workers, and some Jewish workers and artisans whose fate improved under the occupiers welcomed them.

Communists, many of Jewish origin, denounced anti-Soviet Poles, and some Poles did the same. But the overwhelming majority of Jews detested communism. The Soviets, as in the

USSR, suppressed Jewish religious life and institutions. They offered three choices: become Soviet citizens, be sent to labor camps, or return to the German-occupied zone. Orthodox Jews naturally wanted to return to Poland, as did most Zionists, Bundists, and the Jewish middle and upper classes. Jewish socialists abhorred Stalin's brutality and ruthless suppression of all independent leftists. Some 300,000 Jews fled Soviet-occupied Poland in the first months of the war, tragically into the hands of the Germans.

In spite of the anti-Soviet attitudes of the bulk of the Jewish community, rumors swiftly spread among Poles that the Jews welcomed the Soviet invasion. General Grot-Rowecki of the Home Army, the Polish resistance force, reported in September 1941 that Poles believed the Jews had collaborated: "Please take it as an accepted fact that the overwhelming majority of the population is anti-Semitic." But the Polish population in the west knew nothing about Jewish behavior in the east and relied on the popular prewar myth of Judeo-bolshevism. Poles who helped the Soviet security forces were condemned as individual traitors, not as representatives of their race. Ordinary Poles would not acknowledge that Polish hatred and discrimination motivated many Jews who supported the Soviets. The Bolshevik regime continued officially to oppose anti-Semitism until the end of the war, when Stalin no longer needed to appease his allies.

Poles as well as Jews were victims of the ghastly German occupation policies. Of approximately five million Poles who died during the war, close to three million were Polish Jews and the rest Polish Catholics. The Germans killed 30 percent of Poland's technicians, 40 percent of its academics, and 45 percent of its physicians and lawyers, depriving the country of those who might work for an independent Poland. The average wartime diet of Poles caused slow starvation, and they were sometimes shot down in the streets simply because they were Poles.

For all Jews, death was the intended fate. German soldiers as well as Nazis and special killing units used every imaginable form of torture and murder against Jews, sometimes simply for sadistic pleasure. No Polish Quisling government cooperated with the Germans. Unlike other occupied countries, Polish anti-Semites and fascists also hated the Germans, and Hitler had no interest in a puppet government. In the new racial empire there was to be no Poland.

In 1940 General Wladyslaw Sikorski, a moderate, formed a Polish government in exile in London and a *Delegatura* to represent it in Poland. The Allies and the Western Jewish community pressed Sikorski to announce that after the war Polish Jews would be treated with equality and allowed to retain their religion and culture. A high-ranking former official of the Polish government reported from Poland that the announcement made "a disastrous impression." Except for representatives of the Polish Socialist party and tiny democratic groups, the Polish Home Army did not want Jews even as fighters, and most did not want them as part of a postwar Poland. In August 1940 Endek's clandestine publication even maintained that the Germans and the Jews were allies.

Exact figures cannot be known, but about 1,000 Polish rescuers saved some 2,600 Jews, and 200,000 or more Poles helped Jews in various ways. The punishment for such action was death, and neighbors or even relatives might inform on any who helped Jews because they rightly feared a violent German reaction against the entire area. Poles had their own enormously difficult struggle to survive. It required immense courage and humanitarian instincts to transcend the ancient cultural divisions and hostility between the two communities and help Jews. It was far safer to betray them or do nothing.

As the Germans approached some villages, ordinary citizens and town officials slaughtered Jews by the hundreds on their own initiative. There is reason to think there were many such massacres, but to date there is no certain evidence. The government in exile published a clandestine newsletter in Poland expressing sympathy for the plight of the Jews and reported their slaughter by the Nazis to London in 1942, when Sikorski denounced these mass murders. But the British already knew of the killings by the summer of 1941; the Polish underground must have known as well.

There were four hundred Jewish ghettos in Nazi-occupied Poland, all with Jewish councils, Jewish police, and slave-labor factories. The Jews could only hope that the Soviets would defeat the Germans before they were killed, usually a vain hope even for those who produced war materiel for the Wehrmacht. The death rate from starvation and disease alone was staggering. Many individual and group acts of resistance occurred, but they were almost always worse than suicidal; whole blocks might be burned to the ground and all the inhabitants killed in reprisal. Even the Polish Home Army, with vastly more resources and hiding places, did not seriously resist the Germans until early in 1943. By then the overwhelming majority of Polish Jews were dead.

Some priests tried to intervene on behalf of Jewish converts to Christianity, that is, Christians of Jewish origin. Nuns saved about fifteen hundred Jewish children; the Germans shot ten nuns in reprisal. In September 1942 the underground Home Army established Zegota, the Council for Aid to the Jews. Zegota received about $5 million by 1945, largely from the West, made payments to some four thousand Jewish families, and provided false documents for some fifty thousand Jews and safe houses for those able to live outside the ghettos. Zegota wanted to do more, but it was not an important priority for the underground. Zofia Kossak, a major founder of Zegota, lamented the horrors suffered by the Jews and condemned the silence of Poles and the world, adding incorrectly that even international Jewry said nothing. Catholics, she wrote, must condemn the slaughter; God and the Christian conscience did not permit murder. Poles must also denounce those who helped the Germans and punish them severely when possible. But she added that the Jews were Poland's political, economic, and ideological enemies; they hated Poles more than they hated Germans, and held Poles responsible for their sufferings. Her voice was that of an otherwise humane Polish Catholic; one can only imagine what the majority thought.

The Catholic church suffered terribly under the Germans, who murdered 18 percent of all Polish priests, including some bishops. They destroyed churches, looted liturgical objects, forbade the hearing of confession in Polish, closed monasteries and convents, and constantly harassed Polish priests. German priests accompanied the army to replace Polish clergy. Pius XII protested none of this. Bitter at his silence, the clandestine press suggested that after the war the Polish Catholic church should break its ties with the Vatican. Only the anti-communism of the Vatican and the election of the pope restored its moral standing among Polish Catholics.

Of the eight parties in the Polish underground, only the small leftist and miniscule democratic groups concerned themselves with the fate of the Jews. Endek and several fascist groups believed their destruction just. Dmowski had predicted the destruction of Poland if the Jews remained, and Endek believed, as did the Nazis, that both the Western allies and the Bolsheviks were tools of the Jews. In their racist propaganda, the Germans encouraged Poles to loot and kill Jews, and they protected Poles from Zionists and Bundists who fought back. The Polish underground also distributed anti-Semitic leaflets.

Many Poles profited from the destruction of the Jews. After the Germans expropriated 3.5 million Jewish properties, Poles received the leftover land, raw materials, stores, and houses. Many Poles believed it simple justice to loot those who they believed were their former exploiters, and, after all, were not the Jews going to be killed anyway? In August 1943 a high official of the underground reported to the government in exile that after the war the return of any Jews would be seen as wrong and unjust. He was correct, as the killing of hundreds of returning survivors by Poles after the war demonstrated.

The Polish Home Army decided to conduct major operations only when the Germans were retreating, attacked them in force, or began killing large numbers of Poles. To the vast majority, the Jews were a separate community for whom Poles did not feel responsible. Pressured by London, the High Command of the Home Army declared it would help Jews only if it did not endanger other operations; but any significant use of force to save Jews would necessarily weaken other operations. The underground could not have saved the millions of Jews who died, but they would not take risks to save the thousands they might have. They did not even accept Jewish partisan fighters except in some large-scale brutal conflicts between Poles and Ukrainians in the East. Isolated in a hostile environment, some Jewish escapees or partisans seized food and supplies and were shot as criminals if caught. The underground did give or sell some weapons to Jewish units who had served in the Polish military or were known as strict anti-Communists, and a few Jews were accepted in the underground propaganda unit to appease London. But most of the underground regarded Jewish fugitives from the Nazis simply as security risks and even called them criminals and subversives until protests from Polish leftist and democratic underground fighters led to the withdrawal of this outrageous insult.

Vast numbers of Polish extortionists, blackmailers, and informants helped the Nazis. The Home Army punished only a few, despite the belief among many that informers were a danger to all. As in Germany, Nazi anti-Semitic policies would not have been nearly so successful without the large number of civilians who betrayed Jews and those who helped them. Some Polish peasants aided Jews, usually for a price, but far more blackmailed them or raided forests to capture, rob, or kill them, or hand them over to the Germans for a reward, or to Polish police or armed fascist groups who hunted and killed Jews on sight. How many died this way we cannot know. Unlike the Germans, the Poles kept no records, and the witnesses died.

Polish fascists, mostly lower-middle-class urban youth, were pleased that Germans were making Poland *Judenrein*. Anthony Polonsky tells us that the fascistic Confederation of the Nation blamed the Germans and the Jews for the war. Having set the world aflame, they wrote, it was only right that they "burn together." In 1941 the Christian Democratic Party of Labor declared that after the war all Central and Southern Europe would have to be cleansed of Jews. In the death camps, they declared, "Ruthless cunning falls victim to ruthless brutal power," and we do not grieve for the "malevolent" Jews. The prewar National Radical Camp (now called Rampart) wrote that Jews were degenerate revolutionaries who must be cleansed by fire, and noted that the Germans were doing it better than Poles could, as Polonsky also tells us. In September 1943 the prewar Falanga (now Pobudka) exulted: Now we know Poland can survive without the Jews. But of course Poland would not have survived without the defeat of the Germans by the Allies, above all by the hated Soviets.

Until the Warsaw Ghetto uprising of April 1943, many Poles condemned Jews for not defending themselves, ignoring the helplessness of isolated and unarmed ghetto dwellers against the might of the Germans. Even the Home Army, numbering in the hundreds of thousands and relatively well armed, did not rise until 1944. But with only a handful of weapons and no hope of survival, the Jews of the Warsaw Ghetto conducted the largest single European resistance action until then. Even anti-Semites had to admire the hopeless resistance of 750 pitifully armed fighters against 40,000 SS equipped with tanks and flame-throwers. Several Home Army units, again usually moderately leftist or democratic, attacked the Germans to draw them off and helped guide the handful of survivors through the sewers to safety.

In April 1943 Stalin broke with the London government in

exile. He wanted no pro-Allied Poland that claimed former Polish territories in the Ukraine and White Russia. Stalin falsely accused the government in exile of lying when it revealed that the Soviets, not the Germans, had massacred some fifteen thousand Polish officers in the Katyn Forest. Stalin organized a Polish Communist party out of those Communists who survived his murderous purges and in 1942 parachuted them into Poland. In January 1944 the Red Army crossed the prewar borders of Poland; in July it installed a provisional Polish government in Lublin.

On August 1, 1944, the 350,000 men and women of the Home Army rose, mistakenly assuming that the Red Army, at the gates of Warsaw after driving the Germans back in a mighty offensive, had begun a major attack on the city. The brave gamble of the Home Army was necessary if Poland was to be independent of both Germany and the USSR. The Soviets claimed they needed to regroup and renew supplies after their long and exhausting offensive, and did not attack; Stalin even refused to allow the Allies to use Soviet airfields to aid the Home Army uprising until it was too late. Outgunned and outnumbered, the Home Army was defeated; 20,000 died. The Germans rounded up and savagely shot all civilians—close to 250,000—near combat areas. Warsaw was a depopulated city of burned and blasted ruins when the Russians arrived in January 1945. The Soviets dominated Poland until the end of the cold war; Stalin wanted no enemy on Soviet borders and needed control of Poland in order to have access to Germany. His generation had lived through two utterly devastating German invasions; few Russians would have forgiven any leader who allowed Germany to rise again.

In the postwar diplomatic settlements the Soviets moved Poland some 150 miles to the west at the expense of Prussia, reclaiming tsarist territory and preventing any future alliance between Poland and Germany. For the first time Poland was unified ethnically and religiously. The Soviets had taken the

Ukrainians and White Russians, the Jews were dead, and millions of ethnic Germans had been murdered or driven out. The Soviets brutally destroyed any opposition and condemned the fighters of the Polish Home Army as fascist; they praised the Warsaw Ghetto fighters. Many Poles believed that these comments, the disproportionate number of Jews in the government and the Soviet security forces, and Soviet protection of Jews from anti-Semites confirmed the stereotype of Judeo-bolshevism.

More than 90 percent of Polish Jews perished in the Holocaust; about 75,000 survived. Roughly 10,000 Jews were freed from camps in Poland; 13,000 served in a Polish army in the Soviet Union, and about 30,000 returned from Soviet camps. Thousands survived the war by hiding among Gentiles. Many Jews passed as Poles in spite of Nazi racial stereotypes. In general, Poles were notably more "Aryan" looking than the average Prussian, as German scholars had demonstrated in an extensive study in the nineteenth century. Indeed, Himmler personally supervised the kidnapping of Polish children with "Aryan" physical traits to be raised by childless German SS couples. Scholars studied them after the war and found no trace of innate superiority.

In 1946 there were approximately 86,000 Jews in Poland. Anti-Semitism did not end, of course. Police, local officials, and people who held Jewish property, as well as small fascist groups with the slogan "Kill the Jews and Save Poland," murdered some 1,500 to 2,000 Jews who tried to return to their former homes in 1945–1947. Jewish institutions and a residence home for Holocaust survivors were bombed. Nevertheless by 1947, 137,000 Jewish deportees and those who had voluntarily left returned from the USSR, and several thousand more came in 1956–1957. About 125,000 Polish Jews remained in the USSR. Few Jews tried to live where they had lived before or claim their property in Poland; it was far too dangerous, even though the new Communist government ended pogroms—another proof to many Poles of Judeo-bolshevism. But as the cold war intensified in the late 1940s, the Soviets murdered Jewish leaders with ties to the West, broke up Jewish institutions, and ended Polish Jewish connections to American Jewry. When the Polish government began to ease away from Stalinism in 1967, it blamed Jews in the government for its totalitarian excesses and launched an anti-Zionist campaign—35,000 Jews left Poland. We can never know, but it seems likely that without the alliance with the West and the murderous policies of the Nazis toward the Poles, a majority of Poles would have been willing participants and not simply indifferent bystanders during the Holocaust.

TEN

The Italian Exception

Political anti-semitism had no historical basis in modern Italy. Italian fascists were not anti-Semites, and Jews joined their party in proportions equal to their share of the population. Only in 1938 when Mussolini became dependent on Hitler did he take measures against the Jews, measures extremely unpopular among Italians and even among important fascists. Mussolini himself denounced racism afterward, allowed numerous exceptions to the laws, and never turned Jews over to the Germans. During the war Italian bureaucrats, fascist leaders, and military officers refused to hand over Jews and even helped them escape. The vast majority of Italians, including many priests and nuns, rejected racism and many of them, as well as thousands of ordinary people, helped Jews after Italy surrendered in 1943 and the Nazis sought them out.

From Roman times Italian Jews had intermarried to such an extent that notions of racial purity were obviously absurd. Jews had also adopted Italian names and local dialects. Roughly 1 percent of the population in 1500, assimilation reduced them to roughly one-tenth of 1 percent by 1800. Jews mixed well with Italians; even the popes could not prevent it in Rome, though they tried. It helped that no influx of orthodox Jews from the East offered visible targets for hostility. Secular racism was never popular in Italy; Christian anti-Semitism was strong until the last decades of the eighteenth century, but by 1870 it was insignificant outside the Vatican.

Jews had lived in Italy since Roman times as slaves, merchants, or asylum seekers. Many shared in the commercial culture of the Italian Renaissance when banking, commerce, and moneylending were prestigious activities—the Catholic church itself engaged in all three. Economic decline in the sixteenth century, however, led competitors to limit Jewish economic activities, and the Spanish Bourbons, rulers of the Kingdom of Naples and Sicily, expelled the Jews for religious reasons. Italy was spared the religious passions of the Reformation and the Wars of Religion that shattered Europe during the Counter-Reformation. In 1555 Pope Paul IV did establish a ghetto in Rome, ordered torture for any Jews caught outside it after curfew, required them to pay extra taxes, and forbade them to own property. He also tried unsuccessfully to make them wear yellow symbols.

By the eighteenth century most Jews lived in the northern cities of Italy where leading citizens shared the anti-clericalism and religious tolerance of the Enlightenment and undertook significant administrative, educational, and economic reforms. Tuscany granted toleration to the Jews, Trieste abolished its ghetto, and Livorno countenanced no restrictions. Emperor Joseph II, the famed enlightened despot of the Habsburgs who ruled northern Italy, closed half of all monasteries and convents and taxed church possessions. He also decreed religious toleration, opened crafts and professions to Jews, and allowed them to purchase property and send their sons to secular schools. Trade guild monopolies in Tuscany and Lombardy were ended, and they became the best-governed and most prosperous states in Italy.

Napoleon drove the Austrians from northern Italy in 1796, annexed Piedmont, and established an Italian state in north central Italy by 1810. He ended feudal tyranny in the Kingdom of Naples, established constitutions, cut customs barriers, trained Italians for his efficient civil service, and enforced the then progressive laws of the Code Napoleon. To gain middle-class support and raise money for war, Napoleon ended the privileges and tax exemptions of nobles and ecclesiastics, and reduced many restrictions on commerce. He liberated the Papal States from the notoriously corrupt rule of priests, asserting that their temporal power was a hindrance to the spiritual mission of the church. As in Germany, he liberated the Jews. As Raphael Mahler notes, "In no other country did Jewish emancipation so literally mean the destruction of the ghetto walls or arouse such spontaneous demonstrations of sympathy by gentiles as in Italy." Napoleon's reforms and consequent rapid economic growth persuaded the upper middle classes that an enlightened and united Italy was possible, though they rejected the Little Corporal's tyranny. Significantly, unlike the situation in Prussia and France, there was no powerful and militant aristocracy to resist his reforms or label them "Jewish."

When Napoleon was defeated, Austrian troops and Italy's former rulers returned, canceled his reforms, and forced the Jews back into ghettos; the pope restored Christian medieval anti-Jewish restrictions in his Papal States. But such actions merely strengthened the association between anti-Semitism and foreign oppression in Italy. The most influential Italian novel of the nineteenth century, Alessandro Manzoni's *I promessi sposi* (1827), described the brutality of Spanish rule in the seventeenth century, but readers knew the Austrians were the real target, and many others wrote popular tales of the battle against foreign oppressors. Here the foreigners were reactionary Catholics, not liberal Frenchmen or Jews. Secret societies proliferated, fostering reform or revolution; the most famous was the Carbonari of 1796. Jewish printers distributed militant patriotic pamphlets, and Jews joined the revolutions of the 1820s, 1830, and 1848, fighting alongside students and the sons of the professional classes, sharing the fate of many who were bankrupted, imprisoned, exiled, or executed. During their brief rule, revolutionaries closed the ghettos and proclaimed civic equality and religious liberty. As elsewhere, the fate of the Jews was tied to liberalism, but in Italy their enemies were Austria, the Spanish Bourbons, and the Vatican, not powerful indigenous aristocrats.

Many educated Italians joined "Young Italy," formed in 1831 by the famous patriot Giuseppe Mazzini. Unlike German nationalists, he rejected notions of racial superiority or the virtues of autocracy and believed all peoples had a uniquely valuable contribution to make to the development of mankind if democratic republics could be established. Jewish intellectuals were among his closest associates. From exile in London, Mazzini inspired many, including Giuseppe Garibaldi, revolutionary republican and violent anti-cleric. During the 1840s a variety of plans for a united Italy circulated, demanding free speech, equality before the law, freedom of religion, and Jewish liberation, and often calling for an end to the Papal States. Almost everywhere the politically aware middle classes supported either liberalism or the radical republicanism of Mazzini and Garibaldi. In 1847 Metternich was shocked when the new pope, Pius IX, proposed liberal reforms, as did the reactionary Bourbon, King Ferdinand of Naples—both frightened by demonstrations.

The state of Piedmont had the only independent Italian army, and after Napoleon its absolute monarchy was restored. But its educated elites, accustomed to twenty years of French rule and the intellectual influence of the Enlightenment, pressured the king to establish a constitutional monarchy. As revolts spread throughout Italy in 1847, Count Camillo Cavour persuaded King Charles Albert of Piedmont to grant a moderate constitutional monarchy and move against the Austrian occupiers. Cavour admired the French Enlightenment and English institutions, and believed that a moderate constitutional monarchy would persuade the European powers to help force an end to Austrian rule and permit Piedmont to lead the drive for a reformed and united Italy. Radical revolutions, he assumed, would only bring the wrathful opposition of the great powers.

Reluctantly the king declared a constitution that allowed him to name the premier and limit the electorate to 1 percent of the population—landowners, merchants, and professionals. Neither the king nor Cavour trusted the illiterate and apolitical masses. In 1848 Sicily declared independence and adopted a liberal constitution; Garibaldi and Mazzini declared a Roman republic and forced the pope to flee. Jews served on the city council and in the Civic Guard. Everywhere their emancipation was declared. Pius IX appealed to Austria and France to use force to restore his Papal States, causing both Italian moderates and radicals to denounce him as a traitor who would deliver Italy to foreign oppressors.

As revolutions paralyzed the Habsburg Empire, Italians in Milan drove out Austrian troops, and Charles Albert declared war on Austria. In the wake of his defeat, King Louis Philippe, pressured by his Catholic constituency, sent French troops to put down the Roman republic and restore Pius IX, who promptly restored anti-Jewish laws. In all Italy only Piedmont remained independent. England and France refused to allow Austria to destroy a legitimate monarch with a moderate constitution. The constitution stated that all citizens, Catholic or not, enjoyed equal civic and political rights and access to all offices. By now even moderates disdained Austrian concessions, and wanted to be rid of them and the pope's temporal power as well.

To succeed, Cavour needed the armed support of France and British neutrality. With Garibaldi and Mazzini exiled, Cavour believed that liberal economic policies under a constitutional monarchy would win the favor of the two states against both backward Austria and Italian radicals. Minister for trade in 1850, he supervised the building of roads, railways, docks, and tunnels, ended guild privileges, paid the Austrian war indemnity, and attracted foreign investment. Prime minister in 1852, he extended credit and ended tariffs, forcing backward industries to modernize. His policies gained European respect and undermined reactionary Austria.

An agnostic, Cavour detested the papacy and viewed anti-Semitism as sheer superstition. His private secretary, Isacco Artom, was the first Jew to become a prominent public official, and, like other important Jewish leaders, the family was ennobled. Cavour ended the right of the church in Piedmont to its own laws and courts, dissolved monasteries, closed convents, confiscated church lands, pensioned off monks, and subjected seminaries to state control and their students to military service. Declaring that prosperity and public morality were highest where the proportion of clergy was lowest, he ended Jesuit domination of education and obligatory religious instruction in public schools.

Napoleon III's territorial ambitions made him willing to aid Cavour if Piedmont agreed not to attack the Papal States and if Austria could be maneuvered into attacking Piedmont first. Cavour succeeded, and in 1859 Napoleon III defeated Austria but concluded a premature armistice, giving Piedmont only Lombardy—because Piedmont did not contribute enough troops and Cavour had announced that he would try to end the pope's temporal power. Emilia and Tuscany joined Piedmont voluntarily, but the large Papal States still split Italy in half. Pope Pius IX, insisting that his sovereignty over the Papal States came from Christ himself, threatened excommunication because Cavour intended to extend anti-clerical laws to the pope's domains. Thus the only significant source of anti-Semitism in Italy became even more unpopular among politically active Italians. Even the pope's own subjects were unhappy with priestly rule. The Catholic aristocracy, unlike that of France and Prussia, was politically indifferent. The nobles of southern Italy ignored national politics and military careers, content to squeeze profits from their peasants and live in idle luxury.

Garibaldi and his volunteers surprised Europe and Cavour by swiftly liberating the Kingdom of Naples and Sicily. Garibaldi and Mazzini hoped to show there was mass support for a united and republican Italy, not just a monarchy dependent on French armies and a tiny electorate. But to avoid civil conflict, Garibaldi selflessly accepted the sovereignty of King Victor Emmanuel of Piedmont. The road to the Papal States was now open, and Cavour tried to persuade Napoleon III to remove French troops from Rome. Given the sentiments of Catholic France, Napoleon could not allow the pope to be chased from Rome again. Piedmont's army handily conquered the Papal States, but the French denied Cavour Rome. Hoping to make Rome the capital of Italy, Cavour promised to guarantee the pope's spiritual leadership but insisted that he accept religious freedom in return. Rome remained occupied by the French, Austrians still ruled Venetia, but Cavour had the Papal States, seized huge amounts of church property, and closed some seventeen hundred Roman and Neapolitan monasteries. In 1861 parliament met and declared Italy one but did not try to take Rome or Venice and risk the intervention of the great powers. Cavour died in 1861.

In his famous encyclical of 1864, "The Syllabus of Errors," the pope officially condemned progress, science, liberalism, and freedom of religion—as those who believe they possess divine and absolute truth are bound to do. But the Vatican lost all credibility among Italy's political elites, and no government minister in the nineteenth century risked declaring himself a devout Catholic. Even the few parliamentarians who defended the rights of the church never denounced freedom of religion. In 1866 Prussia and Italy jointly attacked and defeated Austria. To finance the war, the Italian government closed 2,382 more convents and monasteries and pensioned off another 29,000 monks and nuns. Italy lost its battles, but Bismarck granted it Venetia, and Italian troops replaced the retreating French in 1870. It is of the utmost significance that liberals and radical republicans—not reactionary anti-Semites, as in Germany—gained whatever prestige accrued to those who united Italy.

The new Italy occasioned no outbreak of mass enthusiasm.

Ordinary Italians played no part in the unification movement and held regional, not national, loyalties. The Piedmontese knew little about the lives of other Italians and their different legal, tax, and administrative systems. In the south the abrupt application of free enterprise, new and onerous consumer taxes, and the cancellation of Bourbon legislation that had kept bread prices low ruined many enterprises and peasants—there were even calls for a Bourbon restoration. But unlike Germans and Austrians, the southerners did not blame "Jewish liberalism" but Piedmontese arrogance, especially because liberals, moderate or radical, dominated parliament and the electorate.

When poverty-stricken peasants revolted, nearly half of the Piedmontese army descended upon them to wage a brutal guerrilla war, slaughtering whole villages. Peasants, mostly agricultural laborers, were always close to revolt, unlike the reactionary peasants and artisans of Germany and Austria. The few Jews in rural or southern Italy were rarely moneylenders, landlords' agents, or middlemen; ethnic differences could not be put into play. The constant denunciations of the Jews by Pius IX and later Leo XIII could have little impact; there was no wave of anti-Semitism as accompanied German unification. The new Italy seemed just another imposed minority and hostile government, brutally enforcing higher prices and conscription, in cooperation with local noble landowners aided by Mafia-like organizations. Moreover, few Italians could identify with a government elected by 150,000 out of 20 million people and a parliament ruled by shifting coalitions of propertied politicians who exchanged favors among themselves and local notables who manipulated elections for them. There were no significant political parties with clearly differentiated programs until socialism in the late nineteenth century. The costs of unification meant that fiscal stability, high taxes, and austerity budgets, not the mitigation of poverty, were the major concerns, bitterly disappointing the idealistic followers of Mazzini and Garibaldi. Indeed, the Piedmontese scarcely seemed Italian after twenty years of French rule. They could hardly claim to be the racial soul of their people, as the Prussian Junkers had done—even Cavour spoke Italian poorly. In addition, mainly French and Prussian armies—excepting the fiery anti-clerical Garibaldi—forged Italian unity. The Piedmontese could not boast of belonging to a superior warrior race. Racist appeals could win no votes, and in contrast with France and Germany there were no politically effective forces to seek them.

In order to pacify Pius IX, in 1871 the pope was given full sovereignty over Vatican City, free of taxes. Nevertheless he called himself "the prisoner of the Vatican" and forbade Catholics to participate in national politics. Consequently no party stood for Christian anti-Judaism. Pius IX instructed the Jesuit journal *Civiltà Cattolica* to label the Jews "an enemy race, hostile to Christianity and society in general." Catholic organizations, allowed to engage in local politics, ignored the remark and worked mainly to help the poverty-stricken, often cooperating with the left to do so. The popes never trusted them.

By the 1890s Jewish assimilation in Italy had surpassed that of any major European nation. In stark contrast to Germany, Jews were prominent in politics, civil service, diplomacy, universities, and the army. Several government ministers were Jewish, including the first Jewish minister of war on the European continent in 1902, the first Jewish prime minister in 1910, and the most highly decorated general in 1914–1918. In 1923, 26 of 350 senators were Jewish. By 1938 close to 45 percent of all married Jews had Christian mates. Jews were entrepreneurs in railway, construction, insurance, banking, and publishing, as well as lawyers, physicians, newspaper owners, and editors. They were an integral part of the Italian liberal elites, who had no anxieties about a Jewish presence in the modern sectors of the economy, unlike the blood-and-soil ultra-nationalists of Central and Eastern Europe. When economic crises struck, the Jewish community was not blamed, as in Germany and Austria after the collapse of 1873. In the 1880s the Italian parliament attempted to cover up bribes taken to allow bankers and industrialists to skim money from state contracts and avoid taxes, but the appropriate government ministers were accused without irrelevant attacks against "Jewish financiers." Naturally the price of Jewish acceptance was a general lack of adherence to Judaism, to the frustration of rabbinical authorities.

In 1882 lower property qualifications gave the vote to 7 percent of Italians, most of them petty bourgeoisie and artisans. Unlike their German and Austrian equivalents, they were not reactionary racists but supported republican and democratic radicals whose electoral strength consequently doubled. In 1891 forty thousand industrial workers attended the first Socialist Congress, but unlike Austria, few Italian Jews were socialists; they were not alienated from society or government and sought no radical change. Unlike German leftists, Italian socialists found significant support in rural areas. Because moneylenders and mortgage holders were overwhelmingly Catholic nobles, race and religion were irrelevant, and class antagonisms favored the left. Moreover, Italian Jews were not as overtly visible in culture as elsewhere—often a consequence of marginal status—or accused of damaging the cultural soul of the Italian people. Verdi was not Wagner.

In 1891 Pope Leo XIII, alarmed by socialism, declared in "Rerum Novarum" that workers' unions were permissible if they were Catholic, did not strike, and rejected socialism. He believed that unrestricted capitalism exploited workers but insisted that restoring the power of the church would renew Christian virtue and bring workers and employers to forge a more just relationship voluntarily. From such ideas a fledgling Christian Democratic movement emerged. Unlike the Austrian and French Christian Social movements, however, it was not anti-Semitic. Moreover, it called for tax relief for the overburdened peasantry and a progressive income tax—a very radical proposal at the time. Parliament supported these measures, but the successive governments of Francesco Crispi and General

Luigi Pelloux (1893–1900) rejected them, and landowner exploitation increased.

In response, destitute agrarian workers demonstrated and rioted; martial law brought more violence. Crispi imprisoned radical democrats and socialists, dissolved their associations, and closed universities, chambers of labor, village banks, and even Catholic organizations, jailing some of their leaders as well. But in 1895 the voters reelected the imprisoned socialists. General Pelloux, who replaced Crispi, tried to rule by royal decree until liberals, republicans, and socialists allied against him and the courts decided in their favor. In new elections in 1898 the left opposition doubled its strength and restored parliamentary rule. As in France during the Dreyfus Affair, moderate socialists and left liberals combined to protect liberal institutions against reactionary authoritarianism, with the crucial difference that anti-Semitism was never involved. In the 1890s, as noted, the German Conservative party, facing the threat of increasing socialist votes and reforms by Chancellor Caprivi, mounted a huge anti-Semitic campaign to protect conservative privileges and powers. In Italy the struggle between liberal and authoritarian views was unencumbered by racial irrelevancies.

In 1900–1901 unprecedented strikes occurred when syndicalists (revolutionary socialists) tried to overthrow the government. Prime Minister Giovanni Giolitti, a clever manipulator and Italy's leading politician until 1914, hoped to co-opt moderate socialists. He offered universal suffrage, the right to organize and strike, higher pensions, a progressive income tax, regulation of corporations, a weekly day of rest for workers, and government neutrality in labor disputes. Left liberals, democrats, republicans, and a few socialists supported Giolitti in the first reformist coalition in Italian history. After bloody police clashes in September 1904, revolutionaries tried to thwart Giolitti by declaring a general strike that paralyzed Italy for five days. But Giolitti refused to use force, assuming correctly that the workers could not hold out.

The violent uprisings caused the Vatican to reconsider its aloofness from Italian politics. For too long government anticlerical ministers under a king thought to be an atheist had been unhindered by pro-Catholic deputies. The parliament had restricted Catholic education, punished clergy who denounced it, ended compulsory payment of tithes, and taken over church charities, claiming they spent their money on their own needs rather than on the poor. The pope did not trust a small Christian Democratic group led by Don Luigi Sturzo, a Sicilian priest, because it supported progressive reforms and sometimes cooperated with the moderate left in rural areas. The pope feared too much enthusiasm for the poor would anger the rich. A tiny minority of Catholic activists wished to restore the temporal powers of the church, and among them were political anti-Semites; but they were ignored or ridiculed, in contrast to the Catholic anti-Semitic aristocrats of France and the ultraracist Austrian Christian Socials.

In 1904 Giolitti held elections in an attempt to defeat the revolutionary left. To gain the support of democratic radicals, he proposed to legalize divorce. Pius X, furious, reluctantly allowed bishops to support government candidates in districts where Catholic votes could help defeat leftists, provided that Giolitti promised to end support for divorce and anticlericalism. Some twenty-six socialists were thus defeated. Italian Catholics, in short, with Vatican support, voted for conservative but nevertheless liberal candidates at a time when most Austrian German Catholics raged against the Jews and voted for virulent anti-Semites.

Giolitti cut taxes on consumer necessities, started public works, improved working conditions and wages for government personnel, and gave workers a weekly day off. Moderate socialists approved but correctly feared they would be thrown out of their party if they joined his government, and they refused to do so. In 1908 revolutionary socialists again tried to overthrow the state, and in the elections of 1909 they made some gains. Radical republicans and socialists became a force in the lower house of parliament; the left governed in several municipalities, and revolutionary extremists defeated moderate Marxists in the Socialist Party Congress of 1910.

As fascists would later, landowners sent motorized volunteer forces to battle leftists and strikers and help the police occupy workers' districts. In 1910 Enrico Corradini founded a Nationalist Association and demanded an authoritarian leader to destroy the left, unite the nation, build a powerful economy, and make Italy a great imperialist power. Throw out these parliamentary "pimps for votes" who pandered to ignorant voters and violent workers, the Nationalists demanded. Although the Nationalists detested the ideals of the revolutionary left, they admired their willingness to fight for them. To Nationalists the truly noble life was sacrifice in the battle for ideals, not that of the timid bourgeoisie, who were satisfied with creature comforts and endless compromises with their enemies. Nationalists found it humiliating that diplomatic intrigue and foreign armies had unified Italy rather than Italian armed might, and that Italy had become just a tourist attraction and source of cheap immigrant labor. Indeed, by 1914 five million of forty million Italians worked abroad.

Unlike the precursors of the Nazis and Eastern European fascists, the Italian Nationalists did not glorify artisans and peasants but praised the modern industrial economy and insisted that Italy support it. That and their opposition to socialism brought subsidies from industry. Nationalists did not venerate a mythical tribal past, as did German pre-fascists. For them Italy's historical greatness lay in Imperial Rome and the cultural creativity of the Renaissance, though they wanted a revolutionary new art to reflect the modern age of steam, industry, power, and speed. The Nationalists did not believe Italians a race, let alone a superior one; they must be taught to be great.

The Italian Nationalists were the first movement of the revolutionary radical right in Europe that was not anti-Semitic.

Their hostilities were directed against the Slavic and German minorities who lived among Italians in Austrian territories that should, they believed, be Italian—the South Tyrol, the Dalmatian coast, Trieste, and Fiume. Until Italy conquered these territories, unification would be incomplete. Above all the Nationalists despised the "barbaric" Africans who inhabited territories that were once part of Imperial Rome and should be again. In 1923 the Nationalist "Blueshirts" naturally enough joined Mussolini.

In 1896 Crispi's government had fallen when his attempt to conquer Ethiopia ended in defeat and the death of six thousand Italian soldiers. In 1911 Giolitti, aiming to rally Italians, attacked the Ottoman province of Libya hoping for an easy victory. As it dragged on, the war divided his liberal following. Socialists and Catholic leaders were angry from the start, though some priests welcomed a crusade against Islam. Citizens tore up the rails carrying troop trains to the coast. Although Italy won what was then a barren desert, the costs were so high that Giolitti feared revealing them and the incompetence of the Italian army.

The disastrous war helped only the extremists of the left, of whom Mussolini was then a prominent member, soon to be editor of the socialist paper *Avanti!* In 1912 the extremists expelled moderate socialists from the party. That same year the passage of universal male suffrage increased the number of voters from roughly three million to nine million. In the 1913 elections Giolitti received Catholic support for any liberal candidates who would allow religious instruction in public schools and oppose the legalization of divorce. But socialists gained close to a third of all seats and some two-fifths of the electorate. Giolitti's liberals lost sixty-two seats, deserted by those angered by the agreement with the Catholics, and he resigned. In "Red Week"—June 1914—battles between peasants and landlords raged as revolutionary socialists declared a general strike; leftist republics were established in various cities. The strikes ended on June 10. Had World War I not intervened, either civil war or a socialist victory seemed likely.

Excluding the extreme left, the Western publics greeted the war enthusiastically. As casualties soared, however, governments encouraged ethnic hatreds to boost morale among drafted civilians and their families, who soon viewed the war as a sacred cause. The vast majority of Italians, however, had no desire for war, nor did parliament, the Vatican, and the socialists. Italy declared neutrality, hence no ethnic group or nationality could be singled out for the hatred of a mobilized population. Although small groups of Nationalists agitated vigorously for war, the Italian government entered it only for practical reasons, knowing that it could gain territory from a defeated Austria.

In May 1915 the government declared war against Austria, in August 1916 against Germany. Most Italians still wanted peace, and Pope Benedict XV called for an end to this "useless carnage." The socialists declared their opposition to the war but would not sabotage it. Mussolini decided for war, ending his socialist career. As casualties mounted in 1916, the Italian public supported a negotiated peace, and the pope spoke of a "people madly oppressed by this regrettable war." Marxists distributed anti-war pamphlets; when German leftists did so they faced a storm of anti-Semitism. General Luigi Cadorna, whom the Nationalists wanted as dictator, blamed anti-war propaganda on socialists and Catholics. Ludendorff and Austrian leaders, of course, blamed the Jews. But Italians, heartsick at mass murder and extreme economic deprivation, blamed no one for "defeatism," and hundreds of thousands dodged the draft or deserted.

The war cost Italy 700,000 dead, immense expenses, a threefold rise in prices, and huge unemployment, including 2.5 million veterans angry because they had not received the land promised to keep them in the trenches. There were bitter complaints that Italy was treated unfairly by the peace settlement, yet it received more territory than any other nation, all at Austrian expense. Above all, the war discredited parliamentary liberalism and opened the way to authoritarian nationalism, but without anti-Semitism. In 1919 Mussolini founded the Fascist party to support the battle of landowners and industrialists against socialists, workers, and peasants. Five Jews were among the founders. Of 45,000 Jews, 5,000 eventually joined. True assimilation allowed Jews to choose whatever their class and inclination dictated.

The two most popular parties in the elections of 1919 were the Socialists and the Catholic Popolari. But they could not cooperate. Socialists detested the church while the Popolari under Don Sturzo ranged from clerical reactionaries to radical democrats, and was forbidden by the pope to form a government with atheistic socialists. The Popolari did not support Christian anti-Semitism; it condemned imperialism, called for the breakup of large estates, and supported agrarian strikers. Sturzo could work with Giolitti's anti-clerical liberals, but Giolitti preferred fascism. In 1920, when riots against the cost of living broke out, the government, afraid of cutting bread subsidies, considered taxing wealth. The Vatican's own considerable wealth was at stake, and the pope instructed the Popolari to refuse support. Reluctant but devout, Sturzo obeyed. The pope still preferred the fascists.

Five governments rose and fell between 1918 and 1922, as fascists supported by industrialists and landowners fought striking workers and peasants. In August 1920 a lockout at the Alfa Romeo automobile plant resulted in workers occupying the factory and running it without management—the ultimate Marxist challenge to private property. Peasants occupied the uncultivated fringes of great estates and forced concessions from landowners. Again Giolitti refused to use force, and industrialists and landowners urged Mussolini to do the job; even the liberal press supported Mussolini's defense of property. Giolitti aided Mussolini by placing his name on the list of candidates he supported. Three hundred fascists and 3,000 opponents were killed in street battles; many local governments instructed the military and the police to cooperate with Mussolini. The socialists called a general strike in August 1922 but failed, outgunned and defeatist.

There were approximately 250,000 fascists in 1922, but unlike the hundreds of thousands of paramilitaries in Germany and Austria, they were not anti-Semites. In the elections of 1921 the fascists won 35 seats while the socialists, the Popolari, and the liberals each received 100 or more. The Popolari wanted to join the socialists in a no-confidence vote against the government for refusing to act against fascist violence, but again the Vatican forbade it while pro-fascist sympathies surged among the church hierarchy.

As a socialist, Mussolini had denounced Austrian Pan German anti-Semitism. In 1919, like many everywhere, he had spoken of the international conspiracy of Jewish Bolsheviks, but he retracted this fantasy in 1920. Hitler gained great public approval for such statements, but the vast majority of Italians found them puzzling if not ridiculous. Mussolini then praised the immense sacrifice of Jewish blood in the war. There was no political advantage to be gained from anti-Semitism in Italy, and he knew it. Moreover he never understood what he once referred to as the "German disease." Italian history had not prepared the people for such fantasies.

The king appointed Mussolini prime minister just before Mussolini's bedraggled forces conducted their "March on Rome" in October 1922. The army, the church, the middle classes, and most of the governing elites approved; parliament granted him dictatorial powers for a year. Two years later parliament passed the Acerbo Law, giving any party that received a plurality—providing it reached 25 percent of the vote—65 percent of parliamentary seats. Violence and the support of Giolitti and other political leaders had assured Mussolini's victory.

Mussolini assured the chief rabbi of Rome that fascists were not anti-Semitic and visited Weimar Germany to assure the German foreign minister that his party did not share the virulent racism of the then powerful Orgesch; the Nazis were not significant at the time. As Mussolini said, "The Jewish problem does not exist in Italy." In secret meetings with Vatican representatives, Mussolini promised to aid the seriously troubled Bank of Rome, which held Vatican funds, and he allowed the return of crucifixes and the catechism to classrooms. When Sturzo protested against liberal and church support of Mussolini as well as fascist electoral terror and brutality, and tried to unite with moderate socialists to oust the fascists, the exasperated pope forced him to resign. In 1924 the socialist Giacomo Matteotti was murdered by fascists after he documented their terror in parliament. Mussolini accepted responsibility for his death in 1925 and began to organize an authoritarian state. The Popolari and the socialists, representatives of the majority of Italians, were no longer obstacles. The Vatican rallied to Mussolini and even allowed him to disband Catholic unions. After all, the fascists supported large families, the subjection of women, and the sanctity of private property. In 1929 the pope recognized the Italian state. In return Mussolini declared Catholicism the state religion, granted tax concessions, and repealed anti-clerical legislation. To show he was not anti-Jewish, he gave rabbinical authorities new powers over the Jewish community.

Many fascists were Jewish or had Jewish wives; Jews were professors, generals, admirals, administrators, fascist journalists, and officers of the fascist militia. Guido Jung, a member of the fascist Grand Council and Mussolini's finance minister in 1932, was Jewish, as was Margherita Sarfatti, Mussolini's mistress, official biographer, and the editor of *Gerarchia*, the fascist journal. In 1932 Mussolini declared that "Italian Jews have always shown themselves good citizens" and that "Nothing will ever make me believe that biological pure races can be shown to exist today." He boasted that wherever he found anti-Semitism he would suppress it; in 1933 he tried to persuade

Hitler to call off his boycott of Jewish businesses. Eastern European Jews were given grants to study in Italy. Mussolini endowed a professorship at the Hebrew University of Jerusalem, allowed the Zionist navy to train in Italy, and even claimed to be a Zionist—undoubtedly to annoy the British. He advised the Austrian government, still dependent on Italian support, to limit its anti-Jewish activities. In 1935 he persuaded Hitler to allow the Jews to leave the Saar with their money when that region was restored to Germany. He also called for League of Nations sanctions against Hitler's violations of the Versailles Treaty, but the French and English refused, and Hitler's forces marched into the Rhineland unopposed. Mussolini realized that the West was unwilling to stop Hitler and drew his own conclusions.

In 1935 Mussolini attacked Ethiopia; the West disapproved but Hitler encouraged him. The Rome/Berlin Axis, formed in 1936, was tested in Spain in 1937 when Mussolini needed and received German help to fight for Franco. Hitler also staged enormous military displays for Mussolini, making Il Duce painfully aware that he was the junior partner. When Jewish groups, along with liberals and leftists, opposed Mussolini's aggression in Ethiopia and Spain, the first anti-Jewish polemics were published in Italy, directed against "international Jewry," though Italian Jewish loyalty was not questioned. Nevertheless Mussolini removed some Jewish fascist journalists from office and warned against intermarriage. But many fascists, some Jewish or married to Jews, protested, and the official position still denied any Jewish problem. In November 1937 Mussolini declared he would not aid Austria if Germany invaded, but he still denounced anti-Semitism. Hitler did not pressure him; he needed an ally and knew that if he won the war Italian Jews would be his.

As Meir Michaelis tells us, Mussolini's regime "did not take on an anti-Jewish character until he became a pawn of the Reich." On July 14, 1938, Mussolini issued his famous "Manifesto on Race." It declared that anyone with two Jewish parents was a Jew by race, regardless of religion. But such a strict definition and the high rate of intermarriage made this far less inclusive than the Nazi definition. Decrees declared Jews inassimilable aliens and excluded them from teaching at or attending public schools and academic or scientific institutions. They were forbidden to marry "Aryans," forbidden to own land or businesses above a certain size, and banned from military service, employing non-Jewish servants, or tutoring "Aryans." They could no longer join the Fascist party. Italians were forbidden to marry Jews or any "non-Aryans"; Mussolini was incensed because some Italian soldiers had returned with Ethiopian war brides. Some Jews were ousted from the civil service, universities, and the fascist militia.

But Mussolini, well aware that anti-Semitism was unpopular in Italy, made many exceptions. Dismissed Jews retained their pension rights; Jewish schools and freedom of worship remained. The law exempted Jewish families of party members who had joined before the March on Rome and Jews who had fought as volunteers or received decorations in Libya, Ethiopia, or Spain. Consequently Jews and half-Jews still served in Mussolini's army at the end of the war. Foreign Jews ordered to leave Italy during the war could remain if they were over 65 or had married Italians before October 1938. The minister of education charged with removing Jews from teaching had a Jewish mother and protected Jews. Intermarriage was common in the fascist hierarchy and in prominent pro-fascist circles, including senior civil servants and diplomats; their children did not qualify as Jews according to the manifesto. Michaelis estimates that close to a quarter of all Jewish families escaped persecution by exemptions. Moreover, there were 4,500 converts after the July 1938 manifesto, and though many were still Jews by fascist law, to the Italian church they were Christians and protected as such—not as in the German church.

Italians were dismayed at the treatment of Jews. In August

1938 when hundreds of foreign Jews were ordered to leave the country, anti-fascist demonstrations erupted. Most fascists disapproved of anti-Semitic legislation, as did the king, and even fascist anti-Semites believed that simply rehabilitating Jews who were anti-fascist in internment camps would suffice. Many Italians complained that the measures were dishonorable and barbarous imitations of the Germans. Pius XI insisted that racist anti-Semitism was incompatible with Christ's universal message, and denounced the regime's newfound racism. Mussolini privately said much the same but added that he needed the measures for reasons of state. In spite of their long campaign against the Jews, Italian Jesuits said that while they opposed Judaism, they rejected racism.

Luigi Federzoni, a former Nationalist leader, argued against the Duce's anti-Semitic measures in the fascist Grand Council meeting in 1938; other highly placed fascists also protested. Frustrated Germans watched as Italian authorities found bureaucratic ways to avoid enforcing racial laws. The Nazis scorned Mussolini's "Kosher fascism"; German Jews had already been reduced to a ghettolike existence, and German plans for the mass murder of Jews when war came were already being considered. *Kristallnacht* upset the king, the Italian public, and many Italian fascists. Unfortunately Pius XI died in February 1939. Pius XII informed Italian Foreign Minister Galeazzo Ciano that he would be more accommodating about racism, as indeed he was. The Nazi regime preferred the new pope, especially when he did not protest when they massacred Polish priests, let alone Jews.

In March 1939 children of two Jewish parents were expelled from the party, universities, the bureaucracy, and the military. Nevertheless the Nazis complained, correctly, that practically all Italian Jews had some Aryan blood and that many would remain in the government and work against Germany. With the war Mussolini depended more heavily on Hitler and hardened his position. In November 1939 a Law for the

Defense of the Italian Race vetoed all marriages between Italians and Jews, including baptized and half- and quarter-Jews. The law desecrated the sacrament of marriage; Christian authorities had always heartily welcomed marriages between baptized former Jews and Catholics. Pius XII remained silent, probably because of concessions Mussolini made to the church, as Michaelis suggests. Mussolini said he would not yet round up Italian Jews but that eventually Europe must be free of Jews—a typical attempt to please the Germans without acting. Even so, the pro-Jewish faction among fascists protested, and in October 1939 Mussolini allowed a book to be published attacking the Nordic theories of the Germans, partly because they referred to "inferior Latin races."

Mussolini was not ready for war; his forces had not yet pacified Ethiopia. When Ribbentrop informed Ciano of the forthcoming invasion of Poland in August 1939—less than a month's notice—Ciano wanted Mussolini to break the alliance or warn Germany that Italy would stay out. To avoid a direct refusal, Mussolini submitted to the Germans an impossibly huge list of war materiel he would need from them. Italians, including most fascists, enthusiastically welcomed the avoidance of war. Ciano insisted that whoever won, Italy would lose, either becoming a German satellite or the victim of the Allies. There were now three thousand illegal Jewish refugees in Italy. They were allowed to remain; ultimately some fifteen thousand Jews found refuge.

When in April 1940 the pope appealed to Mussolini for peace, the circulation of the papal *L'Osservatore Romano* soared, infuriating Il Duce. Hitler's alliance with the Soviet Union and his swift victory over Poland caused Mussolini to take some relatively minor anti-Jewish actions, but Jewish refugees were still allowed to enter Italy. In April Mussolini announced that all Jews must leave Italy, but he gave them eleven years to do so! On June 10, as France collapsed, Mussolini declared war, froze Jewish bank accounts, and opened fifteen forced-labor camps for foreign Jews. But rounding up Jews for the camps proved too difficult because of public and bureaucratic opposition; even Hitler could not have carried out his anti-Semitic policies without wide public support from German civilians. Some local officials reported there were no "dangerous" Jews in their districts; Mussolini had to discipline party members and fire the mayors of Florence, Turin, and Padua for aiding Jews. Jews were expelled from fortified zones; 1,650 Jewish refugees were arrested; and severe restrictions were placed on Jewish business activities.

Orders were given to mobilize all Jews between eighteen and fifty-five for forced labor. But the Germans did not believe that Mussolini would allow Italian Jews to be deported to Germany. Perhaps German military difficulties gave Mussolini pause, because in 1943 he praised a book that attacked the racism of blood and soil and dismissed the ancient Germans as barbaric. In 1943 Ciano persuaded Mussolini not to aid German crimes against the Jews, and an angry Ribbentrop suspected, reasonably enough, that the majority of Italian Foreign Ministry officials—seven had Jewish wives—were aiding the British. By then Mussolini had little support among Italians, and his Grand Council plotted to displace him.

The Final Solution appalled Mussolini and Italian fascists. Meanwhile the SS compiled a lengthy list of complaints against Italian authorities for protecting Jews. Italy and Italian occupation zones remained havens for Jews as late as 1943, and Italian soldiers often guarded synagogues. In the Italian-occupied zone of France, the commander told the Vichy government that Jews would not be forced to wear the yellow star, as it was incompatible with the army's dignity. The commander of the Italian army in Montenegro persuaded Mussolini not to turn over any Jews to the murderous Croatian Ustashi or the Gestapo. In Greece the Italian army issued Jews Italian identity cards if they had the remotest Italian relative or even Italian-sounding names. Many Italian officers falsely swore that Jewish women were their wives. Italian troops protected Jews in Africa; Mussolini proposed a home for the Jews in Ethiopia. In Poland, Italian troops helped Jews with cash, food, or hiding places, sometimes in their barracks, and in 1943 sold arms to the Resistance.

After Italy surrendered in 1943, Mussolini "ruled" a puppet republic of Salò in the north. The SS now controlled Jewish affairs, and Hitler ordered their roundup. Warned by Italian radio, Jews fled Salò. The collection of Jews sickened the overwhelming majority of Italians, and they often demonstrated or passively resisted. Fascist officials designated to carry out racist measures opposed the Final Solution. Bureaucrats destroyed files, fascists insisted that the exemptions provided by Italian law be obeyed, and thousands of Italians provided safety, including priests, monks, and nuns who sheltered more than 4,000 Jews. Some 477 Jews were protected in the Vatican. But the pope made no public gesture when the Jews were taken from Rome, though Cardinal Tisserant and other Catholic leaders appealed to him to do so, and the cardinal of Florence personally intervened. Ernst von Weizsaecker, a high official of the German Foreign Office who tried to pressure the Italian government to surrender its Jews, reported that there was no evidence of anti-Semitism among the Italian public. It has been estimated that Italians saved four-fifths of Italian Jews.

On June 4, 1944, Rome was captured by the Allies. On May 13, 1945, Axis forces surrendered in the north of Italy. Of 6,746 Jews taken from Italy by the Germans after the Italian surrender, only some 830 survived. Seized by Communist partisans in April 1945, Mussolini was executed and his body hung upside down in the main square of Milan.

ELEVEN

Concluding Speculations

THE HOLOCAUST was unique because of its near-total annihilation of the Jews of Europe, and because they were not an enemy of the Germans. In all other attempted genocides there has been a history of mutual conflict. German Jews wished to be accepted as patriotic Germans, and though they formed less than 1 percent of the population, they had made valuable contributions to Germany and fought with distinction in its wars. In short, the illusions of the German anti-Semites were just that. These facts, and the sheer extent and horror of the Holocaust, have persuaded many that it is not only unique but also beyond human comprehension. Hence most studies of the Holocaust focus on remembering the horror while attempts to explain it have been few and inadequate.

Remembering is crucial, but it is not enough. All major historical events—the Great War, the French and Bolshevik revolutions—are unique, but they are also intelligible. So too is the Holocaust. We need to understand why anti-Semitism was so destructive in Germany, and why so many other nationals willingly cooperated with the killers. As we have seen, the key to understanding lies in comparing the relative strengths and weaknesses of anti-Semitic movements in different nations and their access—or lack of it—to political power over many decades. In the history that led to the Holocaust lies the insight necessary to understand its causes and perhaps the means to foresee, intervene, and mitigate future mass murders with different killers and victims and on a lesser scale.

In Western Europe today, including Germany, fascism and political anti-Semitism are dead, notwithstanding the rise of radical right groups in some nations, notably France, Austria, Belgium, Holland, Britain, Switzerland, and even Denmark. Although some of their leaders have made anti-Semitic statements or belittled the Holocaust, their main electoral support comes from those who fear not Jews but immigrants, especially Muslims, who they believe will take their jobs, are responsible for rising crime rates, and may have terrorist connections.

At the same time the conflict between Israel and the Palestinians has intensified the anti-Semitism of Muslim immigrants toward Israel, compounded because Muslim immigrants from the Middle East come from states whose governments have for decades supported the old European image of the vile and conspiratorial Jew. Most Middle Eastern governments routinely publish and distribute the *Protocols of the Elders of Zion*, readily available on the street, and allow religious and secular schools to teach all the old anti-Semitic obscenities, including charges of ritual murder. In many communities, extreme Muslim anti-Judaism—a relatively new phenomenon—is combined with classic European racist ideas in ways that are appallingly similar to the ideas that led to the Holocaust.

Most European immigrants, legal or illegal, are Muslims; Africans are next. It is understood, however, that popular antagonisms focus on all people of color, whether recent immigrants or not. Obviously Jews are irrelevant. Indeed, some leaders of the radical right are pro-Israel and have no interest in anti-Semitism. Consequently almost all anti-Semitic incidents have been carried out by Muslims. Even the notorious extremist Joerg Haider of Austria, who has praised some Nazi policies and defends the "honor" of the SS, concentrates his fire on immigrants; his party's platform demands no anti-Semitic policies. Jean Marie Le Pen, the French rightist who has denigrated Jews and the Holocaust, now avoids such remarks, and his party platform also does not include anti-Semitism.

In short, European rightists rally not anti-Semites, as did the Nazis, but racists that support the deportation of immigrants who, they believe, take their jobs. Supporters also include those who suffer from European economic integration, fearing unemployment and a loss of national identity. German "skinheads" detest Jews but physically attack immigrants; they have no political impact. Because immigrants, unlike the old Jewish communities, hold no prestigious positions in society or the economy, extreme measures are not required; rightists need only demand that immigrants be shipped back to their native lands. All other parties and the general public—conservatives, centrist, or leftist—tend to unite against extremists whenever they make political gains.

Prominent and influential European intellectuals no longer confuse a variety of environmental and social influences with innate racial characteristics or encourage myths of racial superiority. Christian anti-Semitism is far weaker than before the rise of the Nazis; nationalists and those in professional positions no longer vilify the Jews. Threats to the political powers and privileges of the establishment are not identified with the Jewish community. Unlike the old German elites, political leaders condemn racism in all its forms. Socialism and fascism are both politically dead, and farmers and artisans are comfortable now that they have adjusted to the long transition to a modern economic and political society. No European nation, least of all Germany, toys with ideas of building huge armies to conquer territory; economic penetration is far more rewarding, easy, and successful.

In short, the complex of events that caused the Holocaust cannot recur in Europe, and short of nuclear terror the numbers will never be duplicated. Nevertheless elsewhere the slaughter of innocents by religious and ethnic extremists, also motivated by political and economic interests, increases with every year.

The names are familiar: Cambodia, Rwanda, Bosnia, Kosovo, Croatia, Congo, Algeria, Syria, Iraq, Sri Lanka, India, Pakistan, Afghanistan, Kashmir, Malaysia, the Philippines, Nigeria, Sudan, Iraq, Turkey, Indonesia, Chechnya—with more conflicts threatening. At first glance, any comparison with the Holocaust seems false if not indecent. Yet in these lesser horrors religious antagonisms and racist illusions play vital roles. That is why an understanding of the historical causes of the Holocaust can help us understand the causes of "ethnic cleansing" wherever it occurs.

Ethnic and religious conflicts often resulted from the lingering consequences of the collapse of the great empires—Ottoman, Austrian, and Russian/Soviet—where different ethnic and religious groups had been held together by force. Struggling for liberation, these groups cultivated an ethnic nationalism that necessarily threatened any minorities among them. Thus the breakup of the former Yugoslavia was the ultimate consequence of the postwar settlements of 1919 that forced unwilling Croats to join Serbs in one nation to meet Western convenience and Serb ambitions. Tito weakened Serbian and Croatian ethnic conflicts by combining severe repression with rewards for those loyal to the Communist party and to Yugoslavia. After his death, however, ambitious politicians, culminating with Slobodan Milosevic, cultivated these antagonisms for their own power, and in the 1990s the delicate balance exploded in fury.

The consequences of the defeat and breakup of the Ottoman Empire still affect the Middle East, compounded by British and French imperialism and the Western attempt to control oil. France and Great Britain drew the boundaries of all Middle Eastern states, excluding Israel, with no consideration for the wishes of the different ethnic and religious inhabitants. Hence such states—Iraq, Syria, Lebanon, Algeria, and Turkey—often use murderous force to punish indigenous separatist or religious movements, which reply in kind. Saudi Arabia avoids trouble by exporting not only oil but also Islamic fundamentalists, who endanger Middle Eastern as well as Western governments and peoples.

Conflicts and massacres have also broken out where boundaries once drawn by colonial powers included different ethnic and religious groups hostile or indifferent to the European norm of centralized nation-states. Of approximately two hundred ethnic groups in Nigeria, for example, many have broken off to declare themselves independent Muslim regions, initiating bitter conflicts among different religious and ethnic groups. Afghanistan and Somalia are collections of ethnic groups and clans led by semi-feudal warlords who have defeated all attempts to establish a central authority and will probably continue to do so. Elsewhere, ethnic and religious struggles are intensified by attempts to control oil, diamonds, and other forms of natural wealth.

Ethnic and religious groups often concentrate in different social, political, or economic roles because of pre-established ties with their compatriots. This also generates interethnic antagonisms among those who covet their positions, as in Sri Lanka, Cambodia, and parts of Southeast Asia. In Rwanda, for example, the Tutsi minority, favored by European colonialists, dominated politics and thus aroused the anger of the Hutu majority. These situations are roughly comparable to the high presence of Jews in Eastern European commerce and trade that fostered bitter economic antagonisms and racist stereotyping. Thus scholars have referred to the Chinese merchants dispersed throughout Southeast Asia as the "Jews of Asia." During times of economic collapse their communities, as once with the Jews of Europe, are held responsible and often viciously attacked.

Today ethnic and religious conflicts also escalate because of the spread of modern weapons and the struggle for increasingly scarce resources. The world's rapid population growth, from roughly one billion in 1850 to more than six billion today, threatens the biological systems—cropland, forests, fisheries, water—upon which life depends. Meanwhile the gap between rich and poor increases, as does the number of those—now esti-mated at a billion-plus and growing—who live in the kind of poverty that brings daily misery and early death.

Throughout the third world a huge percentage of unem-ployed youth increases yearly; in many regions about half the population is unemployed, uneducated, and under twenty-five—a demographic profile currently valid among many of the "skinheads" and neo-fascists in contemporary Europe who adopt a roughly similar racist reaction. In the third world, how-ever, with its lack of responsibly functioning social systems, ed-ucational institutions, or democratic governments, few among the majority of the poor can expect a reasonable future. Conse-quently extreme religious faith, ethnic nationalism, and its corollary racism are often all that gives their lives purpose and dignity. Many middle-class youth from declining families also feel frustrated, caught as they are between the traditional world of their ancestors, the seductions of the "infidel" West, and in-creasing threats to their status and well-being. They often re-cruit and lead the slum dwellers who can find their only outlet in fundamentalism, ethnic pride, and sometimes terror.

Many in the non-Western world believe, with reason, that colonialism, capitalism, socialism, their indigenous leaders, and the power of multinational corporations have all harmed them. Thus they return to the beliefs of their ancestors or direct their hatred toward their own leaders and the favored West, home of the former colonial powers that for generations treated them with contempt. Many of their own leaders connive with West-ern corporations to extract natural resources without creating jobs or wealth for their own people. Leaders who ignore their own poor, ostentatiously display consumer delights, and share Western secularism aggravate hatred among the miserable and become targets for those who accuse them of betraying their own faith and people in order to increase their bank accounts.

This dangerous situation also feeds on the lack of support for ethnic and religious toleration, values that have little or no cultural strength in much of the third world, as once in Poland and Eastern Europe. In spite of the magnificent achievements of Islamic thinkers and scholars when Europe was but a stagnant backwater, only in the West did the secular humanism and liberalism derived from science and the Enlightenment become the faith of the commercial and professional middle classes, undermining the attractions of extreme racism and religious fundamentalism. Correspondingly, as we know, European liberals, progressives, and social democrats became the strongest opponents of reaction, ultra-nationalism, and racism.

But Westerners should not be arrogant. Civilized Western values are weak and began to prevail only after centuries of bloody history. One need only recall the horrors of the Crusades, the Wars of Religion, the sanguinary conflicts and revolutions that accompanied the end of feudalism, the rise of nation-states and the collapse of empires. Our time has also witnessed the terror of totalitarianism, two world wars, Stalin's purges and the Gulag, and of course the ultimate horror of the Holocaust. A broad historical view tells us that civilized life is frail and may be transient; violent conflict has been far and away the historical norm—it is what mankind seems to do best. Yet Westerners continue to see their "way of life" as permanent and a standard for the non-Western world. We have too easily assumed that non-Westerners will accept our ways, serve our economic needs, and prosper by doing so. Recent events are eroding our complacency.

It is obvious that ethnic and religious violence will stop if democratic liberalism, scientific rationality, and some measure of social justice as well as religious and ethnic tolerance become global norms. Population growth must also be curbed and the environment protected. But it is difficult to reverse potent historical forces and traditions upheld by powerful cultural, political, and economic elites and popular inertia. Such change is the task for this and coming generations.

There has been progress, and in the reasons for that

progress may lie the solutions. In Western civilization, the educated no longer believe in fixed racial differences; sophisticated theologians reject religious fundamentalism; reactionary nationalism is a minority belief; tolerance and even ethnic diversity are slowly becoming accepted virtues. We also know how to protect the environment and share resources and wealth more equally, though we do not do nearly enough of either. Each year brings more pessimistic statistics about the environment and the gap between rich and poor. And unfortunately we take our liberal values for granted even as they are smothered under a wave of doubt, self-concern, and complacency. Some important intellectuals, by twisted reasoning, even hold the Enlightenment responsible for the horrors of our time. There are also signs among us of a renewal of the false comforts of racial and religious absolutism and a growing fear—not entirely unjustified—of the immigrants of other faiths who arrive among us but do not share our history or values.

As rage intensifies, weapons proliferate, and victims increase, the West seems unwilling to intervene to stop "ethnic cleansing." It is an unimaginably difficult task; sacrifice for the sake of other peoples is hardly an easy choice. But as bitterness increases and more seek targets for their rage, it will not be enough to declare war on terror and use the power of a superior technology to strike back. The dialectic of terror and counterforce will escalate—as in the Middle East today—for many in the third world have little to lose and hold religious beliefs that embrace martyrdom. We must find ways to help alleviate reasonable grievances so that the politics of hate cannot recruit supporters from the world's dispossessed. It is hard to face, but even many of Hitler's supporters had legitimate grievances he could exploit—though of course the Jews were in no sense a cause of German distress. If moderation is to succeed, the peoples of the world must have a humanistic and practical education, liberal religious attitudes, and a stake in the well-being of society.

An assistant in Auschwitz once asked the infamous Dr. Mengele, the holder of two Ph.D.s, an accomplished research scholar and mass murderer: "When will all this killing end, when all the Jews are dead?" "Never," he answered, "it will go on and on and on." For Mengele knew instinctively that the ultimate enemy of the Nazis and all "ethnic cleansers" were all those who support an open, tolerant, and humane society—as did the Jews of Western Europe. That is what we must protect and extend. If we know the causes of ethnic and religious slaughter, we will at least have made a start. For that reason, if for no other, the study of the historical causes of the Holocaust is more than a concern of the Jewish community; it is the responsibility of all those who hope to preserve civilization. Without knowing the past, the present is unintelligible, the future a threat, and we are helpless.

A Note on Sources

A BOOK LIKE THIS necessarily depends on a great many secondary works as well as my forty years of teaching modern European history. Many extensive bibliographies on the Holocaust and on the history of anti-Semitism are available, but rare indeed are books that attempt to connect both with the long-term historical development of modern Europe. Excellent and helpful works not mentioned in the notes include the following; others are indicated by an asterisk in the notes to the text.

Yehuda Bauer, *Rethinking the Holocaust* (New Haven, Conn., 2001).

Helen Fein, *Accounting for Genocide* (New York, 1979).

Franklin H. Littell, *The Crucifixion of the Jews* (New York, 1979).

Michael R. Marrus, *The Holocaust in Historical Perspective* (Seattle, 1978).

George Mosse, *Toward the Final Solution: A History of European Racism* (New York, 1978).

Marvin Perry and Frederick M. Schweitzer, *Antisemitism: Myth and Hate from Antiquity to the Present* (New York, 2002).

David S. Wyman, ed., *The World Reacts to the Holocaust* (Baltimore and London, 1996). See especially the articles on Poland by Michael C. Steinlauf, France by David Weinberg, and Italy by Meir Michaelis.

The *Journal of Genocide Research*, edited by Henry Huttenbach and published quarterly by Carfax in the United Kingdom, contains excellent examples of the latest scholarship.

Notes

Chapter 2. Germany to 1914

page

19: Luther quotation from Léon Poliakov, *The History of Anti-Semitism* (New York, 1976), I, 223.

22: Prussian aristocratic views from "Friedrich August von der Marwitz," in Friedrich Meusel, ed., *Friedrich August von der Marwitz* (Berlin, 1913), II, 20–22.

23: Fichte quotation from J. G. Fichte, "Beitrag zur Berechtigung des Urteils des Publikum ueber die Franzoesische Revolution," *Gesammelte Werke* (Stuttgart, 1964), I, 293.

30: "annihilation" from Theodore Zechlin, *Die Deutsche Politik und die Juden im Ersten Weltkrieg* (Goettingen, 1969), p. 44.

31: Ahlwardt call for extermination from *Raul Hilberg, *The Destruction of the European Jews* (New York, 1985), I, 18–19.

34: Langbehn quotation from Fritz Stern, *The Politics of Cultural Despair* (New York, 1965), p. 50.

36: Class quotation from *Richard S. Levy, *Anti-Semitism in the Modern World* (New York, 1991), pp. 129–130.

For a more thorough discussion of Germany, see John Weiss, *Ideology of Death: Why the Holocaust Happened in Germany* (Chicago, 1996).

Chapter 3. Germany: Hitler, the Elites, and the Holocaust

page

39: Pan German protests from Zechlin, *Die Deutsche Politik*, p. 413.

41: Racist League for Defense quote from ibid., p. 212. Kanzler quotation from F. L. Carsten, *Fascist Movements in Austria* (New York, 1977), p. 46.

42: Kapp's second-in-command quotation from George Mosse, *The Crisis of German Ideology* (New York, 1964), p. 255.

45: Nazi poster quotation from Simon Taylor, *Prelude to Genocide* (New York, 1985), pp. 79, 221–222.

48: Hitler quotations from Alan Bullock, *Hitler: A Study in Tyranny* (New York, 1952), p. 81. Nazi election leaflet quotation from Mosse, *Crisis*, p. 255. See also Taylor, *Prelude*, pp. 221–222.

54–55: High Command quotation from *Omer Bartov, *The Eastern Front, 1941–45* (New York, 1986), p. 84.

59: Hitler quotations from Eberhardt Jaeckel, *Hitler's Worldview* (Cambridge, England, 1972), p. 83; and Klaus P. Fischer, *Nazi Germany: A New History* (New York, 1996) p. 439.

60: ghetto administrator's quotation from Hilberg, *Destruction*, I, 222.

Chapter 4. The Austrian Empire Through 1918

page

62: Gentz quotation from Poliakov, *Anti-Semitism*, III, 297.

63: Catholic church journal quotation from *Jacob Katz, *From Prejudice to Destruction* (Cambridge, Mass., 1980), p. 227.

64: *La Civiltà Cattolica* quotation from George Berkley, *Vienna and Its Jews* (Cambridge, Mass., 1993), p. 79.

64: Habsburg Empire quotation from Arthur J. May, *The Habsburg Monarchy, 1867–1914* (New York, 1951), pp. 179, 171.

66: Vogelsang quotation from Rudolf Kuppe, *Karl Lueger und seine Zeit* (Vienna, 1933), pp. 98, 302.

67: Lueger quotation from ibid., p. 153.

73–74: Lueger quotation on the power of the Jews from *Richard S. Geehr, *Karl Lueger, Mayor of Fin de Siècle Vienna* (Detroit, 1990), p. 181. Socialist attitude from Kuppe, *Lueger*, p. 153. Lueger quotation on Marx and Lassalle from ibid., p. 302.

76: Mosse quotation from *Crisis*, p. 239.

77: Christian Social member's quotation from Levy, *Anti-Semitism*, pp. 117, 119.

82: Kunschak quotation from Berkley, *Vienna*, p. 154.

Chapter 5. Austria, 1918–1945

page

83: Pauly quotation from *Bruce F. Pauly, *From Prejudice to Persecution: A History of Anti-Semitism in Austria* (Chapel Hill, 1992), p. 202. I am deeply indebted to Pauly's work.

91: Pauly quotation from ibid., pp. 139, 158.

92: Pauly quotation from ibid., pp. 89, 93.

96: Catholic journals and newspapers quotation from ibid., pp. 151, 161.

98: "clean out the Jews" from *Saul Friedlaender, *Nazi Germany and the Jews* (New York, 1997), p. 242.

99: Kunschak quotations from Berkley, *Vienna*, p. 229.

102: Iverson quotation from ibid., p. 320.

Chapters 6 and 7. France

I am highly indebted to the following excellent works:

*Robert Soucy, *French Fascism: The First Wave, 1924–1933* (New Haven, 1986), and *French Fascism: The Second Wave, 1933–1939* (New Haven, 1995)

*Robert Paxton and Michael Marrus, *Vichy France and the Jews* (New York, 1981)

*David Weinberg, *A Community on Trial: The Jews of Paris in the 1930s* (Chicago, 1977)

Robert F. Byrnes, *Antisemitism in Modern France* (New Brunswick, N.J., 1950)

Chapter 8. Anti-Semitism in Poland to 1918

page

158: Bismarck quotations from Norman Davies, *God's Playground: A History of Poland* (New York, 1982), II, 124–125.

161: Dmowski quotation from *Richard M. Watt, *Bitter Glory: Poland and Its Fate* (New York, 1979), p. 306. Future Pius XI quotation from *David R. Kertzer, *The Popes Against the Jews: The Vatican's Role in the Rise of Modern Anti-Semitism* (New York, 2001), p. 66.

Chapter 9. Poland, 1919–1947

page

177: university students' quotation from Watt, *Bitter Glory*, p. 362. Hlond quotation from David Symet, "Polish State Anti-Semitism as a Major Factor Leading to the Holocaust," *Journal of Genocide Research*, I, no. 2 (June 1999), 170.

184: Grot-Rawecki quotation from *Antony Polonsky, "Beyond Condemnations, Apologetics and Apologies," in Jonathan Frankel, ed., *The Fate of the European Jews* (Oxford, 1997), p. 207.

185: "a disastrous impression" from ibid., p. 209.

189: Falanga quotation from ibid., p. 214–215.

The following books are essential:

*Jan T. Gross, *Neighbors* (Princeton, 2001), recounts the massacre of the Jews of a Polish village by fellow Poles during World War II.

*Yisrael Gutman, Ezra Mendelsohn, Jehuda Reinharz, and Chone Shmeruk, eds., *The Jews of Poland Between Two World Wars* (Lebanon, N.H., 1989), includes excellent essays by leading scholars. See especially Abraham Brumberg, "The Bund and the Polish Socialist Party in the Late 1930s"; Yisrael Gutman, "Polish Antisemitism Between the Wars: An Overview"; Emanuel Melzer, "Anti-Semitism in the Last Years of the Second Polish Republic"; and Edward D. Wynot, "The Polish Peasant Movement and the Jews."

The works of Abraham Brumberg, Antony Polonsky, and Michael C. Steinlauf have been of great use to me.

Chapter 10. The Italian Exception

page

195: Mahler quotation from *Raphael Mahler, *A History of Modern Jewry, 1780–1815* (New York, 1971), p. 118.

201: enemy race quotation from Kertzer, *Popes*, p. 288.

210: Mussolini quotation from *Meir Michaelis, *Mussolini and the Jews: German-Italian Relations and the Jewish Question in Italy, 1922–45* (Oxford, 1978), p. 29.

211: Michaelis quotation from ibid., p. 126.

213: pope's attitude from ibid., p. 251; see also p. 238.

I am heavily indebted to Meir Michaelis's work. See also the excellent book by Susan Zuccotti, *The Italians and the Holocaust* (New York, 1987).

Chapter 11. Concluding Speculations

page

225: Mengele quotation from *Benno Mueller-Hill, *Murderous Science: The Elimination of the Jews, Gypsies, and Mentally Ill, Germany, 1933–45* (Oxford, 1988), p. 9.

See also the excellent booklet by *Robert S. Wistrich, *Muslim Anti-Semitism: A Clear and Present Danger* (American Jewish Committee, New York, 2002). All who wish to understand the Israeli-Palestinian conflict should read it.

Index

Index

Index

Index

Index

Index

Index

Index

Tisserant, Cardinal, 216
Tito, Josip Broz, 220
Tour du Pin, René La, 121
Toussenal, Alphonse, 112, 113
Treaty of Saint-Germain, 84
Treaty of Versailles, 17, 40, 45, 53, 127, 142, 181, 182, 211
Treitschke, Heinrich von, 29, 33
Turkey, 150

Ukrainians: anti-Semitism of, 151; Cossacks and, 154–155; in Poland, post–World War I, 150, 167, 170, 171, 174; in Poland before World War I, 151, 159, 161, 162–163, 164, 167; and Soviet invasion of Poland, 183, 191; World War I and, 165
Union Républicain Democratique, 124
United States, 14, 58, 129, 170
Universities, Austrian, 70, 92–93, 95, 100
Universities, French, 124
Universities, German: before 1914, 23, 29, 32, 33, 70; Nazis and, 54, 55; Weimar Republic and, 43
University of Berlin, 23, 29, 33, 70
University of Vienna, 70, 89, 92–93

Vallat, Xavier, 144
Versailles Treaty, 17, 40, 45, 53, 127, 142, 181, 182, 211
Vichy regime, 110, 113, 119, 144–148, 215
Victor Emmanuel of Piedmont, King, 199
Vienna, Austria, 75–77, 78–81, 88–89, 124, 162
Viviani, René, 126
Vogelsang, Karl von, 65–66, 67
Voltaire, 106, 119

Wagner, Richard, 34–35, 70, 124
Waldeck-Rousseau, Prime Minister, 125
Warsaw, Poland, 162, 189, 190, 191
Warsaw Ghetto uprising (1943), 189, 191
Weimar Republic: anti-Semitism and, 18; compared to French

republicanism, 117, 127; German High Command defense of, 132; parliamentary government and, 117; reactionary hatred of, 41–43, 46, 53, 120, 129
Weizsaecker, Ernst von, 216
Wels, Otto, 53
Westarp, Count Kuno von, 40–41
White Russians: Bolsheviks and, 165; and minority bloc in Poland, 171; in Poland before World War I, 151, 159, 161, 162–163, 164, 167; and Poland post–World War I, 167, 170, 171, 174; Soviet invasion of Poland and, 183, 191
Wiesenthal, Simon, 103, 104
Wilhelm I, Kaiser, 25, 34, 39
Wilson, Woodrow, 81, 84, 165–166
Witos, Wincenty, 163, 169, 170, 175, 176
World War I: Austrian anti-Semitism and, 81–82; Austrian Empire and, 37, 80–82, 150, 165; ethnic nationalism and, 11, 80, 150; Hitler and, 80–81; Italy and, 207–208; origins of, 36–37, 80, 150; Polish nationalism and, 165–166; Serbia and, 37, 80, 150

Young German Order, 41
Yugoslavia, 84, 220

Zegota (Poland), 186
Zionism: anti-Semite approval of, 178; in Austria pre–World War II, 100; Herzl and, 75, 124; and Jewish refugees prior to World War II, 181; and Jews in nineteenth-century Eastern Europe, 151, 164; Mussolini and, 211; Poland's 1967 campaign against, 192; Polish Zionists, 164, 165, 170, 172, 177, 179; Soviet invasion of Poland and, 184; at University of Vienna of 1880s, 70; World War I strikes and, 81
Zola, Émile, 123
Zyclon B, 59

A NOTE ON THE AUTHOR

John Weiss is emeritus professor of modern European history at Lehman College and the Graduate Center of the City University of New York. Born and raised in Detroit, he served in the navy during World War II, then studied at Wayne State University and Columbia University, where he received a Ph.D. and was a university fellow. Mr. Weiss also studied at the University of Innsbruck in Austria and was a Fulbright scholar at the University of Marburg in Germany. He has written extensively on fascism and related topics, including *Ideology of Death: Why the Holocaust Happened in Germany*; *The Fascist Tradition*; and *Conservatism in Europe*. He lives in Nyack, New York.